# Chinese Matters:
# From Grammar to First and Second Language Acquisition

Chris Wilder & Tor A. Åfarli (eds.)

# Chinese Matters:
# From Grammar to First and Second Language Acquisition

tapir academic press

© Tapir Academic Press, Trondheim 2010

ISBN 978-82-519-2536-5

*This publication may not be reproduced, stored in a retrieval system or transmitted in any form or by any means; electronic, electrostatic, magnetic tape, mechanical, photocopying, recording or otherwise, without permission.*

*Layout: Type-it AS*
*Cover Layout: Bjørg D. Wik, Tapir Academic Press*
*Printed and binded by: AIT Oslo AS*

*This book has been published with funding from and in cooperation with The Faculties of Humanities, NTNU*

*Tapir Academic Press publishes textbooks and academic literature for universities and university colleges, as well as for vocational and professional education. We also publish high quality literature of a more general nature. Our main product lines are:*

- *Textbooks for higher education*
- *Research and reference literature*
- *Non-fiction*

*We only use environmentally certified printing houses.*

Tapir Academic Press
NO–7005 Trondheim, Norway
Tel.:   + 47 73 59 32 10
Email:  post@tapirforlag.no
www.tapirforlag.no

*Publishing Editor: mari.nygard@tapirforlag.no*

# Contents

**Introduction** ..................................................................................... 7
    Chris Wilder & Tor A. Åfarli

**The syntax of [+human] terms in Cantonese** ............................. 15
    Joanna Ut-seong Sio

**The syntax of presentative sentences in Norwegian and Mandarin Chinese: Toward a comparative analysis?** .................................. 29
    Tor A. Åfarli & Fufen Jin

**Chinese Relatives and the Coda Construction** .......................... 51
    Chris Wilder

**Nominal Structure in Early Child Mandarin** ............................ 75
    Thomas Hun-tak Lee

**Post-Verbal Locative/Directional Phrases in Child Mandarin: A Longitudinal Study** ........................................................................ 111
    Miao-Ling Hsieh

**Temporal reference of bare verbs in Mandarin child language** ......... 131
    Yi-ching Su

**Pro-drop in Mandarin–Norwegian Bilinguals** ........................... 153
    Fufen Jin, Kristin M. Eide & Tor A. Åfarli

**The L2 Acquisition of the Mandarin Chinese Perfective Marker – *LE* by L1 English Speakers** ................................................................ 171
    Mónica Cabrera & Nicholas Usaj

**Ultimate L2 Acquisition of the Chinese BA Construction: Two Case Studies** ............................................................................................. 191
  Fufen Jin

**Index** ............................................................................................................. 211

# Introduction

Chris Wilder & Tor A. Åfarli
*Norwegian University of Science and Technology (NTNU)*

On April 23-24 2007, the *Workshop on Comparative Chinese – Norwegian Syntax, including Acquisition Topics (CHINOSAT)* took place at NTNU, Trondheim. A collection of articles, with the papers given at the 2007 workshop at its core, was published the following year with the title *Comparative Grammar and Language Acquisition in the Age of Globalization: Norwegian and Chinese* (Åfarli & Jin 2008). In the introduction to that volume we were proud to declare that, to our knowledge, this was the first time Mandarin Chinese and Norwegian were investigated from a comparative and acquisitional point of view to such an extent in Norway and even internationally. A follow-up to the 2007 workshop was organized on October 1-2 2009 with the title *Workshop on Chinese grammar in contrast: syntax and acquisition,* conveniently called *CHINOSAT 2* to mark the continuity. The present book contains nine articles based on papers given at the 2009 workshop.

This time, however, we cannot claim that this is a pioneering enterprise, given the 2007/2008 precedent. Rather, it seems – or at least we hope – that the present book (and the workshop it is based on) should be taken as an indication that a new field of research has established a vigorous foothold at NTNU. Thus, we very much look forward to future comparative and acquisitional investigations and research taking place at NTNU into the syntax of Chinese and its relation to the syntax of other languages like Norwegian and English.

Why should a small country like Norway encourage and actually execute research into Chinese? The "external" reason for this is that China is fast becoming a leading world power both economically and politically, and therefore there is every indication that contacts between Chinese and Norwegian institutions, enterprises, and individuals will be constantly becoming broader and deeper in the future. Understanding of language as a key factor in the understanding of culture is invaluable in this expected ever-broadening and ever-deepening interaction between China and Norway.

The "internal" reason why Chinese matters (or should matter) even in Norway is that Chinese and Norwegian are very different languages both genetically and typologically, and therefore they are particularly interesting from both comparative and acquisitional points of view. For instance, Mandarin Chinese is an isolating language with no inflection of the noun, whereas Norwegian (unlike English, for instance) is a language where nouns show a rich system of inflections. Also, Chinese is a topic prominent language where sentences often seem to lack a subject proper, whereas Norwegian is a subject prominent language with a strict subject requirement. Given this state of affairs, there is every reason to believe that comparative research into Norwegian and Chinese syntax will be extraordinarily fruitful for theoretical linguistics. Furthermore, the linguistic differences between Norwegian and Chinese obviously pose huge challenges for the second language acquisition of Mandarin Chinese by Norwegian natives and of Norwegian by Chinese natives, with corresponding challenges and promises for acquisition research.

In the remaining part of this introduction, we give an overview of the articles that are contained in this book.

## 1. Papers dealing with grammar topics

Research into the syntax of nominal expressions of the past 20 years has been dominated by the Determiner Phrase (DP) hypothesis (Abney 1987), according to which nominal expressions are projections of determiners rather than directly of the noun and DP is the locus of referentiality (cf. Alexiadou et. al. 2007). A much debated issue is whether article-less languages such as many Slavic languages and Chinese, including Mandarin and Cantonese, include a mostly abstract DP in their nominal projections (on Slavic, see e.g. Pereltsvaig 2007 and Bošković 2008). With respect to the Chinese languages, which make extensive use of classifiers, the issue is tied up with the question of whether and to what extent the role of the DP is taken up by the Classifier Phrase (ClP), cf. Cheng & Sybesma (1999). In "Classifying [+human] terms in Cantonese", Sio investigates the Cantonese element *aa* which occurs with nouns having human referents. Sio shows that *aa* is a syntactic marker in a certain subclass of *aa*-nominals which do not contain classifiers, and which show restricted interpretive options, being for example incompatible with predicative use. Sio argues that this 'syntactic' *aa* is best analysed as a D element taking a [+human] noun directly as its complement, and that such *aa*-nominals therefore provide support for positing a DP in Chinese.

It is a feature of many languages having SVO order in simple sentences, that they allow postverbal subjects with indefinite interpretation in certain sentence types, typically identified as 'existential' and/or 'presentative' sentences, and with certain verb-types (verb of existence, (dis)appearance, motion, etc.). Such is the case for both Chinese (cf. Huang 1987) and Norwegian, and this provides the starting point for Åfarli and Jin's paper "The syntax of presentative sentences in Norwegian and Mandarin Chinese: Toward a comparative analysis?" As is so often the case, closer investigation of initial surface similarities reveals a more complex underlying situation. The paper focuses on two cases of presentative sentences, Chinese sentences with existential *you* 'have' (*you* + NP + XP) and their Norwegian counterparts with *vere* 'be' (*det* + *vere* + NP + XP, where *det* is an expletive), and sentences involving motion verbs like Chinese *lai*, Norwegian *komme* (both 'come'). The authors argue that *you*-sentences and *vere*-sentences both involve a postverbal small clause complement (NP + XP), yet Chinese *you*-sentences differ fundamentally from their Norwegian counterparts with *vere* in that they do not involve a dethematized subject position. Sentences with motion verbs and postverbal subjects, on the other hand, are argued to involve a dethematized subject position in both languages, yet to differ in whether the postverbal complement is a small clause (Norwegian) or not (Chinese).

A familiar fact about Chinese constituent order is that it has prenominal relative clauses – like other nominal modifiers, relative clauses carry the nominal marker *de* and precede the noun, as in (1). The Chinese coda construction, exemplified by (2) from Huang (1987), is a virtual paraphrase of (1). In "Chinese Relatives and the Coda Construction", Wilder points out some striking similarities between the construction in (2) and the 'V2 relative clause' construction of German, which was analysed in Gärtner (2001).

(1) Wo    jiao-guo      yi ge          [ hen congming de ] xuesheng
    I     teach-ASP     one CL         very intelligent DE student
    'I have the experience of teaching a student who is (very) intelligent.'

(2) Wo    jiao-guo      yi ge xuesheng              [ hen congming ]
    I     teach-ASP     one CL student              very intelligent
    'I have the experience of teaching a student who is (very) intelligent.'

Wilder argues that the coda expression, bracketed in (2), is best analysed as a restrictive relative clause modifying the preceding noun, hence that Chinese also has postnominal relative clauses. Evidence from the interpretive behaviour of coda sentences is used to argue against alternative conceptions prevalent in the literature – that the construction is paratactic (Li & Thompson 1981), or that the coda is a kind of secondary predicate (Huang 1987 and others).

## 2. Papers dealing with first language acquisition (L1A) topics

The papers by Lee, Hsieh and Su all deal with the monolingual acquisition of Mandarin as a first language. Each seeks to document the emergence of a particular class of structures and their interpretations in the spontaneous production of Mandarin-acquiring children. The paper by Jin, Eide and Åfarli deals with L1A by Norwegian–Mandarin bilinguals.

In "Nominal Structure in Early Child Mandarin", Lee presents a wide-ranging study of nominal expressions in early child Mandarin, based on findings from two longitudinal studies of two individual children covering ages 1;5 to ca. 2;3. The paper examines in depth the way in which the syntactic forms in the child data map to semantic distinctions like argument vs. predicate, including referential distinctions such as specific vs. nonspecific, definite vs. indefinite. The analysis of early child Mandarin nominal structure which he proposes integrates his L1A findings with recent syntactic proposals concerning the status and function of classifiers (e.g. Cheng & Sybesma 1999) and functional nominal structure in general (e.g. Sio 2006), as well as to semantic acquisition issues such as the dependence of the definite / indefinite distinction on the development of a 'theory of mind' in the child (Schafer & de Villiers 2000).

Many Chinese prepositions were historically used as verbs, and the apparent categorial indeterminacy between V and P found with some prepositional items in present-day Mandarin is a familiar issue to linguists investigating Chinese grammar (cf. Huang, Li & Li 2009:25ff). In her paper "Post-Verbal Locative / Directional Phrases in Child Mandarin: A Longitudinal Study", Hsieh investigates one case, the locative preposition *zai* in its postverbal uses, from the perspectives of its syntax and semantics, and how the child acquires it. She documents the complexities of postverbal *zai*-phrases, which may have a locative or directional reading, depending on factors such as the choice of the preceding main verb. Findings from a longitudinal acquisition project indicate that while *zai* appears early, the child only masters the distinctions of the adult target grammar rather late, well into the 6th year. Hsieh suggests that the child initially misanalyses *zai* as a verb (V V NP) rather than a preposition (V P NP).

A much studied phenomenon in child language research is children's use of non-finite root clauses around the ages of two to three years, which includes the use of bare verbs lacking tense and agreement markers in English, the 'root infinitive' phenomenon in Dutch and other European languages, and other types. Recent work has shown that these nonfinite child utterances have present, past and modal interpretations in patterns that vary across languages, and an influential hypothesis is that the interpretation of such non-finite root clauses is governed by aspectual properties (Hyams 2006). Mandarin differs from these languages in that it lacks tense and agreement markers altogether, and it is controversial whether it even has the finite vs. non-finite clause distinction (cf. Hu et. al. 2001). It is thus an interesting question whether Mandarin-acquiring children pass through a phase similar to the 'root infinitive' stage, a topic which is taken up by Yi-Ching Su in her contribution "Temporal Reference of Bare Verbs in Mandarin Child Language". Her preliminary findings indicate that this is indeed the case.

Bilingual first language acquisition is a topic that raises special questions of its own. One such question is whether one grammar influences the other during the acquisition process. That is, do the two grammars develop independently (autonomous development hypothesis), so that the pattern of acquisition of each L1 is the same as for monolinguals? Or can the acquisition of one grammar can affect the development of the other (interdependent development hypothesis), resulting in divergent patterns of acquisition by monolinguals and bilinguals? This forms the backdrop for the paper "Pro-drop in Mandarin–Norwegian Bilinguals" by Jin, Eide and Åfarli. Their study focusses on Mandarin-Norwegian differences concerning the pro-drop phenomenon, i.e. the occurrence of null arguments with pronominal interpretation, which are licensed relatively freely in subject and object positions in Mandarin, while being quite restricted in Norwegian (topic drop in main clauses). The authors examined transcripts of spontaneous production of children born into Chinese families living in Norway who are becoming Mandarin–Norwegian bilinguals, at ages ranging from 3;9 to 6;10. They report both quantitative evidence and evidence of transfer to indicate that there is indeed cross-linguistic influence in the domain of pro-drop. These findings lend support to the interdependent development hypothesis.

## 3. Papers dealing with second language acquisition (L2A) topics

The papers by Jin and Cabrera & Usaj both deal with the learning of Mandarin as a second language, focussing on points where Mandarin grammar is markedly different from the relevant L1 (English, Norwegian). Both papers also address issues of general interest for L2 acquisition research, namely, the effects of external factors in the acquisition process – L1 vs. L2 setting (Cabrera & Usaj), and age of onset of the L2A process (Jin).

In their contribution "The L2 Acquisition of the Mandarin Chinese Perfective Marker *–LE* by L1 English Speakers", Cabrera & Usaj focus on a basic tense-aspect difference between English (L1) and Mandarin (L2). Mandarin does not have overt tense markers, and it employs a perfective aspect marker *-le* in many but crucially not all situations where English employs the simple past tense. As the authors point out, this difference is typically remarked upon but not properly explained in teaching materials, thus the use of *-le* forms a natural area for transfer errors to occur (incorrect use of Chinese *-le* for English past tense). The investigation seeks to elucidate whether the acquisition of *-le* by college-level English L1 speakers is affected by the context of learning. The authors compared students who have spent time in China on a 'study abroad program' (L2 setting) with students who have only studied 'at-home' (L1 setting only). By means of a multiple-choice translation test, the two groups were compared with respect to their correct and incorrect use of *-le*. The authors show that the 'at-home' group displayed error patterns consistent with the predicted L1 transfer effect (more incorrect uses of *-le*), while the 'study-abroad' group performed more like native speakers.

The topic of Jin's paper "Ultimate L2 Acquisition of the Chinese BA Construction: Two Case Studies" is a well-studied speciality of Chinese grammar, the *ba* construction, which involves the pattern S + *ba* + OV corresponding to ordinary SVO sentences, cf. (3)-(4).

(3) Wo ba men guan le.   (S + *ba* + OV)
    I BA door close ASP
    'I closed the door.'

(4) Wo guan le men.   (SVO)
    I close ASP door
    'I closed the door.'

As Huang et al. (2009: 153) note, "[t]he basic facts about *ba* are deceptively simple". The construction is governed by a complex set of conditions; for instance, the NP following *ba* must be understood as 'affected', and it cannot be a nonspecific indefinite. In view of its uniqueness and subtle complexities, the construction makes an interesting object for L2A investigation. While previous studies have focussed on the early stages of the acquisition of *ba*, Jin's goal is to explore the ultimate attainment of L2 learners, i.e. the extent to which the complexities of *ba* are fully acquirable in L2A. She presents two case studies involving subjects with Norwegian L1, both of whom are highly fluent speakers who have arguably reached the final state of their learning. One of the subjects began learning Chinese in early childhood, while the other began in adulthood. This difference allows Jin to pose a second question, namely, whether the age of onset of L2A affects the final outcome. Jin obtains clear answers to both questions:

certain aspects of the *ba* construction were not acquired by the subject who began learning Chinese in adulthood, whereas all aspects tested were acquired by the subject who began the learning process in childhood. Whether these results will be replicated in further studies remains to be seen.

Like Jin's paper, most of the contributions to this volume deal with matters that have hardly begun to be investigated properly and hence end with open questions – an invitation to continuing research.

## Acknowledgements

Both the 2009 workshop and the publication of the present book were supported by *the Globalization Programme* at NTNU, more specifically by the focus area *Intercultural Dynamics: Communication, Responsibility and Development* (formerly called *Cultural Translation*). We are deeply grateful for this support; in fact, neither the workshop nor the book would have come into existence without it.

We would also like to thank the authors, and Heidi Brøseth (NTNU), Francesca Del Gobbo (University of California, Irvine), Paul Law (City University of Hong Kong), Peppina Lee (City University of Hong Kong), Mila Vulchanova (NTNU), Ben Au Yeung (Chinese University of Hong Kong), and Xiaolu Yang (Tsinghua University), for their valuable help in preparing this volume.

## References

Abney, S. 1987. The English Noun Phrase in its Sentential Aspect. PhD., MIT.
Åfarli, T.A. & F. Jin. 2008. *Comparative Grammar and Language Acquisition in the Age of Globalization: Norwegian and Chinese*. Trondheim: Tapir.
Alexiadou, A., L. Haegeman & M. Stavrou. 2007. *Noun Phrase in the Generative Perspective*. Mouton de Gruyter, Berlin.
Bošković, Željko. 2008. What will you have, DP or NP? In: Proceedings of the North East Linguistic Society 37. GLSA, University of Massachusetts, Amherst. 101-114.
Cheng, Lisa & Rint Sybesma. 1999. Bare and not-so-bare nouns and the structure of NP. *Linguistic Inquiry* 30:4. 509-542.
Gärtner, Hans-Martin. 2001. Are there V2 relative clauses in German? *Journal of Comparative Germanic Linguistics 3*, 97-141.
Hu, Jianhua, Haihua Pan, & Liejiong Xu. 2001. Is there a finite vs. nonfinite distinction in Chinese? *Linguistics*, 39. 1117-1148.
Huang, C.-T. James. 1987. Existential sentences in Chinese and (in)definiteness. In: E. Reuland & A. ter Meulen (eds.) *The Representation of (In)definiteness*. MIT Press, Cambridge Mass. 226-253.

Huang, C.-T. James, Y.-H. Audrey Li & Yafei Li. 2009. *The Syntax of Chinese*. Cambridge: Cambridge University Press.

Hyams, Nina. 2006. Aspect matters. In K. Deen, J. Nomura, B. Schulz, & B. Schwartz (eds.) Proceedings of the Inaugural Conference on Generative Approaches to Language Acquisition – North America (GALANA). University of Connecticut Occasional Papers in Linguistics 4. 1-18.

Li, Charles. & Sandra Thompson. 1981. *Mandarin Chinese: a functional reference grammar.* University of California Press, Berkeley/Los Angeles.

Pereltsvaig, Aysa. 2007 The Universality of DP: a view from Russian. *Studia Linguistica* 61, 59–94.

Schafer, R. and J. de Villiers. 2000. Imagining Articles: What a and the can tell us about the emergence of DP. In S.C. Howell, S.A. Fish and T. Keith-Lucas (eds.), BUCLD 24 Proceedings, 609-620. Somerville, MA: Cascadilla Press.

Sio, Ut-Seong Joanna. 2006. Modification and reference in the Chinese Nominal. Doctoral dissertation, University of Leiden.

Email: christopher.wilder@hf.ntnu.no , tor.aafarli@ntnu.no

# The syntax of [+human] terms in Cantonese[1]

Joanna Ut-seong Sio
*Hong Kong Baptist University*

## 1. Introduction

Two signature properties of Chinese nominals are the lack of articles and the use of classifiers. The former is the impetus for the debate whether a Determiner Phrase (DP) (Abney 1987) should be postulated for Chinese. DP is the locus of referential properties. Even without such a layer, referential properties have to be encoded somehow. It has been proposed that the Classifier Phrase (ClP) in Chinese takes up the deictic function of the DP layer (Cheng & Sybesma 1999). Assuming that referential properties are encoded in a syntactic projection, whether there is DP in Chinese or ClP is its functional equivalent hinges on whether we can find referential nominal expressions that lack ClP. In this paper, we argue that such nominals do exist.

In Cantonese, there is a nominal element *AA*, which only appears with [+human] nouns, namely, common nouns (1a), kinship terms (1b) and proper names (1c).[2,3,4]

(1) a. aa sigei      (AA driver)
    b. aa sailou     (AA younger brother)
    c. aa ming-jan   (AA Ming-Jan)

The element *aa* has received very little attention in the literature. Lyons (1999:153) assumes that *aa* is a vocative marker, on a par with the Albanian *o*, the Egyptian

---

[1] The research study reported here was carried out within the context of Sze-Wing Tang's project 'A comparative study of definiteness in Chinese dialects' (General Research Fund, Hong Kong Research Grants Council, PolyU5476/06H). I am grateful to comments from the anonymous reviewers. All remaining mistakes are mine.
[2] By [+human] we refer to nouns the references of which are human beings.
[3] Phrases with *aa* often give an air of informality.
[4] *Aa* is not compatible with pronouns.

Arabic *ya*, etc. However, phrases with *aa* can also be used designatively, as shown in (2), showing that *aa* cannot be a vocative marker.

(2)  aa sailou  heoi-zo  bin le?
     AA younger brother go-ASP where SFP[5]
     "Where did (our) younger brother go?"

Yip (1992) treats *aa* as an infix inserted to satisfy an iambic foot template: [*aa* σ], a language specific requirement for Cantonese when a familiar human term is monosyllabic. This phonological insertion account of *aa* seems promising at first sight. Monosyllabic proper names and kinship terms are not used on their own. They either undergo reduplication or *aa* has to be added.[6] This supports the existence of an iambic template for [+human] familiar terms.

(3)  a.  Proper names (reduplication): *man-man, wai-wai*
     b.  Proper names (with *aa*): *aa man, aa wai*
     c.  Kinship terms (reduplication): *ba-ba* (father), *ma-ma* (mother)
     d.  Kinship terms (with *aa*): *aa ba* (father), *aa ma* (mother)

However, *aa* can also be followed by familiar human terms (i.e. proper names and kinship terms) containing more than one syllable:

(4)  a.  aa Pittaa   (AA Peter)
     b.  aa go-go    (AA older brother)

In (4), both nouns that *aa* attaches to are already disyllabic. If *aa* is inserted for prosodic reason, it is unclear why *aa* is allowed in (4). This suggests that *aa* does not always form an iambic foot with the following noun. The fact that *aa* sometimes seems to function as a template filler while sometimes not indicates that *aa*-nominals do not form a homogenous group (Sio & Tang 2008).

Other than the heterogeneous status of *aa*-nominals, the categorical status of *aa* is another knot to be untied. *Aa* has no substantial semantic content and its meaning is only "complete" when taking its "complement" (i.e. the [+human] noun) into consideration. This suggests that *aa* is a functional element. However, at least at first

---

5  SFP stands for Sentence Final Particle.
6  For men at least, another possibility is to add *lou* 'old' in front of a monosyllabic surname, e.g. *lou can* '(lit.) old Chan'.

sight, *aa* does not seem to belong to any of the regular nominal functional categories in the Chinese nominal domain (e.g. classifiers, numerals, quantifiers, etc.).

To recapitulate, the brief overview above uncovers two interesting issues regarding *aa*: (i) *aa*-nominals do not form a homogenous group; (ii) it is unclear what kind of functional element *aa* is.

The goal of this paper is to investigate the syntactic status of the Cantonese *aa* and its theoretical implication on Chinese nominal structures. We argue that *aa* is a D element taking a [+human] NP directly as its complement, thus providing support for the postulation of DP in Chinese.

(5)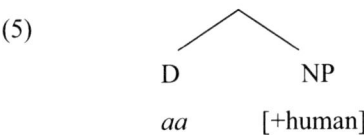
      D         NP
      *aa*      [+human]

The paper is organised in the following manner. In section 2, we present the observations in Sio & Tang (2008), arguing that there are two types of *aa*. One (*aa1*) is part of a lexical item while the other one (*aa2*) is part of syntax. In section 3, we argue that *aa2* is a D head directly selecting an NP as its complement. We conclude the paper in section 4.

## 2. Two types of *aa*

Sio & Tang (2008) observe that the properties of *aa*-nominals are sensitive to the number of syllables of the noun *aa* attaches to. They observe two differences between [*aa* σ] nominals (henceforth disyllabic *aa*-nominals) and [*aa* σ σ…] nominals (henceforth multisyllabic *aa*-nominals). The first difference has to do with possessor reference of kinship terms (KTs). Consider the sentences below:

(6) a. Pittaa joek-zo          aa-mui          heoi sik-faan.
Peter make appointment-ASP AA-younger sister go eat-rice
'Peter is meeting his younger sister / the speaker's younger sister for a meal.'
b. Pittaa joek-zo          aa-saimui       heoi sik-faan
Peter make appointment- ASP AA -younger sister go eat-rice
'Peter is meeting the speaker's younger sister for a meal.'

c. Pittaa joek-zo saimui heoi sik-faan.
   Peter make appointment-ASP younger sister go eat-rice
   'Peter is meeting his younger sister / the speaker's younger sister for a meal.'

The possessor reference variation is summarized in the table below:

(7)

| Form | | Possessor reference possibilities |
|---|---|---|
| (a) *aa-mui* | [aa σ] | the subject's younger sister or the speaker's younger sister |
| (b) *aa-saimui* | [aa σ σ...] | the speaker's younger sister |
| (c) *sai-mui* | [bare KT] | the subject's younger sister or the speaker's younger sister |

The possessor reference possibility in the above examples indicates that disyllabic *aa*-nominals behave like bare kinship terms while multisyllabic *aa*-nominals don't.

The second difference has to do with the abilities for kinship terms to act as predicates. Just like bare kinship terms, disyllabic *aa*-nominals with kinship terms can act as predicates while multisyllabic *aa*-nominals with kinship terms cannot. This is illustrated below:

(8) ngo dong keoi aa-mui gam gaa
    1SG treat 3 SG AA-younger sister like-that SFP
    'I treat her like a younger sister.'

(9) ?? ngo dong keoi aa-saimui gam gaa
    1SG treat 3SG AA-younger sister like-that SFP
    Intended reading: 'I treat her like a younger sister.'

(10) ngo dong keoi saimui gam gaa
     1SG treat 3SG younger sister like-that SFP
     'I treat her like a younger sister.'

(11)

| Form | | Predicate? |
|---|---|---|
| (a) *aa-mui* | [aa σ] | YES |
| (b) *aa-saimui* | [aa σ σ...] | NO |
| (c) *sai-mui* | [bare KT] | YES |

Again, it shows that disyllabic *aa*-nominals are like bare kinship terms while multisyllabic *aa*- nominals have different properties.

Based on the above observation, Sio & Tang (2008) conclude that there are two types of *aa*-nominals. In particular, *aa* in disyllabic *aa*-nominals is indeed a prosodic template filler in the sense of Yip (1992). We will refer to it as *aa1*. It is part of the lexical item, as shown in (13). It does not affect the grammatical properties of the noun it attaches to. As a result, disyllabic *aa*-nominals behave like bare nouns, (12).

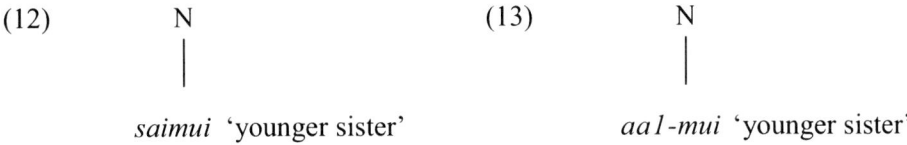

(12)    N
         |
     *saimui* 'younger sister'

(13)    N
         |
     *aa1-mui* 'younger sister'

*Aa* in multisyllabic *aa*-nominals is, however, not a template filler. It alters the grammatical properties of the noun it attaches to. We will call it *aa2*. We will discuss its grammatical properties in the next section, which would in turn motivate its syntactic treatment.

## 3. *Aa2*

In this section, we present a syntactic analysis of *aa2*. We argue that *aa2* is base-generated in D and selects an NP directly as its complement. We will provide empirical evidence to show that firstly whenever *aa2* is attached to a noun, the resulting phrase is rigidly referential. This indicates that *aa2* is related to referential properties. We will then argue that *aa2*-phrases do not contain a Classifier Phrase. The combination of the two will argue positively for a DP projection in Cantonese.

### 3.1 *The referential property of* aa2- *phrases*

*Aa2* can be attached to common nouns, kinship terms and proper names. Example (1) is repeated here as (14):

(14) a.  aa sigei         (AA driver)
     b.  aa sailou        (AA younger brother)
     c.  aa ming-jan      (AA Ming-Jan)

We will discuss each type of nouns in turn. We will begin with common nouns. Generally, Chinese only allows definite subjects. Bare common nouns in Cantonese cannot have a definite reading (Cheng & Sybesma 1999) and thus are banned from the subject position.[7]

(15) * saufong-jyun   ci-dou
      sales person    late
      Intended reading: 'The sales person is late.'

When *aa2* is added to the [+human] common noun in (15), the resulting expression is definite and can then be used in the subject position.

(16) aa-saufong-jyun ci-dou
     AA-sales person late
     'The sales person is late.'

The translation of (16) is not exactly accurate as even though *aa*-common nouns have a definite reading, the reading is not simply 'the *common noun*' ('the sales person' in the above case). To see the difference, consider the following sentences:

(17) I went to the new corner shop yesterday…

(18) a.  The sales person was very pretty.
     b.  go saufong-jyun hou leng gaa
         CL sales person very pretty SFP
     c.  ??aa saufong-jyun hou leng gaa
         AA sales person very pretty SFP

Consider the situation set up in (17) with (18a) as a follow-up sentence. In such a situation, even though the hearer probably cannot identify the sales person, a definite noun phrase can still be licensed by association with the corner shop (see Lyons 1999). In this setting, only (18b), but not (18c), would be a natural corresponding Cantonese follow-up sentence. In (18b), the [Cl-N] noun phrase in the

---

7   Common nouns can appear in the subject position if the intended reading is a generic one.

subject position has a definite reading. The subject *aa2*-common noun in (18c) also has a definite reading, The inappropriateness of (18c) indicates that *aa2*-common nouns are not simple definite noun phrases. *Aa-saufong-jyun* can only be used naturally in a setting where it points rigidly to a particular person. Consider the following sentence:

(19) ngo gamjat jau gin-dou aa saufong-jyun
1SG today again see-ASP AA sales person
'I saw "sales person" again today.'

Example (19) would be appropriate in a setting where both the speaker and the hearer can recognise a particular sales person but they don't know his/her name. Then, they can use *aa-saufong-jyun* 'aa sales person' to refer to that particular sales person they have in mind. Furthermore, it has to be the case there is only one sales person that they are referring to as *aa-saufong-jyun* 'aa sales person'. The reference of *aa-saufong-jyun* 'aa sales person' cannot fluctuate with the context. It has to refer to the same person across contexts. In this sense, *aa2*-common nouns have a rigidly designating reading, like the interpretation of proper names.

Now, we move on to the differences between bare kinship terms and *aa2*-kinship terms. Both bare kinship terms and *aa2*-kinship terms can have a definite reading:

(20) saimui / aa saimui                    hai bin le?
     younger sister/AA younger sister      be.at where QP
     'Where is (our) younger sister?'

Both *saimui* and *aa-saimui* in (20) refer rigidly to the speaker's and the hearer's younger sister. Any previous mentioning of the reference is not necessary for the use of *saimui* or *aa-saimui* in the above example, indicating that they are not simple definite nominal expressions. Both of them are interpreted like proper names, just like *aa2*-common nouns.

Bare kinship terms, however, can also have an indefinite reading while *aa2*-kinship terms cannot.

(21) a.  ngo jau saam go saimui
         1SG have three CL younger sister
         'I have three younger sisters.'
     b.  *ngo jau saam go    aa    saimui
         1SG have three CL   AA    younger sister
         Intended reading: 'I have three younger sisters.'

This shows that *aa2*-kinship terms are rigidly referential. They are always interpreted like proper names.

As for proper names, even though proper names have rigid designation, it is still possible to coerce a proper name into having a common noun reading. Imagine a situation where three men named Peter are in a room. The following sentence could be used to describe the situation:

(22)  fong-japmin jau saam go Pittaa
      room-inside have three CL Peter
      'There are three Peters in the room.'

When *aa2* is added to the proper name, coercion becomes impossible:

(23)  * fong-japmin jau saam go aa Pittaa
      room-inside have three CL AA Peter
      Intended reading: 'There are three Peters in the room.'

The above observations can be summarized as follows. Common nouns are always indefinite. Kinship terms can have either a definite or an indefinite reading. Once *aa2* is added, the resulting phrase is always definite and has rigid designation, like the interpretation of proper names. Proper names generally have rigid designation but can be coerced into having a common noun reading. However, once *aa2* is added, coercion is no longer possible. The above indicates that once *aa2* is added to a [+human] noun, the resulting phrase is *always* rigidly designating.

## 3.2 The lack of a Classifier Phrase

It has been proposed that the Classifier Phrase (ClP) in Chinese takes up some of the functions of D, among them the deictic function (Cheng & Sybesma 1999). Given that *aa2* always gives rise to rigid designation, it is a potential candidate to head the Classifier Phrase. *Aa2* poses semantic selection, i.e. [+human], on the following noun. Assuming that selection is done via a head-complement structure, this means *aa2* directly selects the head noun. Chinese NPs are generally assumed to be immediately dominated by the Classifier Phrase, which would fit the structural requirement for selection. If *aa2* heads the Classifier Phrase, it would also explain why the classifier is not compatible with phrases with *aa2*, as illustrated below:

(24) a.  ngo go saimui
         1SG CL younger sister
         'my younger sister'
     b.  *ngo go aa      saimui
         1SG CL AA       younger sister
         Intended reading: 'my younger sister'

Despite the above, we have good reasons to believe that *aa2* does not head the Classifier Phrase. The selection for [+human] noun and the incompatibility with the classifier can be explained in another way.

Classifiers are generally assumed to be related to division/partition and counting (Sybesma 2007). *Aa2*, however, is unrelated to any of these functions. This is the first reason why we think it is unlikely for *aa2* to be base-generated in the classifier head. Another reason for arguing against *aa2* being base-generated in the classifier head is not as straightforward. It has to do with modification. In brief, modifiers in Cantonese are merged at the level of the Classifier Phrase (Arsenijevic & Sio 2009). *Aa2*-phrases resist modification, suggesting the absence of the Classifier Phrase. We present the detailed argument below.

Common nouns, kinship terms and proper names can be modified by modifiers. However, once *aa2* is added the noun, modification is no longer possible. The underlined portion in each of the following examples is the modifier. The final element of the modifier, *ge*, is a modification marker. *Ge* is obligatory in modification. [8]

(25) <u>hou leng ge</u> saufong-jyun        / *aa saufong-jyun
     very pretty GE sales person            / AA sales person

(26) <u>hou leng ge</u> saimui              / *aa saimui
     very pretty GE younger sister          / AA younger sister

(27) <u>hou leng ge</u> Pittaa              / *aa Pittaa
     very pretty GE Peter                   / AA Peter

Arsenijevic & Sio (2009) argue that the modification marker *ge* merges with the head of the Classifier Phrase, as both of them have a partitive feature. They give two pieces of evidence, one semantic, one syntactic. The semantic argument goes

---

8   Some simple adjectives can be used to modify nouns without the presence of *ge*. For discussion, see Sio (2006).

as follows. All nouns come out of the lexicon with the denotation of mass (Borer 2005). When a classifier is in the Cl head, it partitions the mass based on the unit specified by the classifier. With modifiers, Arsenijevic & Sio (2009) suggests that there is also partition but the effect is slightly different. The modifier divides the denotation of the NP into two parts, one of which has the property specified by the modifier, and the other does not. The modifier then restricts the predicate of the nominal expression to only the former part, yielding an effect of portioning out a part of the denotation that fits the modified expression. In this sense, both classifiers and modifiers are related to partition. As modifiers in Cantonese are consistently marked by the modification marker *ge*, Arsenijevic & Sio (2009) argue that just like classifiers, *ge* also has a partitive feature.

Arsenijevic & Sio (2009) also provide a piece of syntactic evidence to argue for the similarities between *ge* and classifiers. They argue that they both contain a partitive feature. The evidence comes from Noun Phrase Ellipsis (NPE). In Cantonese, both *ge* and the classifier can license NPE (see also Cheng & Sybesma 2009 for similar discussion). This is illustrated below:

(28) nei go saam bun syu bei     ngo go saam bun syu hou tai
     2SG that three CL book compare 1SG that three CL book good read
     (the original sentence)
     'Your three books are more interesting than my three books.'

(29) *nei go saam bun syu bei     ngo go    hou tai
     2SG that three CL book compare 1SG that good read
     (ellipsis after the demonstrative)

(30) *nei go saam bun syu bei     ngo go saam    hou tai
     2SG that three CL book compare 1SG that three   good read
     (ellipsis after the numeral)

(31) nei go saam bun syu bei     ngo go saam bun  hou tai
     2SG that threeCL book compare 1SG that three CL  good read
     (ellipsis after the classifier)

(28) is the original sentence. Sentence (29), (30) and (31) are sentences with different portions of the nominal containing the NP elided. All intended to mean 'your three books are more interesting than my three books'. As shown above, a classifier, but not other nominal elements (demonstrative, numeral), can license NP ellipsis. Interestingly, *ge* can also license NPE, as illustrated below:

(32) nei ge syu    bei          ngo ge hou tai
     2SG GE book compare 1SG GE good read
     'Your books are more interesting than mine.'

Based on their similar ability in licensing NPE, Arsenijevic & Sio (2009) argue that classifiers and *ge* contain the same feature. In particular, they argue that both the classifier and *ge* have a partitive feature, which has been proposed to license NPE (Alexiadou & Gengel 2008). Arsenijevic & Sio (2009) propose that in structure-building, *ge* merges with the classifier head, as indicated below:

(33)

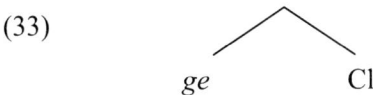

Note that modification is also possible when an overt classifier is not present. In (25), (26) and (27), there are no overt classifier and yet modification is possible. This indicates that as long as a Classifier Phrase is present, *ge* can be merged, even with a covert classifier head. Assuming the above, the impossibility of modification for *aa2*-phrases indicates the absence of the Classifier Phrase.

To recapitulate, *aa2* lacks semantic content and *aa2*-phrases are rigidly referential. These two together indicate that *aa2* should head a functional projection that is related to referential properties. If there is a projection dedicated to the encoding of referential properties, i.e. a Determiner Phrase (DP), *aa2* should head such a projection. In Chinese, the presence of a DP layer is controversial due to the lack of articles. Instead of postulating a layer that is most of the time invisible, it has been proposed that the Classifier Phrase (ClP) in Chinese takes care of the deictic function that DP does in languages with articles (Cheng & Sybesma 1999). Our treatment of *aa2*, if correct, shows that there are referential nominals that lack a ClP. This argues against having ClP as the locus of referential properties and supports the presence of a Determiner Phrase in the Chinese nominal. We propose the following structure for *aa2*-phrases:

(34)

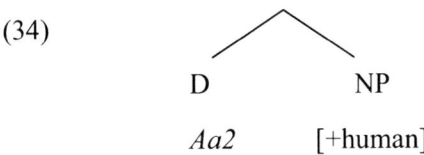

In (34), D takes NP directly as its complement, facilitating the semantic selection of [+human] nouns. As there is no Classifier Phrase, the structure is naturally incompatible with classifiers, explaining the ungrammaticality of (24b), partially repeated here as (35):

(35) *ngo go aa saimui
1SG CL AA younger sister
Intended reading: 'my younger sister'

As for *aa1*, since it is merely a prosodic template filler for familiar human terms and thus part of the lexical item, *aa1*-nominals are just like bare nouns. As expected, both bare kinship terms and *aa1*-kinship terms are compatible with classifiers:

(36) a.   ngo go saimui
          1SG CL younger sister
          'my younger sister'
     b.   ngo go aa mui
          1SG CL AA younger sister
          'my younger sister'

The possessums in (36a) and (36b) have the following structure:

(37)
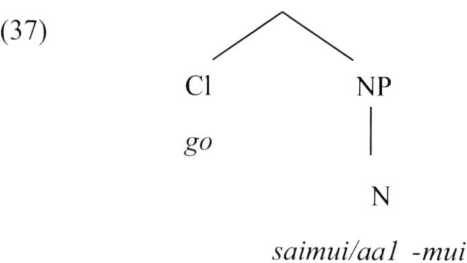

## 4. Conclusion

In this paper, we have proposed an analysis for the Cantonese *aa*, an element that selects for [+human] nouns. There are two types of *aa* in Cantonese (Sio & Tang 2008). *Aa1* is a prosodic template filler (Yip 1992), added to [+human] nouns to form an iambic template. *Aa2*, on the other hand, is part of syntax. We argue that it is base-generated in D. It takes an NP directly as its complement. *Aa1*-nominals behave no differently from a regular bare noun and are compatible with classifiers. *Aa2*-nominals are always rigidly designating and are resistant to modification. Assuming that modifiers are merged at the level of the classifier,

(Arsenijevic & Sio 2009), this indicates the lack of a Classifier Phrase. The lack of a classifier projection will naturally explain why *aa2*-phrases are incompatible with classifiers. This analysis, if correct, provides support for the presence of a DP layer in Chinese.

# References

Abney, Steven. 1987. The English noun phrase in its sentential ASPect. MA: MIT dissertation.

Alexiadou, Artemis & Gengel, Kirsten. 2008. NP ellipsis without focus movement/projections: the role of Classifiers. Universität Stuttgart manuscript.

Arsenijevic, Boban & Joanna Ut-Seong Sio. 2009. 'Mediating Merge: evidence from Cantonese'. Presented in the Seventh Glow in Asia Conference, Hyderabad, India.

Borer, Hagit. 2005. *Structuring Sense I: In name only*. Oxford: Oxford University Press.

Cheng, Lisa & Rint Sybesma. 1999. Bare and not-so-bare nouns and the structure of NP. *Linguistic Inquiry* 30:4. 509-542.

Cheng, Lisa & Rint Sybesma. 2009. De as an underspecified classifier: first explorations. *Yǔyánxué lùncóng* 39. 125-156.

Lyons, Christopher. 1999. *Definiteness*. Cambridge, UK: Cambridge University Press.

Sio, Joanna U.-S. 2006. Modification and reference in the Chinese nominal. Doctoral dissertation, Universiteit Leiden.

Sio, Joanna U.-S. & Sze-Wing Tang. 2008. The Cantonese aa. Paper presented at the 13th International Conference on Cantonese and Yue Dialects. City University of Hong Kong, Hong Kong.

Sybesma, Rint. 2007. Běifāng fāngyán hé Yuèyu zhōng míngcí de kěshubiāojì (Markers of countability on the noun in Mandarin and Cantonese)". *Yǔyánxué lùncóng* 35. 234-245.

Yip, Moira. 1992. Prosodic Morphology in Four Chinese Dialects. *Journal of East Asian Linguistics*. 1:1. 1-36.

Email: neosome@gmail.com

# The syntax of presentative sentences in Norwegian and Mandarin Chinese: Toward a comparative analysis?

Tor A. Åfarli & Fufen Jin
*Norwegian University of Science and Technology (NTNU)*

## 1. Introduction[1]

This paper was originally motivated by an observation that there seem to exist certain striking similarities between presentative sentences in Norwegian and their counterparts in Mandarin Chinese, and by the hope that the prospects for a nice comparative analysis therefore were good. However, after taking several closer looks at the data we have realized that the differences are at least as striking as the similarities, and it has dawned on us that the picture is more complicated than we thought originally. Still, the topic of presentative sentences in the two languages is very intriguing, and even more so now when the hopes for a seamless comparative analysis appear to be dashed. Therefore, we will try in this paper to penetrate into this topic in a more exploratory manner, seeking to identify research problems and putting forth potentially fruitful hypotheses, rather than definite analyses. We still hope that our examination may contribute to a more developed comparative analysis of presentative sentences in the two languages in the future.

## 2. Presentative verbs and sentences in Chinese and Norwegian

Presentative sentences, which is the term used by Li & Thompson (1981: 509), are referred to as existential sentences in Huang (1987: 226) and as existential/presentative sentences in Li (1990: 134). This sentence type "performs the function of introducing into a discourse a noun phrase naming an entity" (Li & Thompson 1981: 509). The noun phrase is typically indefinite (representing new information), and it typically occurs in a position that seems to be an object position, i.e. the postverbal position both in Norwegian and Chinese.

---

[1] We would like to thank Francesca Del Gobbo for useful comments to a previous version of this article. Shortcomings are of course our own responsibility.

As a point of departure for the syntactic analysis, (1) displays the general template for presentative (existential) sentences in Chinese, given in Huang (1987: 226). To some degree, this linear structure also seems to be relevant for Norwegian presentative sentences.

(1) Basic structure of presentative (existential) sentences:

    (NP) V NP (XP)
     1   2  3   4

In Huang's words: "Position 1 is the position of the subject, and position 3 that of the NP whose existence is being asserted. The phrase in position 4 is an expression of predication, generally a descriptive clause or phrase, semantically associated with the NP in position 3."

Particular semantic classes of lexical verbs occur in presentative sentences in Chinese. According to Li (1990: 134) these are verbs of presence, appearance, and disappearance, cf. (2) (Li's examples).

(2)   a.  *Presence*: you 'have', zhan 'stand', zuo 'sit', tang 'lie', gua 'hang', fang 'place', etc.
    b.  *Appearance*: lai 'come', chu 'come out', qi 'emerge', xia 'fall', jin 'enter', dao 'arrive', etc.
    c.  *Disappearance*: qu 'go', si 'die', pao 'run', tao 'escape', guo 'pass', etc.

Li & Thompson (1981) distinguishes between existential/positional verbs (i.e. Li's presence verbs) on the one hand, and verbs of motion (i.e. Li's appearance and disappearance verbs), on the other. Among the presence/existential/positional verbs, Li & Thompson (1981) singles out *you* 'have' for special treatment. This is also done in Huang (1987), who distinguishes between four types of verbs that can occur in presentative (his existential) sentences:

(3)   a.  *you* 'have'; the closest counterpart to "there be"-sentences
    b.  verbs of appearance/disappearance
    c.  locative verbs (Li's presence verbs, except *you* 'have')
    d.  verbs expressing existence of event or experience

Generally, cognates of the same verbs that occur in Chinese presentative sentences, also occur in presentative sentences in Norwegian. Disregarding Huang's type

(3d) (because it has no presentative counterpart in Norwegian), there are three interesting classes of verbs that occur in presentative sentences both in Norwegian and Chinese, shown in (4).[2]

(4) a. The *be*-type: *vere* 'be' in Norwegian and *you* 'have'/'exist' in Chinese.
b. Motion verbs (appearance/disappearance verbs), e.g. *komme* 'come' in Norwegian and *lai* 'come' in Chinese.
c. Position verbs (Huang's locative verbs), e.g. *ligge* 'lie' in Norwegian and *tang* 'lie' in Chinese.

Generally, it seems that Norwegian is a little more permissive than Chinese in allowing motion and position verbs to occur in presentative sentences, but this difference of frequency will not concern us here.

## 3. The structure of presentative sentences in Chinese and Norwegian

Li (1990: 134) suggests that presentative verbs are ergative verbs, i.e. verbs that do not assign any external role, only an internal one. Thus, the phrase structure shown in (5) could be appropriate for presentative verbs.

(5)
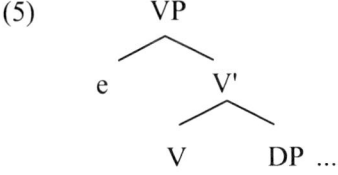

In fact, the structure in (5) neatly seems to fit all three classes of presentative verbs in Norwegian, as indicated by the examples in (6), where *ein elg* 'a moose' is the postverbal DP (see also Åfarli & Eide 2003: Chapter 15). Notice that an expletive subject (*det* 'it') must fill the semantically empty subject position in Norwegian.

---

2  Notice that all Norwegian data are given in the *Nynorsk* written standard.

(6) a. Det er ein elg under treet.
 there is a moose under tree-the
 b. Det kom ein elg (frå under treet).
 there came a moose (from under tree-the).
 c. Det låg ein elg under treet.
 there lay a moose under tree-the

Also, as expected given the existence of an empty subject position, the postverbal DP may move to fill that position, thus creating non-presentative counterparts to each of the example sentences in (6). See (7).

(7) a. Elgen er under treet.
 moose-the is under tree-the
 b. Elgen kom (frå under treet).
 moose-the came (from under tree-the).
 c. Elgen låg under treet.
 moose-the lay under tree-the

Thus, it seems that presentative sentences of all three types show a common basic structure in Norwegian.

Now, the situation may seem to be similar in Chinese at first sight, as e.g. indicated by the alternation shown in (8), with a motion verb (from Li 1990: 136). However, a closer look reveals a more complicated pattern, as we will see later.

(8) a. Lai-le keren.
 (there) came (some) guests
 b. Keren lai-le.
 (the) guests came

In what follows, we shall concentrate on the *be*-type verbs and motion verbs. This is due to space limitations, and these are also the two verb types that strike us as the most interesting ones for a comparison between Norwegian and Chinese. Of course, this is not to say that position verbs are not intriguing, and in particular a comparison between sentences with position verbs and *be*-type sentences would be interesting, but we will leave this for future work.

We shall start with an examination of the *be*-type sentences (*you*-sentences in Chinese) in section 4, turning to presentative sentences with motion verbs (*lai*-sentences in Chinese) in section 5. Throughout, we will put our main emphasis on Chinese, but we will also keep an eye on Norwegian in order to highlight both differences and similarities between the two languages. For a useful general examination of the syntax of Chinese, see Huang et al. (2009).

## 4. Presentative *be*-type sentences

### 4.1 Chinese data

According to Li & Thompson (1981: 510), presentative *you*-sentences always signal the existence of the referent of the presented noun phrase at some locus.

Taking into account the verb, the presented DP and the locus XP, Li & Thompson further claim that there are basically three different word orders shown by *you*-sentences: *you+DP+PP*, *PP+you+DP*, and *locus-DP+you+DP*. All possible permutation patterns are shown in (9) and (10), where (9) shows patterns with a locus PP, and (10) shows patterns with a locus DP-subject. As already suggested, only three of the patterns correspond to grammatical sentences, namely (9a), (9e), and (10e).

(9) a.  you DP PP
    b.  * DP you PP
    c.  * DP PP you
    d.  * you PP DP
    e.  PP you DP
    f.  * PP DP you

(10) a.  * you DP locus-DP
     b.  * DP you locus-DP
     c.  * DP locus-DP you
     d.  * you locus-DP DP
     e.  locus-DP you DP
     f.  * locus-DP DP you

The grammatical patterns are exemplified in (11)-(13).

(11) Examples of (9a) *you DP PP*:
    a.    You yixie shu zai zhuozi-shang
         exist some books at desk-on
    b.    You yi-zhi gou zai yuanzi-li    (Li & Thompson 1981: 511)
         exist one-CL dog at yard-in

(12) Examples of (9e) *PP you DP*:
    a.    Zai zhuozi-shang you yixie shu
         at desk-on exist some books
    b.    Zai yuanzi-li you yi-zhi gou    (Li & Thompson 1981: 510)
         at yard-in exist one-CL dog

(13) Examples of (10e) *locus-DP you DP*:
    a.    Zhuozi-shang you yixie shu
         desk-on exist some books
    b.    Yuanzi-li you yi-zhi gou    (Li & Thompson 1981: 510)
         yard-in exist one-CL dog

## 4.2 Norwegian

Huang (1987: 226) says that *you*-sentences are the closest counterpart to English "there be"-sentences, thus also the closest counterpart to the corresponding Norwegian "det er"-sentences, see (14).

(14) Det er ein mann i gangen.
     there is a man in entrance-the

The structure here is the same as for (6a). Notice that the presence of an expletive subject indicates that the subject position is a dethematised position, which predicts that a postverbal DP can move to the subject position, resulting in (15a), cf. also (7a). (15b) is also possible, but slightly less natural for discourse reasons (an indefinite DP often sounds pragmatically awkward in initial position).

(15)    a.    Mannen er *t* i gangen.
             man-the is in entrance-the
      b.    Ein mann er *t* i gangen.
             a man is in entrance-the

There are strong reasons to believe that the postverbal DP+PP in (14) is a small clause. First, several linguists have argued that the corresponding sequence in presentative sentences in English and other languages is a small clause, see Sabbagh (2009: 676) and references cited there. Second, Nordgård (2002) argues extensively for a small clause analysis of the postverbal sequence in Norwegian presentative sentences like (6a) and (14).

For instance, according to the rules for anaphora in Norwegian, an anaphor must be part of a predicate that has the antecedent of the anaphor as its subject (Hellan 1988: 73-74). Thus, (16) indicates that the PP *i huset sitt* 'in house-the SELF-POSS' is a small clause predicate with the postverbal DP as its predication subject. This follows on Hellan's analysis, since the antecedent of the possessive anaphor *sitt* 'SELF-POSS' has to be the postverbal DP *ein mann* 'a man'.

(16) Det er ein mann i huset sitt.
    there is a man in house-the SELF-POSS

Therefore, a typical presentative *be*-sentence like (14) in Norwegian has the following postverbal structure (see also Hoekstra 1988):

(17)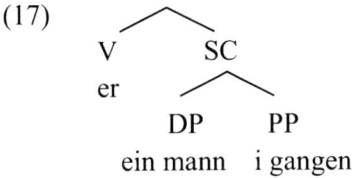

Notice however that the small clause predicate must be a locational predicate in Norwegian presentative *be*-sentences (as in English). Thus, (18) is ungrammatical. This is different from Chinese where the translation of (18) is grammatical. An analysis of this difference is beyond the scope of this paper, but see Wilder (this volume) or Del Gobbo (2010) for some illumination.

(18) *Det er ein mann sint.
    there is a man angry

Before we proceed, we will give a sketch of the basic structural representation of clauses that we assume both for Chinese and Norwegian, see (19).

(19) [ TOPIC ... [ SUBJECT ...[ MIDDLE FIELD [ V [ POSTVERBAL FIELD ]]]]]

The middle field is the position for sentential adverbials/adjuncts in Norwegian and for all adverbials/adjuncts in Chinese.

## 4.3 The structure of Chinese you-sentences

Is the structure of Norwegian *be*-type sentences a clue to the analysis of Chinese *you*-sentences? Consider first the patterns with a locus PP in (9), repeated below:

(9)  a.  you DP PP
     b.  * DP you PP
     c.  * DP PP you
     d.  * you PP DP
     e.  PP you DP
     f.  * PP DP you

Notice that (9a) seems to violate the so-called Postverbal Constraint (Sybesma 1999: 1) which says that a verb in Chinese may be followed by only one constituent, but, as argued by Sybesma, a postverbal small clause counts as one constituent for the Postverbal Constraint. Therefore, we suggest that (9a) has the same postverbal structure as e.g. (20) (from Sybesma 1999: 1), which by assumption contains a postverbal small clause.

(20) Wo fang-le yixie shu zai zhuozi-shang
     I put-LE some books at table-on

In other words, the adoption of a small clause analysis for the postverbal DP+PP sequence in (9a) would explain why there is an apparent violation of the Postverbal Constraint in such cases. We therefore suggest that the postverbal structure of (9a) constitutes a small clause, cf. (21), which is the same as in the corresponding example in Norwegian.

(21)
```
        /\
       V  SC
      you /\
         DP PP
```

It is not otherwise important to us that a small clause analysis is adopted, see e.g. Fang & Lin (2008) for an alternative analysis of *you*-sentences, but, given that the small clause analysis offers a straightforward solution to the seeming Postverbal Constraint violation, we will assume that the small clause analysis is correct.

A small clause analysis also explains why (9d) is ungrammatical. Here the postverbal sequence is PP+DP, which is not a well formed small clause word order in Chinese.

Now, the small clause subject DP can raise to the matrix subject position in Norwegian, producing structures like (7a) and (15a, b). However, judging from the ungrammaticality of (9b), this is impossible in Chinese. Why? One possible explanation is that a DP in the front position must be definite in Chinese, and that Chinese *you*-structures do not tolerate definite DPs. However, this is essentiallly a stipulation, so we will suggest another explanation.

What we want to suggest is that *you*-sentences, in contrast to Norwegian *be*-type sentences, do not have a dethematised matrix subject position, i.e. they have a thematic subject position. If that is the case, there is no possible landing-site for a raised small clause subject DP. This would explain why (9 b, c, f) are ungrammatical.

Evidence for the assumption that *you*-sentences have a thematic subject position is as follows. Huang (1987: 227) gives the example in (22) (his (7a)), with the structure *PP+(SU+)you+DP*. Notice that the two alternative translations are those given by Huang.

(22) Zai zheli (wo) you yi-ben shu.
　　 at here (I) have one-CL book
　　 'I have a book here' (or 'There is a book here')

We suggest that the PP is the topicalized small clause PP-predicate in (22), and further we suggest that in case the subject *wo* 'I' is left out, the sentence still contains a referential pro subject, which blocks raising of the small clause DP-subject.

Henne at al. (1977: 143) suggests that (23), which they translate as "he has money," is better rendered as "as for him, there is money" in order to capture "the basic existential relationship" implied.

(23) Ta you qian.
    he has money

We would like to suggest the following paraphrase: "As for him, he has money at/with himself," and similarly we would like to suggest the following paraphrase for (22) when *wo* 'I' is left out: "Concerning at here, someone has a book here." Generally, we suggest that the type (9a) should be paraphrased as follows (*mutatis mutandis*): "As for someone, this someone has something (DP) somewhere (PP)." Thus, even though it is perfectly natural in most cases to translate *you*-sentences with their existential counterparts in English or Norwegian, we forward as our hypothesis that Chinese *you*-sentences are always essentially possessive sentences, and in those cases where there is no overt subject, there is a pro possessor subject which is a semantically indefinite argument pro, which therefore blocks DP movement from below, notably excluding (9b, c, f). Notice that this means that the alternative 'there is' translation of (22) is strictly speaking never correct, even though it may give a very rough indication of the meaning of the version with an indefinite possessor pro subject.

Our hypothesis receives circumstantial support from Li & Thompson (1981) who remarks that the fact that Chinese *you*-sentences are sometimes translated as existentials (*be*) and sometimes as possessives (*have*) "should not keep us from seeing their essential similarity," cf. Li & Thompson (1981: 513). In both types, something is claimed to exist, the difference being "whether it is said to exist with respect to a place or to another entity" (ibid.). Accordingly, they offer two possible translations of an example sentence like (24) (their (16); notice that this sentence has a locus-DP as subject, see next section).

(24) Shujia-shang    you      yi-ge da zhanglang
     bookcase-on     exist    one-CL big cockroach

The two translations that they give are "There's a big cockroach on the boookcase" and "The bookcase has a big cockroach (on it)." The last alternative is a very close paraphrase of what we take to be the general structure of a *you*-sentence, whether it is translated as an existential (*be*) or a possessive (*have*).

Why is (9e) grammatical? (9e) is exemplifed by (22) (with *wo* 'I' left out). It is also exemplified by (25) (from Huang 1987: 227, his (7b)) with *wo* 'I' left out.

(25) Wo zai Taipei you yi-ge pengyou hen youqian.
I at Taipei have one-CL friend very rich

(22) and (25) show that the PP may be topicalized or occur in the middle field, i.e. in a "middle" adjunct position. In the absence of an overt subject, both analyses are open for (9e), it seems.

Notice that the small clause predicate is non-locative in (25). As mentioned at the end of section 4.2, this is quite common in Chinese, cf. also e.g. Huang (1987: 227), but in English and Norwegian *be*-type sentences must have a locative small clause predicate. As stated earlier, an analysis of this difference is beyond the scope of this paper.

## 4.4 Chinese *you*-sentences with a locus DP-subject

Now, consider Chinese *you*-sentences with a locus DP-subject, as seen in the type (10e). The complete permutation pattern given in (10) is repeated here.

(10) a.  * you DP locus-DP
     b.  * DP you locus-DP
     c.  * DP locus-DP you
     d.  * you locus-DP DP
     e.    locus-DP you DP
     f.  * locus-DP DP you

(13), repeated here, exemplifies the grammatical pattern (10e).

(13) Examples of (10e) *locus-DP you DP*:
     a.  Zhuozi-shang you yixie shu
         desk-on exist some books
     b.  Yuanzi-li you yi-zhi gou         (Li & Thompson 1981: 510)
         yard-in exist one-CL dog

First, we assume that such locus DPs are structural subjects, as argued in Li (1990: 137). The locus DP-subject in such cases is a so-called "unselected" subject. Lin (2001) explains the existence of unselected subjects by assuming a light verb analysis, where the unselected subject is the specifier, not of the main verb, but of an appropriate covert light verb, thus making the subject seem "unselected" by the main verb. We do not take a final stand on Lin's analysis, but a potential weakness of his analysis is that several types of covert light verbs must be postulated, corresponding to each type of the many types of unselected subject that

Lin (2001) identifies. A potential revision of Lin's analysis would be to assume that there is just one light verb, i.e. the familiar small v heading a vP, and that the "unselected" effect is a result of V not being raised to v in Chinese. In such an analysis, the different semantic types of unselected subjects would be derived from the conceptual semantics associated with the structure.

Is the locus-DP in (10e) raised from below? We will assume that it is not, since, as assumed in section 4.3, the subject position of *you* is not a dethematized position. What we would like to suggest is that the subject locus-DP should be analysed as a base-generated subject on a par with subject locus-DPs in English and Norwegian *swarm*-type verbs, see Salkoff (1983). The following is an example from Norwegian.

(26)  Lufta dirrar av varme.
      air-the vibrates from heat

We assume that the subject locus-DP is base-generated in place in such examples, the basic meaning being that the air has the property that it vibrates for some reason, where the reason is specified as the heat in the adjunct PP. Notice that the subject in (26) seems to be an "unselected" subject similar to unselected subjects in Chinese. We leave open the problem of how this should be analysed in Germanic, and to what extent a version of Lin's (2001) proposal could be brought to bear on Germanic *swarm*-type sentences with locus subjects.

As for the Chinese structure (10e), it is exemplified by (27), in addition to the corresponding examples in (13).

(27)  Zhuozi-shang you yi-ben shu.
      desk-on exist one-CL book

(27) should be paraphrased as follows: "The desk has a book on it." Notice that the subject locus-DP is the possessor here.

We assume that the small clause predicate (corresponding to *on it* in the paraphrase) is abstract in (27), but it is somehow "controlled" by the subject locus-DP. This is sketched in (28).

(28)  Locus-DP$_i$     you     [ DP  XP-pred$_i$ ]

This type of control is not unlike what we find in Norwegian inalienable constructions like (29).

(29) Han kasta Ola ein ball i magen.
    he threw Ola a ball in stomach-the

(29) can only be interpreted as (30).

(30) Han kasta ein ball i magen på Ola.
    he threw a ball in stomach-the of Ola

In other words, the stomach in (29) can only be Ola's stomach. One possible analysis of this is that *magen* 'the stomach' in (29) contains an abstract possessor element that is controlled by the indirect object *Ola* in (29). Thus, we hypothesise that Chinese structures like (28) are partly similar to the Norwegian inaleniable construction in (29).

Why are (10 a, b, c, d, f) ungrammatical? (10 a, b, d) are ungrammatical because the locus-DP, being a (matrix) subject, is too low in the structure (positioned to the right of *you*). (10 c, f) are ungrammatical because the "existential" DP cannot be a matrix subject, i.e. cannot occur preverbally, for reasons already explained. This is also another reason why (10b) is excluded.

In order to further elucidate our approach to the analysis of *you*-sentences, it is interesting to consider two examples given by Cheung et al. (1994: 64), see (31a, b), along with the translations they provide (in 31 a', b').

(31) a.   Women you san-ge laoshi.          (contains animate subject)
          we have three-CL teacher
    a'.   'We have three teachers.'
    b.    Zhongwen xi   you san-ge laoshi.   (contains inanimate subject)
          Chinese department have three-CL teacher
    b'.   'There are three teachers in the Chinese Department.'

They say that if the subject is animate, as in (31a), the appropriate interpretation is possessive, but when the subject is inanimate, as in (31b), the interpretation is existential. It seems to us that the animacy/inanimacy of the subject is irrelevant for the syntactic structure, which is the same in both examples. Our hypothesis is that the translation in (31a') best renders the basic structural meaning, and that the translation for (31b) is more appropriately given as "The Chinese Department has three teachers in it." Arad (1998: Chapter 5) advances a similar line of thought regarding psych predicates, which are often assumed to have special syntactic structure. She argues, contrary to standard analyses, that psychological and corresponding non-psychological verb phrases have parallel structures. Our claim regarding the possessive and existential interpretations of Chinese *you*-sentences is fully in line with Arad's general approach here, since we too assume a common underlying structure for the two interpretations under discussion.

Summarizing, we have given reasons to believe that both possessive and existential *you*-sentences are essentially of the possessive type. Thus, there are basically two types of structure, both with a possessive *you*, which may be glossed *HAS*, namely *Someone HAS something at/on some place* and *Some place HAS something at/on it*. A similar unified analysis of the two interpretations of *you*-sentences is in fact suggested in Lin (2008: 87).

## 5. Presentative motion sentences

### 5.1 Parallels and differences between Norwegian and Chinese

Presentative motion sentences are presentative sentences that contain verbs of appearance/disappearance, i.e. verbs of motion. A paradigmatic example is provided by verbs meaning 'come,' *komme* in Norwegian and *lai* in Chinese. As verbs that can occur in presentative sentences, this is a quite big class in Norwegian, but in Chinese fewer verbs seem to belong to this class. However, presentative motion verbs both in Norwegian and Chinese seem, at the outset, to exhibit strikingly similar syntactic behaviour (as observed in the beginning of this paper).

Consider the Norwegian motion verb *komme* 'come,' shown in (32).

(32) a. Det kom nokre gjester.
      there came some guests
   b. Gjestene kom.
      guests-the came

The corresponding sentences in Chinese are shown in (33) (cf. Li 1990: 136).

(33) a. Lai-le keren.
      came some guests
   b. Keren lai-le.
      (the) guests came

In the presentative a-versions there is of course a difference as to the obligatory presence of an expletive subject in Norwegian, and its obligatory absence in Chinese, but apart from that the examples seem to be parallel. The presented DP is postverbal and it is subject to the Definiteness Effect (DE). Also, the (non-presentative) b-versions indicate that the subject position is non-thematic, since the postverbal DP can move to that position in both languages. Also, this movement cancels the DE in both languages. A parallel analysis suggests itself whereby presentative motion verbs are analysed as unaccusative verbs in both languages, see (34) and (35); see also Li (1990: 134 ff.) for the analysis of Chinese.

(34)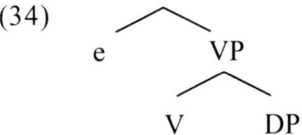

(35)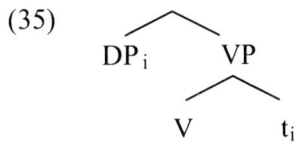

However, there are still some differences between the two languages. Notably, there is reason to believe that the complement of presentative motion verbs is a small clause in Norwegian, whereas that is not the case for Chinese presentative motion verbs. In Norwegian, evidence for a postverbal small clause is seen by considering the distribution of anaphora (see also section 4.2). Thus, like in the Norwegian *be*-sentences, an anaphor included in a locative XP in a presentative motion sentence can take the presented DP as its antecedent, cf. (36) where the possessive anaphor *sine* 'SELF-POSS' takes *nokre gjester* 'some guests' as its antecedent.

(36) Det kom [ nokre gjester i bilane sine ]
    there came some guests in cars-the SELF-POSS

This leads us to conclude that the presented DP and the locative PP constitute a small clause, as indicated by the bracketing.

As seen in (32a), the locus XP is, strictly speaking, not obligatory in Norwegian, but in fact, the example in (32a) is exceptional, because the vast majority of presentative motion sentences in Norwegian strongly prefer a locative XP in addition to the presented DP (Nordgård 2002). On the other hand, a locus XP in the corresponding position is bad in Chinese, so that (33a) is a representative example in Chinese. In fact, Li & Thompson (1981: 517) says that there is typically no locus mentioned with presentative motion verbs in Chinese. This indicates that there is an important structural difference between Norwegian presentative motion sentences and the corresponding sentences in Chinese, despite the apparent similarities.

We will now take a closer look at Chinese *lai*-sentences in order to try to characterize this difference more accurately.

## 5.2 Chinese lai-*sentences*

The grammaticality of both examples in (33) shows that both *lai-le DP* and *DP lai-le* are good, where the preverbal DP in the latter is assumed to be raised from the postverbal DP position of the former, see the representations in (34) and (35) above.

Now, although a locus PP is not easily added to *lai*-sentences, as mentioned above (cf. Li & Thompson 1981: 517), a locus PP is not completely excluded, and in fact presentative motion sentences in Chinese sometimes allow a locus PP (with a restricted set of prepositions, e.g. *dao* 'to' and *cong* 'from'). The basic permutation pattern of *lai*-sentences with a locus PP is shown in (37).

(37) a. \* lai-le DP PP
 b. \* DP lai-le PP
 c. DP PP lai-le
 d. \* lai-le PP DP
 e. PP lai-le DP
 f. \* PP DP lai-le

(38) Examples of (37c) *DP PP lai-le*:
 a. Keren cong jia-li lai-le
 guests from home-in come-LE
 b. Na-ge ren cong ta jia lai-le (Li 1990: 139)
 that-CL man from his home come-LE

(39) Examples of (37e) *PP lai-le DP*:
    a.   Cong jia-li lai-le keren
          from home-in come-LE guests
    b.   Cong ta jia lai-le yi-ge ren
          from his home come-LE one-CL man

This pattern shows that a locus PP is not always excluded in principle, cf. the grammaticality of (37 c, e), but crucially it indicates that a locus PP is excluded in any postverbal position, cf. (37 a, b, d). (37 a, b) are important since they (in particular (37a)) show that presentative motion sentences are very different from presentative *you*-sentences, where the structure corresponding to (37a) is fully grammatical, cf. (9a). In other words, not only is a locus PP marginal in presentative motion sentences in Chinese, but if a locus PP is present, it cannot occur in the postverbal field, but has to occur preverbally.

The possibility of a postverbal DP+PP sequence in *you*-sentences led us to assume that *you*-sentences allow a postverbal locus small clause, see section 4.3. The impossibility of a corresponding postverbal DP+PP sequence in *lai*-sentences leads us to hypothesize that presentative *lai*-sentences do not allow a postverbal locus small clause. We therefore hypothesize that whereas *you* has a postverbal locus small clause, that is not allowed with presentative motion verbs like *lai*, and we assume that the presented DP in *lai*-sentences is a direct object in Chinese. Thus, Norwegian *komme*-sententences have the structure in (40), whereas Chinese *lai*-sentences have the structure in (41).

(40)
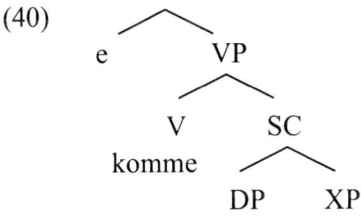

(41)
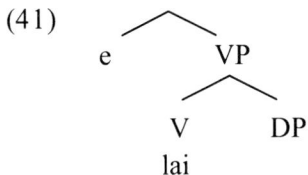

Actually, this conclusion may not be very surprising in a universal perspective. Sabbagh (2009) argues that existential (presentative) sentences in some languages may contain postverbal small clauses, whereas they contain a sole direct object in other languages (e.g. in Tagalog, as argued by Sabbagh). If our analysis is on the right track, the division between a small clause structure vs. a direct object structure cuts right through the class of presentative sentences in Chinese, so that *you*-sentences belong to the small clause type, whereas the *lai*-sentences belong to the sole direct object type. In Norwegian, on the other hand, all types of presentative sentences belong to the small clause type. Notice that the reasoning here applies to locus small clauses. Non-locus DP+XP sequences in postverbal position are beyond the scope of this article, but we speculate that these do not constitute small clauses, but rather complex DPs, see Wilder (this volume) or Del Gobbo (2010) for discussion.

Given the analysis suggested above, (37a) and (37d) are both excluded by the Postverbal Constraint, and the same goes for (37b) since the only source for (37b) would be a structure where the DP is moved from a postverbal position.

Now, to proceed, consider the two grammatical patterns with PP in Chinese, i.e. (37 c, e), repeated here.

(37) c.   DP PP lai-le
     d.   PP lai-le DP

These seem to be easily analysed as follows. (37c) is the type (33b) with the DP moved to the dethematised subject position and with the adverbial locus PP in the standard middlefield position. (37e) is the type (33a) with the presented DP in situ, and again with the adverbial locus PP in the standard middlefield position. Also, in this latter case, one might possibly assume that the PP should be analysed as topicalized (i.e. moved from its base-generated middle position), but as suggested in the next paragraph, that possibility may turn out to be excluded.

What about the ungrammaticality of (37f), i.e. the order \**PP DP lai-le*? Actually, (37f) should have been grammatical under an analysis where the DP is moved from the postverbal position to the subject position, and where the PP is topicalized. We know that the postverbal DP can be moved to the subject position, so the fact that (37f) is ungrammatical therefore indicates that the designated locus PP in a *lai*-sentence cannot be topicalized, but that it has to occur in the middle field between subject and verb, cf. (37c). This will be our tentative hypothesis. Notice that this seems to be unlike locus PPs in *you*-sentences, which may apparently be topicalized, as indicated by e.g. (22) in section 4.3. Possibly, this difference between locus PPs in *you*-sentences and locus PPs in *lai*-sentences might be related to the more fine-grained semantics of the locus PPs involved in the two sentence types (locational in *you*-sentences vs. directional in *lai*-sentences), but this is just a conjecture, and we will not pursue this problem further in this paper.

## 5.3 Chinese lai-*sentences with a locus DP-subject*
We now turn to presentative motion sentences with a locus DP-subject instead of a locus PP. Consider the pattern in (42).³

(42) a.  * lai-le  DP  locus-DP
     b.  * DP  lai-le  locus-DP
     c.  * DP  locus-DP  lai-le
     d.  * lai-le  locus-DP  DP
     e.    locus-DP  lai-le  DP
     f.    locus-DP  DP  lai-le

The clearly grammatical (42e) is exemplified in (43), whereas (42f) is exemplified in (44). Notice that the order in (42e) is slightly better than the order in (42f), but still (42f) must be counted as grammatical. (42f) improves if an adverb like *yijing* 'already' is added: *locus-DP DP yijing lai-le*.

(43) Example of (42e) *locus-DP lai-le DP*:
     Ta jia lai-le yi-ge ren                    (Li 1990: 140)
     his home come-LE one-CL man

(44) Example of (42f) *locus-DP DP lai-le*:
     Ta jia keren lai-le
     his home (the) guest come-LE

We will first concentrate on (42e), which is the typical word order of motion presentative sentences with a locus DP-subject discussed in the literature. This type is exemplifed in (43); an additional example is given in (45), from Li (1990: 137).

---

3   Even though (42b) is ungrammatical, the following word order (with a postverbal locus-DP and a sentence final aspectual morpheme *le* non-adjacent to the verb) seems to be grammatical: *DP lai locus-DP le*. We have no explanation for this fact, which remains a mystery to us at this point.

(45) Jia-li lai-le keren.
home-in come-LE guests

Here, the DP is in the postverbal object position, whereas the locus-DP seems to occupy the subject position, at least if we assume that the locus-DP in *lai*-sentences is a subject (i.e. occupies the subject position, cf. Li 1990: 137), like the locus-DPs of *you*-sentences. However, in the *you*-sentences we argued that the locus-DP bears a semantic role, but *lai*-sentences have a non-thematic subject position, so the locus-DP cannot receive a semantic role in the subject position. Thus, the locus-DP in *lai*-sentences might be analysed as a topic. If the locus-DP in (42e) is a topic and not a subject, it would follow that (42f), i.e. the order *locus-DP DP lai-le*, is grammatical, which in fact it is. Actually, the grammaticality of (42f) shows that it must be possible to analyse the locus-DP as a non-subject (since the raised DP must occupy the subject position here). We therefore tentatively conclude that the locus-DP in both (42e) and (42f) is a topic, not a subject.

Notice that the grammaticality of (42f) contrasts with the ungrammaticality of (37f), i.e. *\*PP DP lai-le*, where we concluded that the designated locus-PP in a *lai*-sentence cannot be topicalized, and we also conjectured that the reason for this could possibly have to do with the fine-grained semantics of the locus PP. However, this idea seems to be undermined by the fact that a corresponding locus-DP in a *lai*-sentence may be a topic. Clearly, further investigation is in order to dig deeper into these intriguing matters.

What about the ungrammaticality of (42 a, b, c, d)? Given that we hypothesize that a locus-DP must be a topic in *lai*-sentences, (42 a, b, d) are ungrammatical because the postverbal locus-DP is clearly too deep down in the structure to be a topic. (42 c) is ungrammatical basically for the same reason, even though here the locus-DP is preverbal. Here the initial DP must be moved from the postverbal object position to the subject position, so that the only possible position for the locus-DP is the middlefield position, which is prohibited for a locus-DP, hence the ungrammaticality.

## 6. Conclusion and further work

At the outset, presentative constructions in Norwegian and Chinese seem to be structurally quite similar, but a closer examination revealed that there are also important differences. In our view, perhaps the most striking difference concerns the *be*-type sentences. Although presentative *be*-sentences both in Norwegian and Chinese are often naturally translated into English as existential *there be*-sentences, we concluded that only Norwegian presentative sentences of this type are properly analysed as existential *there be*-sentences with an unaccusative verb. In contrast, the corresponding Chinese sentences are sentences with an overt or covert possessive subject, i.e. with a base-generated thematic subject, which means that they are not *there be*-sentences in any structural sense.

On the other hand, we found evidence that Norwegian and Chinese *be*-type sentences are similar in containing a postverbal small clause, and we also concluded that Norwegian presentative sentences of the motion type contain postverbal small clauses, just like their Norwegian presentative *be*-type counterparts. Furthermore, we found that both *be*-type and *motion*-type presentatives in Norwegian contain unaccusative type verbs.

We also found evidence that Chinese presentative motion-sentences contain unaccusative verbs, like their Norwegian counterparts. However, whereas Norwegian presentative motion-type sentences contain locus small clauses in their postverbal field, we found evidence that Chinese presentative motion-type sentences contain just a direct object and therefore no postverbal locus small clause. In other words, there is an unexpected Chinese-internal partition in that Chinese *be*-type presentatives contain a postverbal small clause structure, whereas Chinese motion-type presentatives contain just a direct object. Thus, whereas Norwegian *be*-type and motion-type presentatives are structurally very similar, Chinese *be*-type and motion-type presentatives are structurally quite different, both as regards the status of the subject position and the structure of the postverbal field.

As for future research, it is clear from our explorations that there is much to investigate further in this area. Some and perhaps most of our conclusions are tentative or hypothetical and are in need of further support (or perhaps falsification). Also, the significance of definiteness effects and other matters bordering on semantics should be looked closely into. In this effort, the insights in Li (1997) regarding existential sentences in English and Chinese should be taken into account, something that we have not been ready to do in the present article. Furthermore, the prospects for an explicit and theoretically based parametric analysis of presentative sentences in Norwegian and Chinese should be explored more vigorously than we have been able to do at this stage, hopefully resulting in a more developed parametric analysis in the future. Last but not least the presentative sentence type containing position or locative verbs (type (4c) in section 2) has not been investigated at all in this paper, but is an obvious topic for further research.

# References

Åfarli, Tor A. & Kristin M. Eide et al. 2003. *Norsk generativ syntaks*. Oslo: Novus.
Arad, Maya. 1998. *VP-Structure and the Syntax-Lexicon Interface*. London: University College London dissertation.
Cheung, Hung-nin Samuel in collaboration with Sze-yun Liu & Li-lin Shih. 1994. *A Practical Chinese Grammar*. Hong Kong: The Chinese University Press.
Del Gobbo, Francesca. 2010. On Secondary Predication and Specificity in Mandarin Chinese. Ms., UC Irvine and UCLA.
Fang, Huilin & T.-H. Jonah Lin. 2008. The Mandarin *you* existential: A verbal analysis. *USTWPL* 4. 43-56.
Hellan, Lars. 1988. *Anaphora in Norwegian and the Theory of Grammar*. Dordrecht: Foris Publications.
Henne, Henry, Ole Bjørn Rongen & Lars Jul Hansen. 1977. *A Handbook on Chinese Language Structure*. Oslo: Universitetsforlaget.
Hoekstra, Teun. 1988. Small clause results. *Lingua* 74. 101-139.
Huang, C.-T. James. 1987. Existential Sentences in Chinese and (In)definiteness. In: Eric J. Reuland & Alice G.B. ter Meulen (eds.), *The Representation of (In)definiteness*. Pp. 226-253. Cambridge, Mass.: The MIT Press.
Huang, C.-T. James, Y.-H. Audrey Li & Yafei Li. 2009. *The Syntax of Chinese*. Cambridge: Cambridge University Press.
Li, Yen-hui Audrey. 1990. *Order and Constituency in Mandarin Chinese*. Dordrecht: Kluwer.
Li, Yen-hui Audrey. 1997. Types of Existential Sentences in English and Chinese. Ms, University of Southern California.
Li, Charles N. & Sanda A. Thompson. 1981. *Mandarin Chinese: A Functional Reference Grammar*. Berkeley: University of California Press.
Lin, Tzong-Hong. 2001. *Light Verb Syntax and the Theory of Phrase Structure*. Irvine, CA: University of California dissertation.
Lin, T.-H. Jonah. 2008. Locative subject in Mandarin Chinese. *Nanzan Linguistics* 4. 69-88.
Nordgård, Kari Anne. 2002. Presenteringssetninger i en småsetningsanalyse. Trondheim: NTNU MA thesis.
Sabbagh, Joseph. 2009. Existential sentences in Tagalog. *Natural Language and Linguistic Theory* 27. 675-719.
Salkoff, Morris. 1983. Bees are swarming in the garden. *Language* 59. 288-346.
Sybesma, Rint. 1999. *The Mandarin VP*. Dordrecht: Kluwer.
Wilder, Chris. This volume. Chinese Relatives and the Coda Construction.

Email: tor.aafarli@ntnu.no; fufen.jin@ntnu.no

# Chinese Relatives and the Coda Construction

Chris Wilder
*Norwegian University of Science and Technology (NTNU)*

## 1. Introduction[1]

The Chinese 'coda construction' illustrated in (1) has the general format (2). The 'coda phrase' (*hen congming* in (1), XP in (2)), is linked interpretively to the italicised postverbal noun phrase (NP* in (2)).[2, 3]

(1) Wo   jiao-guo    *yi ge xuesheng*   [ hen congming ]
    I    teach-ASP   one CL student     very intelligent
    'I have the experience of teaching a student who is (very) intelligent.'

(2)   ... V(-ASP) NP* XP

Though an optional constituent, the coda is central to the construction in that sentences having a coda show an array of properties lacking in corresponding coda-less sentences.

This paper presents evidence that the coda is a type of relative clause which restrictively modifies NP* – in disagreement with the earlier proposals outlined in (3).[4]

---

1   I am indebted to Niina Zhang for pointing out to me similarities between the coda construction and the German IV2 construction. All Chinese data, except where indicated, were kindly provided by her. In glosses to the Chinese examples, ASP = aspect marker, CL = classifier and DE = relative clause marker *de*.
2   The term *coda* is sometimes applied to XP in English sentences of the form 'there be NP XP' and provides a theory-neutral designation for XP in (2). Other terms for the Chinese coda are *descriptive clause* (Huang 1987) and *realis descriptive clause* (Li & Thompson 1981). Example (1) is from Huang (1987).
3   NP* in (2) can be the object or the postverbal subject of the matrix predicate. A coda is generally possible only with an NP that is postverbal. With eventive verbs, a coda is sometimes only possible if the verb takes an aspect marker such as *le* or *guo*.
4   To my knowledge the only previous analysis which treats the coda as a (type of) relative clause is Zhang (2008). Zhang proposes that the coda together with NP* forms a type of internally headed relative clause.

(3)   a.  *Parataxis*: the construction is paratactic, XP is an independent clause containing a zero pronoun linked to NP* by mechanisms of intersentential anaphora (Li & Thompson 1981).
   b.  *Secondary predication*: XP is a secondary predicate which takes NP* as its subject (Huang 1987, Li 1997, Tsai 1999, Del Gobbo 2009).

The possibility that the coda is a restrictive relative clause is explicitly rejected by Li & Thompson and by Huang. Both point out that relative clauses in Chinese, illustrated in (4), like other NP modifiers, are pre-nominal (separated from the noun by the morpheme *de*).

(4)   Wo      jiao-guo     yi ge     [ hen congming de ]     xuesheng
      I       teach-ASP    one CL    very intelligent  DE    student
      'I have the experience of teaching a student who is (very) intelligent.'

However, neither of the proposals (3a,b) is convincing. Part of the reason for not recognising the coda as a relative clause may lie in an implicit assumption that Chinese relative clauses must be *uniformly* prenominal. The evidence presented below indicates that in addition to prenominal *de*-relatives, Chinese also has *de*-less finite relatives that are postnominal.

If the coda is a relative clause in the syntactic sense, then it forms a constituent at some level with the NP* which it modifies. This is something that I do not try to establish in this paper. Rather, I focus on semantic evidence that indicates that the coda is a restrictive modifier of NP*, and general considerations that argue against alternatives to the relative clause hypothesis (in particular, against the idea that the coda is a secondary predicate).

The Chinese coda construction shows striking similarities with the *Integrated Verb Second* (IV2) construction of German analyzed in Gärtner (2001), illustrated by (5a). IV2 involves a sequence of two finite clauses showing finite-verb-second (V2) order, of which the second, the *IV2 clause*, appears to be a relative clause modifying an NP in the first clause. Thus (5a) is synonymous with the ordinary relative clause construction (5b). Both involve fronting of a pronoun of the same type, a so-called *d*-pronoun, in the bracketed clause, but differ in the placement of the finite verb in that clause. Having the finite verb in second position as in (5a) normally signals root clause status, while standard relative clauses display the finite verb-final order common to (most) subordinate clauses in German.

(5) a. Ich suche jemanden, [ den nennen sie Wolf ]   *IV2*
       I    seek  someone    D-PRON call  they W.
    b. Ich suche jemanden, [ den sie Wolf nennen ]   *RC (V-final)*
       I    seek  someone    D-PRON they W.   call
    Both: 'I am looking for someone who they call Wolf.'

A striking property of IV2 is that it displays an *indefinites-only* restriction – the nominal modified by the IV2 clause is required to be indefinite. Replacing *jemanden* ('someone') in (5a) with the definite *denjenigen* ('that one') yields an ill-formed sentence (6a). This restriction is triggered by the presence of the IV2 clause; the object of *suchen* ('seek') need not be indefinite otherwise, even if modified by a V-final relative clause (6b).⁵

(6) a. *Ich suche *denjenigen*, [ den    nennen sie Wolf ]   *IV2*
       I    seek  that-one       D-PRON  call   they W.
    b. Ich suche denjenigen, [ den    sie  Wolf nennen ] *RC (V-final)*
       I    seek  that-one     D-PRON they W.   call
    'I am looking for the one who they call Jürgen.'

The Chinese coda construction displays a similar restriction. NP* in (2) is required to be an indefinite of a certain type (Li & Thompson 1981, Huang 1987, Tsai 1999). Replacing the numeral *yi* ('a', 'one') in (1) with the demonstrative *na* ('that') yields an ill-formed sentence (7a). This restriction is dependent on the presence of the coda. The object of *jiao-guo* ('have taught') in the corresponding coda-less sentence need not be indefinite, whether or not it is accompanied by a prenominal relative clause (7b).

(7) a. *Wo jiao-guo    na ge    xuesheng         [ hen   congming ]
       I   teach-ASP  that CL  student            very  intelligent
    b. Wo  jiao-guo   na ge    ( hen congming     de )  xuesheng
       I   teach-ASP  that CL   very intelligent  DE    student
    'I have the experience of teaching that student (who is (very) intelligent).'

---

5  The IV2 construction shows a specific intonation pattern which distinguishes it from string-identical two-sentence sequences (see section 2.3). The judgement in (6a) thus holds modulo intonation. The Chinese coda construction is also characterised by a specific intonation pattern distinguishing it from string-identical two-sentence sequences. The judgement in (7a) thus also depends on the specific intonation.

Clearly, this restriction calls for an explanation. Given how it depends on the occurrence of a coda, any explanation will require a proper understanding of the relation between the coda XP and the nominal NP*. Further comparison with German IV2 can shed light on this issue. Gärtner suggests an interesting explanation of the indefinites-only restriction in IV2, which I suggest may also apply to the Chinese case, in terms of a requirement imposed on NP* by the coda. Suppose the coda is a finite relative clause that is constrained not to be interpreted as presupposed material, i.e. it may only be 'assertional'. Then, the only kind of NP which a coda can modify must itself be nonpresuppositional, i.e. an indefinite. The incompatibility of codas and definites or 'strong' QNPs follows from the presuppositional nature of such noun phrases.

The paper is organized as follows. Section 2 reviews further properties of the Chinese coda. Section 3 argues that the semantic relation between the coda and NP* is one of restrictive modification. Section 4 argues against the analysis of the coda as a secondary predicate, and section 5 addresses the indefiniteness requirement. Section 6. concludes with some brief comments on the syntax of the construction.

## 2. Descriptive aspects of the coda construction

### 2.1 Definiteness effects in Chinese

The 'indefinites-only' restriction in the coda construction was investigated in Huang (1987) as part of a broader inquiry into definiteness effects in Chinese. Huang showed that two classes of Chinese sentences without a coda display a definiteness effect in postverbal NP positions:

(8) (i) existential sentences with *you* (*you*+NP...) similar to the English existential *there+be* construction

(ii) sentences with verbs expressing the coming into or going out of existence ('die', 'escape', 'go', ...) of their postverbal subject argument

In sentences with a coda in the pattern (2), the V + NP sequence may belong to one of these two classes. The definiteness effect found in such cases are similar to what is found in other languages, and the retention of the effect when a coda is added in such cases is not surprising. However, codas occur with a wider range of V-NP sequences that do not display a definiteness effect independently. For example, Huang contrasts *you*-NP sentences with the 'XP *you* NP...' type with preverbal locative XP, whose post-*you* NP need not be indefinite (9). The addition of a coda forces this NP to be indefinite (10).⁶

(9) Zhuo-shang    you     nei ben    shu
    table-top     have    that CL    book
    'On the table is that book.'

(10) Zhuo-shang    you    yi ben shu        / *nei ben shu    *hen youqu*
     table-top     have   one CL book       / that CL book    very interesting
     'On the table is a book / *that book that is very interesting.'

Codas are also found in transitive constructions like (1) above, where NP* is the object of the matrix verb. In these cases, too, the definiteness effect is triggered by the coda (cf. (7) above). It is the pattern in (1) vs. (7) and (9) vs. (10) that demonstrates that codas are associated with their own indefiniteness requirement.

## 2.2 Codas as finite CPs involving null operator movement to SpecCP

There are numerous indications that codas are clausal constituents. I shall assume that categories like 'finite' vs. 'nonfinite' are relevant for clause-typing in Chinese⁷ and propose that codas are (the Chinese equivalent of) finite CPs. Though this cannot be verified directly given that Chinese lacks finite verbal inflection or other marking of finiteness (e.g. complementizers), indirect support comes from considering meaning. For Li & Thompson (1981), codas are *realis* descriptive clauses, and they juxtapose these (p. 618) with 'irrealis descriptive clauses' (11) similar to English purpose infinitives (the NP linked to the irrealis clause can be definite):

(11) Women    zhong    nei zhong cai           chi
     we       raise    that kind vegetable     eat
     'We raise that kind of vegetable to eat.'

Li (1997) presents evidence that codas which appear to contain only an adjective or verb phrase in fact involve silent functional layers of clause structure (IP, CP).⁸ For example, the coda can include expressions like a modal verb (12) or sentential

---

6  Also, sentences involving (state-denoting) verbs of location ('lie', 'stand', etc) permit postverbal subjects that show no definiteness effect, unless a coda is added.
7  See however Hu et. al. (2001) for critical discussion.
8  The traditional labels IP, CP are used here as cover terms for functional clausal projections. Precise details, for example whether Chinese has TP, are not crucial for the argument in this paper.

adverbials which can be taken to signal the presence of clausal structure beyond the core predicate.

(12)  You    yi ge    hushi    *yinggai    zhaogu*    Lisi
      have   one CL   nurse    should     care       L.
      'There's a nurse that should take care of Lisi'

The coda of English *there*-sentences, often treated as a small clause predicate lacking its own CP / IP structure, does not tolerate individual-level predicates (*\*There is someone [intelligent]* / *\*There is someone [a student]* ). Li (1997) notes that a Chinese coda be an individual level predicate (ILP), as in the *you*-sentence (13). ILPs have been claimed to require IP-structure; cf. Diesing's 1992 control analysis of sentences like *John is intelligent*. If so, cases like (13) are evidence that codas are at least IPs.[9]

(13)  You    yi ge    xuesheng    *hen conming*
      have   one CL   student     very intelligent
      'There's one student who is (very) intelligent.'

Li concludes from (12)-(13) that the coda in *you*-NP sentences is at least IP "in order to accommodate the occurrence of IP-level constituents between *you* NP and the VP", leaving open whether the coda is a full-fledged CP. Additional evidence that the coda can involve an IP-layer comes from cases like (14)-(15), in which the coda contains a preverbal subject of its own and NP* is linked to a gap deeper in the clause. Taking codas to be a full-fledged finite CPs, they can be analysed generally in terms of A'-movement of a null operator (*Op*) from the subject ((12)-(13)) or object position ((14)-(15)) inside the coda, landing in SpecCP.[10]

(14)  You    $ren_j$    [ $Op_j$ Zhangsan   bu renshi $t_j$ ]
      have   person              Z.        not know
      'There's someone Zhangsan doesn't know.'

---

9   The possibility for what appears to be a bare AP to function as a clause can be traced back to the fact that simple finite assertions with a predicative AP lack an overt copula (as in *Na ge xuesheng hen conming*, lit: 'that student very intelligent'). A simple assertion with a nominal predicate requires an overt copula (*shi*), cf. *na geren \*(shi) xuesheng* (lit: 'that person is student') as does the corresponding coda (i).
    (i)   wu-li       you yi ge ren [ *(shi) xuesheng ]
          room-in     have one cl person (be) student
          'there is one person in the room that is a student'
10  Example (14) is from Li (1997), (15) is from Li & Thompson (1981).

(15) Ta chao le [yi ge cai]$_j$ [ Op$_j$ wo hen xihuan chi t$_j$ ]
     she fry ASP one CL dish      I very like eat
     'She fried a dish that I like to eat.'

Under the null operator analysis for *de*-relatives, the relative clauses in (16) are structurally parallel (ignoring the particle *de*) to the codas in (14)-(15). Similarly, if one adopts the null operator analysis of topic constructions, the sentences in (17) contain CPs of the same form.[11]

(16) a. Wu-li you [ Op$_j$ Zhangsan bu renshi t$_j$ de ] ren$_j$
       room-in have     Z.      not know   DE person
       'There's someone in the room that Zhangsan doesn't know.'
   b. Ta chao le [ yi ge [Op$_j$ wo hen xihuan chi t$_j$ ] de cai]$_j$
       she fry ASP one CL     I very like eat     DE dish
       'She fried a dish that I like to eat.'
(17) a Na ge ren$_j$ [ Op$_j$ Zhangsan bu renshi t$_j$ ]
      that CL person   Z.      not know
      'that person, Zhangsan doesn't know'
   b. Na ge cai$_j$ [ Op$_j$ wo hen xihuan chi t$_j$ ]
      that CL dish     I very like eat
      'That dish, I like to eat.'

The internal structural parallel between codas, *de*-relatives and topic constructions is further shown by the fact that all three show the same extraction patterns. To take one example: Chinese permits relativization out of a *de*-relative modifying an NP, in apparent violation of the Complex NP Constraint (Li 1999). In (18a), the relative operator of the clause modifying *ren* is extracted out of the relative clause modifying *yifu* 'clothes'. However, relativization out of an NP in this pattern is possible only if that NP precedes the main predicate (verb, adjective) of its clause, as in (18a) (*chuan de yifu* precedes *hen piaoling* '(are) very pretty'). Relativization out of a *de*-relative is not possible if the NP in question is in postverbal position, as in (18b) (*chuan de yifu* follows *xihuan* 'like'). The same pattern is displayed by topicalization (19), and also by the coda construction (20).[12]

---

11  Example (17a) is taken from Li (1997).
12  It is immaterial whether the extraction analysis itself is correct. What is important is the fact that codas show same pattern as *de*-relatives and topicalizations. For clarity's sake, the operator-trace pair belonging to the internal relative clause is omitted from (18)-(20). The ill-formed (b)-examples are possible if the trace *ti* is replaced by the overt pronoun *ta* 'he/she/they'.

(18) a.  [ *Op*$_j$ [ [ *t*$_j$ chuan de ] yifu]   hen piaoling de ] na ge ren
                     wear DE   clothes very pretty  DE   that CL person
         'the *person* that the clothes *he* wears are very pretty'
     b.  * [ *Op*$_j$ wo xihuan [ [ *t*$_j$ chuan de ] yifu ]  de ] na ge ren$_j$
             I  like  wear DE              clothes DE that CL person
         'the *person* that I like the clothes *he* wears'

(19) a.  Na ge ren$_j$ [ *Op*$_j$ [ [ *t*$_j$ chuan de ] yifu ]  hen piaoling ]
         that CL person         wear DE clothes very pretty
         '*That person*, the clothes *he* wears are very pretty.'
     b.  * Na ge ren$_j$ [ *Op*$_j$ wo xihuan [ [ *t*$_j$ chuan de ] yifu ] ]
         that CL person       I  like        wear DE  clothes
         '*That person*, I like the clothes *he* wears.'

(20) a.  Nar zhan-zhe yi ge ren$_j$ [ *Op*$_j$ [ [ *t*$_j$ chuan de ] yifu ] hen piaoling ]
         there stand-ASP one CL person wear DE  clothes very pretty
         'over there is standing *someone* that the clothes *he* wears are very pretty'
     b.  *Nar zhan-zhe yi ge ren$_j$ [ *Op*$_j$ wo xihuan [ [ *t*$_j$ chuan de ] yifu ] ]
         there stand-ASP one CL person I like wear DE clothes
         'Over there is standing *someone* that I like the clothes *he* wears.'

## 2.3 The role of intonation

Gärtner (2001) identifies *intonational integration* of S2 and S1 as a central property of the German IV2 construction. An IV2 sentence consists of a sequence of two V2 clauses in the format (21), where S2 contains a fronted pronoun of the *d*-series, and S1 and S2 together form a single intonational unit.

(21)  [$_{S1}$ ... NP*$_j$ ... ] (/) [$_{S2}$ D-PRONOUN$_j$ V$_{fin}$ ... ]

The notation (/) signals "a high boundary tone [...] or other [prosodic] devices marking non-final boundaries". Crucially, "IV2 may not be preceded by final boundary markings", shown by (\). The role of intonation is demonstrated by the paradigm in (22):

(22) a.  Ich kenne einen Norweger,  (/) der spricht chinesisch.  *IV2*
         I know   a Norwegian       D-PRON speaks Chinese
     b.  Ich kenne einen Norweger,  (/) der chinesisch spricht. *restrictive RC*
         I know   a Norwegian       D-PRON Chinese speaks
     c.  Ich kenne einen Norweger,  (\) der chinesisch spricht. *appositive RC*
         I know a Norwegian         D-PRON Chinese speaks
     d.  Ich kenne einen Norweger.  (/) Der spricht chinesisch.  *text (S1. S2)*
         I know   a Norwegian       D-PRON speaks Chinese

The IV2 sentence differs from the ordinary restrictive relative only in the position of the finite verb. (22a,b) both mean 'I know a (male) Norwegian that speaks Chinese', and the IV2 clause and the V-final relative clause are preceded by a non-final intonation boundary. A V-final RC that is not intonationally integrated on the other hand has a non-restrictive (appositive) reading; (22c) means 'I know a Norwegian, who (by the way) speaks Chinese'.

A *d-pronoun* can function both as a demonstrative and as a relative pronoun. An V2 clause introduced by a *d-pronoun* functions in isolation as a simple assertion (main clause), in which case the *d-pronoun* is a demonstrative signalling the topic of the sentence. Thus the IV2 clause of (22a) can be used independently to mean 'He speaks Chinese', as in the second clause of (22d). The indefinites-only restriction holds only of (22a) with (/), and not of (22d) with (\) – the indefinite *einen Norweger* can be replaced by a definite in (22d).

Intonational integration plays a similar role in defining the Chinese coda construction: "a realis descriptive clause is actually no different from two sentences juxtaposed together, except that it is pronounced with one single intonation contour" (Li & Thompson 1981:614). This is shown in (23)-(24), using the (/) notation to indicate integration within a 'single contour'.

(23) Ta   chao le  [ yi / *na ge cai]$_j$ (/) [Op$_j$  wo  hen xihuan  chi $t_j$]  *Coda*
     she  fry ASP    one / that CL dish            I   very like     eat
     'She fried a / *that dish that I like to eat.'

(24) Ta   chao le  [ yi / na ge cai]$_j$ (\) [Op$_j$  wo  hen xihuan  chi $t_j$]
     she  fry ASP    one / that CL dish           I   very like     eat
     'She fried a / that dish. That (dish), I like to eat.'

Like an IV2 clause in German, the coda clause must be integrated with S1. Used in isolation, S2 can usually function as an independent clause with a zero topic; e.g. *wo hen xihuan chi* means 'that (dish etc), I like to eat'. In that case, the null operator functions as a topic pronoun, picking up a referent from some antecedent in the preceding discourse, such as the indefinite *yi ge cai* or the definite *na ge cai* from the preceding sentence in (24). Only when the second clause is integrated (23) does the indefinites-only restriction emerge.

## 3. Meaning: the coda restrictively modifies NP*

Section 3.2 presents the argument (based on Gärtner 2001) that the coda is a restrictive modifier of NP*. First, I review what earlier analyses have said about the idea that the coda is a restrictive modifier or relative clause.

### *3.1 Previous analyses*

Li & Thompson (1981:611-619) describe the coda construction as a "presentative" construction whose function is to "introduce a NP to be described", with the coda ('realis descriptive clause') being a clause that provides an incidental description of the object of the first clause. They note the similarity of the coda to a *de*-relative: "Semantically, [this] construction might appear to be rather similar to a relative clause construction ... in fact both types of constructions can be given the same English translation." (p.612) However, they proceed to claim that the coda is not in fact a relative clause:

> the manner in which the realis descriptive clause and the relative clause provide information about the noun phrases they are describing, however, is different in a subtle but significant way: the message conveyed by the realis descriptive clause is that the property it names is entirely incidental, while the message conveyed by the relative clause is that there is a preestablished class of such items. (p.614)

While *de*-RCs and coda XPs differ in the way they 'present' the information they provide, my contention is that it is wrong to characterize this difference in these terms. The property named by XP is not 'entirely incidental'; as a restrictive modifier of NP, it is crucial for establishing truth conditions of the whole sentence.

Li & Thompson further state that

> [t]he semantic principles for interpreting sequences of sentences .. are exactly the same as those for interpreting a descriptive clause sentence ... [S]emantically, a descriptive clause simply adds another assertion to the first one. (p.614)

If a coda construction is interpreted like a sequence of two clauses, this would predict that the gap in the coda and the indefinite NP in the first clause are related by intersentential anaphora. The discussion in section 3.2 indicates that this is not the case.

Huang (1987:233ff) also considers and rejects the possibility that the coda is a restrictive modifier of NP. Addressing the perceived difference in meaning between *de*-relatives and codas, Huang follows Li & Thompson in claiming that codas "have a *descriptive* but not a *restrictive* function", unlike prenominal modifiers, which "have a restrictive function". Thus, in (25a), "what is being asserted is specifically the existence ... of an interesting book (and not just a book)", while the coda 'very interesting' in (25b) "is a continuative description of the existing book" (p.235).

(25) a. Zhuo-shang you yi ben *hen youqu* de shu
table-top have one CL very interesting DE book
'On the table there is a very interesting book.'
b. Zhuo-shang you yi ben shu *hen youqu*
table-top have one CL book very interesting
'On the table there is a book (which is) very interesting.'

He proceeds to claim that "if such an XP is to be represented as a postnominal modifier in accordance with the bare NP analysis, then it must be represented as a nonrestrictive modifier". The discussion in section 3.2 indicates that the difference between *de*-relatives and codas is not restrictive vs. nonrestrictive; semantically, the coda restrictively modifies the NP, like a *de*-relative.

Huang makes a further suggestion which might shed light on the real nature of the perceived meaning difference between codas and *de*-relatives. He compares the relation between the coda and the *de*-relative in (25) with that between a prenominal AP (26a) and a postnominal depictive adjunct (26b):

(26) a. He ate the raw meat. b. He ate the meat raw.

As in (26b), "the relation it [the coda] has with the preceding NP is [...] that between subject and predicate, or between topic and comment [...] a postnominal XP makes a comment about the preceding NP" (p.235).

This idea is taken up by Li (1997) in discussing coda constructions introduced by *you*+NP. Li proposes that *you*+indefinite NP introduces a 'topic', which needs a coda as 'comment' in order to be pragmatically well-formed. Li notes that a *you*-sentence lacking a coda like (27b) is felt to be semantically or informationally incomplete, suggesting that this is because it involves a topic that lacks a comment.

(27) a.  You    ren      lai    le
        have   person   come   ASP
        'Someone has come.' / 'There's someone who has come.'
    b.  ?? You   ren
        have person

Li's suggestion is that a sentence like (27a) is structured as (28a) in the discourse, corresponding semantically to (28b). Semantically, the existential verb *you* corresponds to nothing more than the existential quantifier, with the following NP providing a variable which it binds. The comment is then predicated of that variable:

(28) a.  you [$_{Topic}$ ren ] [$_{Comment}$ lai le ]
    b.  ∃x (person(x) ∧ came(x))

The intuition that *you*+NP is somehow incomplete without a coda holds equally of English *there*-sentences. The contrast in (27) is reproduced in (29). Here, however, the role of the comment in 'rescuing' the construction is taken by an ordinary restrictive relative clause.

(29) a.  ?? There's someone.
    b.  There's someone who is singing.

It seems reasonable to attribute the oddity of (27b) and (29a) to lack of 'informativity'. However, if *you*-sentences are to be analyzed in terms of topic-comment structuring, then that analysis should also apply to (29b), with the relative clause playing the role of 'comment'. Thus, the analysis should be embedded in a theory in which a relative clause is permitted to play the role of the 'comment'. That would then be compatible with an analysis of the coda in (27a) as a relative clause modifying the nominal that provides the 'topic'.[13]

Tsai (1999) and Del Gobbo (2009) follow Huang (1987) in taking the Chinese coda to be secondary predicate functioning like a depictive adjunct. The secondary predicate analysis is addressed in section 4 below.

---

13  Zhang (2008) argues that the coda is in fact an internally headed relative clause which contains NP* as a left-peripheral topic constituent inside it.

## 3.2 Gärtner's test for restrictive modification

Gärtner (2001) identifies a way of testing for restrictive modification of indefinites that involves scalar implicatures. This test shows that a German IV2 clause is not related to the indefinite NP of the preceding clause via intersentential anaphora, nor as a non-restrictive modifier. The test exploits the apparent anomaly of examples like (30):

(30)  # That sheet of paper has one side.

At first blush, assuming that numerals have the 'at least $n$' reading, the meaning of (30) (=31a) is not in itself anomalous. The oddity of (30) is due rather to the scalar implicature (31b) triggered by the numeral, which creates the 'exactly $n$' reading: 'the sheet has at least one side *and not more than one side*'. This 'at most one' implicature conflicts with the common-sense assumption (31c):[14]

(31) a.  'That sheet of paper has at least one side'   *Assertion*
     b.  'That sheet of paper has not more than one side'   *Scalar implicature*
     c.  All sheets of paper have exactly two sides.   *World knowledge*

The contrast between (32) and (33) shows that adding a restrictive relative clause *that is black* eliminates the oddity, while adding a second sentence (*it* referring back to *one side*) does not.

(32)  That sheet (of paper) has one side that is competely black.

(33)  # That sheet (of paper) has one side$_j$. It$_j$ is completely black.

This contrast arises because the meaning of the indefinite in (32) is dependent on the relative clause, while the indefinite in (33) is interpreted independently of the second sentence. In (32), the relative clause restricts the domain to which the indefinite determiner applies – 'sides that are black' instead of simply 'sides' as in (30). The scalar implicature triggered ('the sheet has not more than one black side') does not conflict with world knowledge. The link between the indefinite

---

14  Gärtner points out that the implicature (31b) is strengthened by the fact that (31a) on its own, being entailed by (31c), is not informative at all: "The strength of the implicature ... follows from a higher-order Gricean effect. ... [(31a)] is entailed by common-sense knowledge ... [O]nly the Horn-scale implicature [i.e. (31b)] ... restores informativity ... This, in turn, requires costly revision of the hearer's knowledge base ..." (Gärtner 2001:112). Also, if the sheet of paper under discussion is in fact a Moebius strip, the anomaly of (30) simply disappears – as predicted.

and the pronoun in (33), on the other hand, is a case of intersentential anaphora, established after the first clause has been semantically evaluated. The first sentence in (33) therefore gives rise to the same absurd implicature as (30).

A German IV2 clause behaves like a restrictive relative clause with respect to this diagnostic. The relevant paradigm (Gärtner, 2001:112) is given in (34)-(35).

(34) a. Das Blatt hat eine Seite$_j$, (/) die$_j$ ist ganz schwarz. *IV2*
the sheet has one side D-PRON is quite black
b. Das Blatt hat eine Seite$_j$, (/) die$_j$ ganz schwarz ist *RRC*
the sheet has one side D-PRON quite black is

(35) # Das Blatt hat eine Seite$_j$. (\) Die$_j$ ist ganz schwarz. *text*
the sheet has one side D-PRON is quite black

The interpretation of the indefinite is dependent on the IV2 clause in the same way as it depends on a V-final relative clause – both examples translate as (32). In other words, the IV2 clause is interpreted as a restrictive modifier, so the implicature is '...not more than one black side'. (35) on the other hand behaves like (33), with the same oddity-inducing implicature.

The Chinese coda construction behaves in precisely the same fashion as German IV2 with respect to this test. (36)-(37) provide a relevant minimal pair (cf. Zhang 2008:38 for further examples).

(36) Zhe ben shu you yi ye (/) shi kongbai *Coda*
this CL book have one page be blank
'This book has one page that is blank.'

(37) # Zhe ben shu you yi ye (\) shi kongbai *Text*
this CL book have one page be blank
'This book has one page. It is blank.'

The coda sentence (36), with the 'single intonation contour' identified by Li & Thompson, has the 'sensible' implicature that the book has at most one blank page, indicating that *shi kongbai* is a restrictive modifier. The same string pronounced as two independent clauses, as in (37), is associated with the absurd implicature 'the book has only one page'. The contrast shows that the link between a coda and the preceding indefinite is not mediated by intersentential anaphora; which argues against an analysis of the coda as an independent clause (contra Li & Thompson 1981).

The same argument can be used to argue that the coda is not a non-restrictive modifier (appositive relative clause) of the indefinite NP. Appositive relatives do not contribute to the computation of truth-conditions or informativity of their host clause. The link between an appositive relative and its host NP is in this respect identical to intersentential anaphora.

(38) # That sheet of paper has one side, which (by the way) is completely black.

Thus, if the Chinese coda is a modifier of the indefinite NP, its function is that of a *restrictive* modifier (contra Huang's suggestion).

## 4. The secondary predicate analysis

The facts just reviewed argue against the analysis of the Chinese coda as an independent clause, or as a non-restrictive modifier of the indefinite NP. The scalar implicature associated with (36a) indicates that the coda restricts the denotation of the indefinite NP. This is of course what we expect if the coda is a restrictive relative clause modifying the NP. But it is not incompatible with a different hypothesis, that the coda is a VP-adjunct linked to the NP as a secondary predicate. In section 4.1, I consider why the scalar implicature test fails to distinguish the secondary predicate analysis from the restrictive modifer analysis. Section 4.2 offers reasons why the secondary predicate analysis is nevertheless wrong.

### 4.1 Non-distinctness of readings with symmetric quantifiers

Comparing a secondary predication such as the depictive (39a) with a case of intersentential anaphora (40a), it is immediately apparent that the scalar implicatures are different. (40a) implies that Mary discovered not more than two students in total. The implicature in (39a) is that Mary discovered not more than two *drunk* students (she may have discovered additional sober students). Thus (39a), with *drunk* as a secondary predicate, has the same implicature as (41a), with *drunk* as an adnominal modifier.

(39) a.   Mary discovered two students drunk          *depictive adjunct*
     b.   'Mary discovered not more than two drunk students' *scalar implicature*

(40) a. Mary discovered two students (and they were drunk)    *independent S*
     b. 'Mary discovered not more than two students'    *scalar implicature*

(41) a. Mary discovered two drunk students    *restrictive modifier*
     b. 'Mary discovered not more than two drunk students' *scalar implicature*

The secondary predicate restricts the denotation of the indefinite in a similar fashion to an attributive adjective. The reason for this is that the quantificational structure of the sentences is non-distinct in relevant respects. In both, the variables introduced by the adjective *drunk* and the noun *students* are bound by the numeral quantifier so that they are interpreted conjunctively (intersectively) within the scope of the quantifier. The meaning of (39a) can be represented as in (42) – which is non-distinct from the meaning of (41a).[15]

(42) TWO$x$ [ Mary discovered $x$ ∧ student($x$) ∧ drunk($x$) ]

Since the meanings of (39a) and (41a) are the same in the relevant respect, they both give rise to the same scalar implicature.

This near-synonymy between secondary predication and restrictive modification arises when the nominal is headed by a *symmetric* quantifier, like *two*.[16] Whether *drunk* modifies the noun, interpreted as part of first argument ('restrictor') of *two*, or is a secondary predicate, interpreted as part of its second argument ('nuclear scope'), the resulting meanings are equivalent.

With a *non*-symmetric quantifier like *every*, it does make a difference whether *drunk* is evaluated as part of the first or second argument of the quantifier. The truth conditional difference is seen by considering models in which not every student is drunk, e.g. a model including five drunk students and five sober students. In such models, (43) can be true but (44) must be false.

(43) a. Mary discovered every drunk student.    *restrictive modifier*
     b. $\forall x$ [ student($x$) ∧ drunk($x$) ] → [ Mary discovered $x$ ]
     c. If there are 10 students, 5 drunk and 5 sober, then (a) may be true.

---

[15] The result is the same if the indefinite article is treated as a cardinality predicate, with the variable introduced by the noun bound by existential closure:
(i) $\exists x$ [ Mary discovered $x$ ∧ student($x$) ∧ card($x$)=TWO ∧ drunk($x$) ]

[16] A quantifier Q is symmetric if 'Q As are B' = 'Q Bs are A', and non-symmetric if 'Q As are B' ≠ 'Q Bs are A'; see e.g. Keenan (1987).

(44) a. Mary discovered every student drunk. *depictive adjunct*
 b. $\forall x\ [\text{student}(x)\ ] \rightarrow [\ \text{Mary discovered } x \wedge \text{drunk}(x)\ ]$
 c. If there are 10 students, 5 drunk and 5 sober, then (a) cannot be true.

In the case at hand, however, asymmetric quantifiers cannot be brought to bear. The NP* in the coda construction is restricted to symmetric quantifiers.[17] Therefore the reading determined by a 'secondary predicate' analysis of a coda sentence is always, in the relevant respect, non-distinct from the one determined by a 'restrictive modifier' analysis.

## 4.2 How the coda differs from secondary predicates

There are two further considerations which indicate that the secondary predicate analysis of the coda construction is not correct. One is that that analysis offers no explanation of the indefinites-only restriction on NP* in the coda construction, while the restrictive relative clause analysis does so. This is addressed in section 5.

The other has to do with assumptions about syntax-semantics correspondence. If the coda is a secondary predicate, it is presumably an adjunct, adjoined to the VP or IP. A common though often implicit assumption is that an adjunct semantically modifies its host.

(45) *Adjunct interpretation*:
 If YP is base-generated as an adjunct to XP, YP semantically modifies XP.

Thus, an attributive adjective semantically modifies its host NP; an adverbial semantically modifies its host VP. In the coda construction, the coda modifies a noun phrase within VP. If the coda is generated as an adjunct to the VP or IP, we expect there to be an *additional* modification relation between the coda and its host, on the basis of (45).

The interpretive difference between depictive predication and restrictive nominal modification illustrates the point. While the depictive adjective in *Mary met two students drunk* restricts the denotation of the noun like the attributive adjective in *Mary met two drunk students*, there is a semantic difference in another respect. Unlike an adnominal modifier, a depictive predicate is linked in a specific way to the event of the matrix VP. To capture the meaning of (39a) more precisely than

---

17 Certain indefinite quantifiers like *many* and *few* are asymmetric in their proportional readings. Li (1997) notes that the post-*you* NP in Chinese *you*-NP-XP sentences always has a symmetric reading, for example there is no proportional reading of *hendao* 'many'. This is not true of IV2 in German; Gärtner (2001: 113-114) discusses examples involving the quantifier *viel* 'many' in its proportional reading.

is done in (42), it is necessary to add the condition that the two students were drunk *at the point in time when Mary discovered them*.[18] In other words, depictive predication involves an additional temporal dependency over and above 'argument sharing'. It is by virtue of this temporal dependency that depictives satisfy (45). No such additional dependency is found with a restrictive NP modifier. Nor is there evidence for such an additional dependency in the Chinese coda construction. The absence of a direct modification relation between the coda and the matrix VP / IP makes this construction an exception to (45) under the 'secondary predication' analysis.[19] Under the relative clause hypothesis, of course, the coda is no exception to (45).

There is a second generalisation which the coda construction counterexemplifies under the secondary predicate analysis. Certain adjunct types display a thematic or control relation with an argument of the verb, in addition to the modification of the event or proposition which falls under (45). As well as depictives, these include controlled temporal adjuncts and purpose infinitives (where the control relation is mediated by an A'-dependency within the adjunct).[20]

(46) a. Mary$_j$ read it [ while e$_j$ travelling to London ].
 b. Mary bought it$_j$ [ to give e$_j$ to John ].

In all cases involving such an additional link to an argument of the verb, the adjunct itself is *non-finite*. Finite adverbial adjuncts generally do not involve an additional link to an argument of V. There are for example no finite causal or

---

18 Rothstein (2000) provides an explicit event-based analysis. Assuming that the secondary predicate introduces an event variable distinct from that introduced by the matrix VP, the depictive interpretation is licensed as a summing of the two events. Thus the event of 'Mary discovering John drunk' is an event that is composed of an event of 'Mary discovering John' and an event of 'John being drunk'. Event summation is subject to two conditions: (i) the two events must share a participant; (ii) the run-time of the matrix event must be contained within the run-time of depictive event. The meaning of (i) emerges as (ii), where τ(ej) is the 'run time' of the event ej, and 'part-of' is temporal containment.
 (i) Mary discovered John drunk
 (ii) $\exists e \exists e_1 \exists e_2$ [ e=(sum of e$_1$,e$_2$) ∧ discover(e$_1$) ∧ Ag(e$_1$)=Mary ∧ Th(e$_1$)=John ∧ drunk(e$_2$) ∧ Arg(e$_2$)=John ∧ τ(e$_1$) is-part-of τ(e$_2$) ]
19 Chinese has a construction, illustrated in (i), distinct from the coda construction, which appears to be a true depictive secondary predication (Zhang 2003). The secondary predicate (a preverbal adjective) is predicated of a postverbal NP, and shows the same temporal dependency as its English translation, i.e. (i) entails the tea was hot when Akiu drunk it.
 (i) Akiu rere de he le yi bei cha / na bei cha
  Akiu hot de drink prf one cup tea / that cup tea
  'Akiu drank a / that cup of tea hot.'
20 Whether the link to an argument of the matrix verb is mediated by a control relation or by a direct thematic relation, as in Rothstein's analysis of depictives, is immaterial to the point being made here.

temporal adjuncts that involve internal operator movement of the type found in purpose infinitives.[21] If the Chinese coda is a finite clause, the secondary predicate analysis renders it exceptional in this respect too. On the other hand, finite clauses that modify (only) an argument of the verb and yet surface in right-adjoined positions are attested in many languages. These are (extraposed) relative clauses.

## 5. The 'indefinites-only' restriction

The relative clause analysis of the Chinese coda construction provides a promising perspective for understanding the indefinites-only restriction. The idea sketched here is essentially Gärtner's (2001) proposal for the German IV2 construction.

### 5.1 Strong vs. weak NPs and presuppositionality

Broadly speaking, the division between NP-types that can figure as NP* in the coda construction and those that cannot matches the distinction between strong NPs and weak NPs (see e.g. Diesing 1992). The same is true of German IV2.[22]

Strong NPs are *presuppositional*. For example, the use of the definite NP *the man who is called Wolf* presupposes there is a man called Wolf (or, it recalls the already-established discourse entity 'man called Wolf'). Weak NPs on the other hand are not presuppositional: the use of *a man who is called Wolf* does not presuppose that there is a man called Wolf, but asserts this (or, it introduces a man called Wolf as a new discourse entity). In the case of QNPs, the presupposition ensures that the domain they quantify over is not empty. In the case of definite expressions, this is the existential presupposition, or Heim's (1988) familiarity condition.

In German, V2 order is generally a mark of main clauses; a finite declarative with V2 order is typically used to make a simple assertion. A central property of assertions is, put simply, that the content of an assertion may not be presupposed or already given in (entailed by) the context. Gärtner suggests that in IV2 clauses,

---

21 Finite adjuncts may involve an optional link with a matrix argument realised by binding of a pronoun, as in *Mary kissed John[j] because / though / while he[j] was drunk*. Such a link lacks the obligatory character of the control relations in (46).

22 Weak NPs in English and German include bare mass nouns and bare plurals in existential readings, and those introduced by indefinite determiners (*a*, numerals, *some*, *many* etc.), while strong NPs include definites, proper names, personal pronouns and those introduced by strong quantifiers (*every*, *all*, *most* etc.). In Chinese, weak NPs include 'numeral+classifier+noun' and bare nouns in existential readings, while strong NPs include 'demonstrative+classifier+noun', names, personal pronouns, bare nouns in definite readings, and strong quantified NPs. It has been observed that non-specific bare N does not support a coda (Huang 1987, Tsai 1999); however bare nouns apparently can support a coda in sentences with *you*; cf. (14) above, from Li (1997).

V2 order is a reflex of a special mood specification which requires that the clause be 'assertional', and that this is the key to understanding the indefinites-only restriction.

Suppose that the Chinese coda is a finite relative clause whose mood specification requires that it be 'assertional'.[23] As such, it cannot occur in contexts which require it to form part of a presupposition. The exclusion of strong quantifiers and definite expressions is then explainable in terms of the fact that such NPs are presuppositional. Because the coda is a restrictive relative clause, its content is computed as part of the presupposition of NP*. The nature of the determiner in (47a) requires that (47b) be presupposed, while the [+assertional] specification of the relative clause requires that (47c) be asserted (which includes not being entailed by the presupposition). The presuppositional nature of NP* automatically conflicts with the anti-presuppositional nature of the coda.

(47) a. \* Wo jiao-guo  *na ge xuesheng*  [ hen congming ]
        I   teach-ASP   that CL student   very intelligent
   b. $\exists x.\ student(x) \wedge intelligent(x)$
   c. $\exists x.\ intelligent(x)$

This line of explanation is not open to analyses that do not treat the coda as a restrictive modifier. If the coda is not a restrictive modifier of NP*, then the presupposition associated with NP* is limited to $\exists x.\ student(x)$, so that no conflict would arise.[24,25]

---

[23] This could be a way of cashing out the idea that *de* in ordinary relatives marks subordination (like V-final order in German), while the lack of *de* in the coda marks 'insubordination' (like V2 in German). It may also accommodate the intuition (Huang 1987, Li 1997) that the relation NP* – XP is like a 'topic – comment' relation.

[24] This is also essentially the difference between a NP*-coda nexus and a topic sentence like (i).
   (i) [ [topic *na ge xuesheng* ] hen congming ]
       that cl student very intelligent
   That a student exists is presupposed by the topic NP and (47c) corresponds to comment of the assertion. The topic NP is not subject to an indefinites-only restriction; indeed, the opposite is true – in Chinese, a topic NP may not be *in*definite.

[25] Tsai's (1999) secondary predicate analysis of the coda highlights the fact that secondary predicates trigger specificity on their NP 'subjects' (Percus 1996). However, secondary predicates do not limit their subjects to indefinites. It is not clear how Tsai's analysis can explain the indefinites-only restriction.

## 5.2 'Even' and 'only'

The prosodic integration of the German IV2 construction goes hand in hand with the fact that the two clauses form a single 'information unit'; for example, the main clause and the IV2 clause together form a single focus-background domain. Gärtner (2001) exploits this as a way of independently verifying the anti-presuppositional nature of the IV2 clause.

In ordinary restrictive relative clause constructions (in which the relative clause is also prosodically integrated) a focus-sensitive particle like *even* or *only* in the main clause can associate with a focussed constituent in the relative clause, as in (49a,b), both of which could be a natural response to an utterance of (48). (The focus-sensitive particle is italicised, small capitals indicate the focus).

(48)  I know someone that can speak three languages.

(49)  a.  I *even* know someone that can speak FOUR languages.
      b.  I *only* know someone that can speak TWO languages.

Horn (1969) analysed *even* and *only* in terms of presuppositions, whereby *only* presupposes the content of its scope, while *even* asserts the content of its scope, as indicated in (50)–(51). *Even*, in this analysis, presupposes a focus-derived alternative to its scope, while *only* asserts a focus-derived alternative to its scope:

(50)  a.  I *even* know someone that can speak FOUR languages.
      b.  *assertion* = "the speaker knows someone who can speak 4 languages"
      c.  *presupposition* = "less than 4 ", i.e.
          "the speaker knows someone who can speak $n$ languages, $n < 4$ "

(51)  a.  I *only* know someone that can speak TWO languages.
      b.  *assertion* = "not more than 2 ", i.e.
          "the speaker does *not* know someone that can speak $n$ languages, $n > 2$ "
      c.  *presupposition* = "the speaker knows someone that can speak 2 languages"

With *even*, the content of the relative clause is part of the *asserted* meaning (and the presupposition involves the 'less than' alternative to the relative clause). With *only*, the content of the relative clause is part of the *presupposition* (and the asserted meaning involves the '(not) more than' alternative to the relative clause).

As Gärtner (2001) points out, if Horn's analysis is on the right track, a clear prediction emerges, namely that an IV2 relative, which cannot be presupposed, can contain a focus associated with *sogar* 'even' in the main clause, but not a focus associated with *nur* 'only'. The prediction is borne out, cf. (52) (with *nur* 'only' a regular verb-final relative clause can be used):

(52) Ich kenne sogar / *nur jemanden der kann DREI Sprachen sprechen.
     I know even / *only someone D-PRON can three languages speak
     'I even / *only know someone who can speak three languages.'

The same test can be applied to the Chinese coda, and it yields the same result. A focus inside a coda can associate with *shenzhi* 'even' in the main clause (53b). A focus inside the coda cannot associate with *zhi* 'only' in the main clause (53c). The *de*-relative sentence (54) is however judged to be natural.

(53) a. Akiu renshi yi ge ren [ neng shuo san zhong yuyan ]
       A. know one CL person can speak three kind language
       'Akiu knows someone who can speak three languages.'
   b. Lao Li *shenzhi* renshi yi ge ren [ neng shuo SI zhong yuyan ]
       L.L. even know one CL person can speak four kind language
       'Lao Li even knows a person who can speak FOUR languages.'
   c. * Baoyu *zhi* renshi (yi ge) ren [ neng shuo LIANG zhong yuyan ]
       B. only know one CL person can speak two kind language

(54) Baoyu *zhi* renshi [ neng shuo LIANG zhong yuyan de ] ren
     B. only know can speak two kind language DE person
     'Baoyu only knows someone who can speak TWO languages.'

In term of Horn's analysis, the coda in (53b) with *shenzhi* 'even' provides part of the asserted content (and not part of the presupposition); while the coda in (53c) with *zhi* 'only' provides part of the presupposition. The contrast between (53b) and (53c) thus provides independent evidence for the 'anti-presuppositionality' of the Chinese coda.

## 6. Syntactic issues

In sections 3.-5. above, the claim that the coda is a restrictive modifier of NP* was supported by semantic arguments. It may still be argued that whether the coda is *syntactically* a relative clause construction is a different issue. Indeed, Gärtner (2001) proposes that the German IV2 construction is *not* a relative clause construction in the syntactic sense (even though the IV2 clause is semantically a 'relative clause'). Rather, he argues that IV2 sentences are syntactically paratactic. He suggests the IV2 clause is the complement of an abstract head π whose specifier is the first clause containing the indefinite NP*.

(55) [$_{πP}$ CP1 [ π CP2 ] ]

This allows an explanation inter alia of why the IV2 clause is constrained to appear at the right edge of the first clause (unlike a V-final RC); and is consistent with the absence of evidence that the IV2 clause is c-commanded by positions within the first clause (for example, nothing may be moved out of the IV2 clause into CP1).

There are considerations that speak against such an approach to the Chinese coda. For example, Zhang (2008:30) suggests that a constituent may be extracted out of the coda clause to become the topic of the main clause, as in (56). If this kind of example indeed involves extraction, the coda must be c-commanded by the topic position within the first clause.

(56) [Zhe zhong chou-tofu]$_j$ wo renshi yi ge laowai [ hen xihuan chi t$_j$ ]
    this type stinky-tofu  I  know  one CL foreigner very like eat
    'This type of stinky tofu, I know a foreigner who likes to eat (it) very much.'

If the coda is a relative clause in the syntactic sense, then it forms a constituent at some level with the NP* which it modifies. To establish this would however require a closer analysis of the syntactic properties of the construction than is attempted here (for relevant discussion, see Zhang 2008 and Del Gobbo 2009).

# References

Del Gobbo, Francesca. 2009. On secondary predication and specificity. Handout of talk given at IACL, Paris, 2-4 July.

Diesing, Molly. 1992. *Indefinites*. MIT Press, Cambridge Mass.

Gärtner, Hans-Martin. 2001. Are there V2 relative clauses in German? *Journal of Comparative Germanic Linguistics* 3, 97-141

Heim, Irene. 1988. *The Semantics of Definite and Indefinite Noun Phrases*. Garland, New York.

Horn, Laurence. 1969. A presuppositional analysis of ONLY and EVEN. In: R. Binnick, A. Davison, G. Green & J. Morgan (eds.) *Papers from the Fifth Regional Meeting of the Chicago Linguistics Society*, 98-107.

Hu, Jianhua, Haihua Pan & Liejiong Xu. 2001. Is there a finite vs. nonfinite distinction in Chinese? *Linguistics* 39, 1117-1148.

Huang, C.-T. James. 1987. Existential sentences in Chinese and (in)definiteness. In: E. Reuland & A. ter Meulen (eds.) *The Representation of (In)definiteness*. MIT Press, Cambridge Mass. 226-253.

Keenan, Edward. 1987. A Semantic Definition of 'Indefinite NP'. In: E. Reuland & A. ter Meulen (eds.) *The Representation of (In)definiteness*. MIT Press, Cambridge Mass. 286-317.

Li, Charles. & Sandra Thompson 1981. *Mandarin Chinese: a functional reference grammar*. University of California Press, Berkeley/Los Angeles.

Li, Y.-H. Audrey. 1997. Types of existential sentences in English and Chinese. Ms., USC.

Li, Y.H. Audrey. 1999. Word order, structure and relativization. Ms. USC.

Percus, Orin. 1996. Consequences of a predication-based analysis of semantic partition. In: J. Camacho, L. Choueiri & M. Watanabe (eds.), *Proceedings of WCCFL 14*. CSLI, Stanford. 415-429

Rothstein, Susan. 2000. Secondary Predication and Aspectual Structure. *ZAS Papers in Linguistics* 17, 241-264.

Tsai, W-T. Dylan. 1999. *On Economizing the Theory of A-bar Dependencies*. Garland, New York.

Zhang, Niina. 2003. The asymmetry between depictives and resultatives in Chinese. In: Anna Maria Di Sciullo (ed.), *Asymmetry in Grammar, Volume I: Syntax and Semantics*. John Benjamins, Philadelphia. 165-185.

Zhang, Niina. 2008. Existential Coda Constructions as Internally Headed Relative Clause Constructions. *The Linguistics Journal* 3: 8-54. [http://www.linguistics-journal.com/2008articles.php]

Email: christopher.wilder@ntnu.no

# Nominal Structure in Early Child Mandarin[1]

Thomas Hun-tak Lee
*Chinese University of Hong Kong*

## 1. The status of DP in early child language

It has been widely reported that in early grammatical development, the first nominals used by children comprise proper names, demonstratives and bare nouns, with the determiner noticeably missing. In the earliest stage of nominal development, determiner use is either absent or not productive. This phenomenon has been observed for many languages, including English (Brown 1973, Radford 1990), Mandarin Chinese (Min 1994), Dutch (Hyams 1996), German (Penner and Weissenborn 1996), Cantonese (Wong 1998), and Greek (Marinis 2003).[2] Various analyses have been proposed to reconcile the late appearance of determiners with the nativist assumption that syntactic categories and representations are available to children from the earliest stages of their development.

Some scholars argue that the functional category D is present in early language, but may be underspecified, resulting primarily in deictic reference (Hyams 1996). In her analysis, adopting the semantic analysis of Heim (1982), the syntactic repre-

---

[1] I wish to thank the participants of the Hunan Chinese Early Language Acquisition (CELA) project for their help in building the Hunan child language corpus, in particular Ai Zhaoyang, Huang Aijun, Ning Chunyan and Zeng Tao. I wish also to thank Hu Yajuan for her classification of the nominal data of LSY and AJR in a MA thesis I supervised as part of the CELA project. Earlier versions of the paper have been read at workshops at Nanzan University, National Tsinghua University, Beijing Language and Culture University, Workshop on Cantonese 7, and the 16th Annual Meeting of the International Association of Chinese Linguistics. I am indebted to various participants of those events for their comments, in particular Stephen Crain, Fan Li, Fang Li, Hu Jianhua, Keiko Murasugi, Thomas Roeper, and Xiaolu Yang, though any fault that remains is mine. Finally, I am grateful to Tor Åfarli and Christopher Wilder for inviting me to contribute to this volume, and for their editorial comments. The support of CERG grant CUHK4583/06H is hereby acknowledged. In this paper, the following abbreviations are used: CL=classifier; NUM= numeral; NOM= nominalizer; MOT= mother; INV= investigator; CHI= child. The age of the child is given in years and months, or years, months and days, represented as 'y;mm' or 'y; mm; dd'.

[2] In Mandarin and Cantonese, languages without an article system, enumeration and determination require the presence of classifiers, and the studies of Min (1994) and Wong (1998) show clearly the relative later onset of classifiers than proper names or bare nouns.

sentation of DPs such as 'the boy' or 'a boy' consists of a D-operator binding a variable, which has as its default range the contextually salient and presupposed entities in the discourse domain. The D may be specific, carrying the index of the D-operator, and picks out a familiar NP; or it may be non-specific, bearing an index different from that of the D-operator, and introduces a novel NP. In early grammar, besides the co-indexing and contra-indexing options of adult grammar, the child has the additional option of an unindexed D, which is assigned a familiar, deictic interpretation.[3]

Other scholars have also proposed that DPs are available to children in the early stage. Based on child Dutch data, Hoekstra and Jordens (1994) argue that determiners may appear first as adjuncts to NPs rather than as head, taking as supporting evidence the apparent left branch violations of Dutch children in the scrambling of the specifier of an object DP to a position before the negator. The violations can be understood if the scrambled DPs are seen as adjuncts to NPs, which do not form a barrier to movement. The existence of DPs is supported by the fact that in the language of Dutch two-year-olds, proper names and pronouns scramble, but determinerless nominals do not. While DPs are available to children, the determiners that head them are optional.[4] In another proposal espousing the Strong Continuity view, Penner and Weissenborn (1996) report evidence for N-to-D raising in the early language of German children, as reflected in their early use of dative possessives and expletive definite articles.[5] While the functional projection of DP is available in early child grammar, its manifestation may not be fully adult-like from the start because of properties of the triggering information, which may vary in salience depending on the richness of the morphological

---

3   Hyams (1996) tries to capture the parallel between underspecified D and underspecified I. Just as unindexed D refers deictically and to familiar entities, underspecified I refers to the deictic present. While the underspecification of D results in determinerless nominals, the underspecification of I gives rise to root infinitives and null subjects.
4   As observed by Hyams (1996), once determiners appear in nominals in child Dutch, these nominals with determiners will scramble as well as proper names and pronouns.
5   Penner and Weissenborn (1996) report use of possessive pronouns as place holders for $D^0$ and complete dative possessives consisting of both possessor and possessum in their Swiss German subject before two years of age (examples (a-b)). The expletive definite article appeared at 1;7 (example (c)), and became productive around 2;4.
    (a)   Nomi mis (J, 1;07;02)
          Naomi mine: 1:SG|NEUT:SG
          'Naomi's' (points to Naomi's alarm clock)
    (b)   Nadaw sis Ue [=Uhr] (J, 1;10;19)
          Nadaw: NEUT:SG watch:FEM:SG
          'Nadaw's watch'
    (c)   d'Outo ab (J, 1;07;13)
          the car down

markings of D.⁶ In a study of the acquisition of Modern Greek, Marinis (2003) reports that definite articles have become productive in child Greek from 2;0, when number marking on nouns and case marking on nouns and articles appear, as do indefinite articles. These facts are taken as evidence for an elaborate DP involving three layers of functional structure.⁷

A large body of literature has taken the Weak Continuity view, arguing that functional categories and structures may not be available to children before two years of age (Lebeaux 1988, Radford, 1988, 1990, Guilfoyle and Noonan 1992, among others). With respect to the development of nominals, the recent proposal of Schafer and de Villiers (2000) has pointed to deficiencies in young children's interpretation of articles, reaffirming the view that DPs are absent in early child English. It is well known that conflicting findings have been reported on the acquisition of articles. While the early experiments of Maratsos (1976) have demonstrated early mastery of the distinction between definite and indefinite articles, the later studies of Karmiloff-Smith (1979) and Warden (1981) have revealed complexities in the use of nominals for referent introduction and referent tracking. The experimental data of the latter scholars highlight young children's failure to correctly use DPs to mark information structure. The experiments of Schafer and de Villiers, carried out with preschoolers, have replicated some of these early results, showing children's grasp of the specific/non-specific uses of the indefinite article.⁸ At the same time, as in earlier studies, their findings reflect children's

---

6   Penner and Weissenborn (1996) argue that triggering information may vary in terms of its accessibility. Thus the dative possessive head is regarded as more accessible than the expletive definite article since the former is embedded in a richer agreement configuration than the latter. While D is available, the implementation of expletive insertion in $D^0$ will involve language-specific idiosyncracies.
7   Marinis (2003) postulates the functional projections FP and NumP as constituents of DP, with F hosting the definite article, and NumP the structure for numerals. In Modern Greek, the definite article, unlike the indefinite article, is not in complementary distribution with demonstratives, which require the presence of the definite article, as illustrated below. The demonstrative would occupy the D position whereas the definite article will be in F.
    (a)   *Aghorasa afto ena vivlio
          bought this a/one book
    (b)   Aghorasa afto to vivlio
          bought this the book
    (c)   *Aghorasa afto vivlio
          bought this book
8   Schafer and de Villiers (2000) used a linguistic context to elicit children's verbal answers in the absence of visual cues. Children aged between 3;6 and 5;6 performed well on the following task which required children to use an indefinite article to signal non-specific reference: "Cindy is going to the pond. She wants to catch some fish. What will she need?" Children also did well on a task that required the use of an indefinite article to signal specific reference (an entity known only to the speaker but not the hearer): "I'll bet you have something hanging on the wall of your room at home. What is it?"

failure to make use of the indefinite article when referring to a member of a plural set of entities of the same kind.[9] To account for their data, Schafer and de Villiers propose that children's early use of the definite article is semantically limited to unique referents that they are familiar with, best represented not with DP, but a projection labelled 'theP'.[10] The indefinite articles are captured by the projection of NumP, whose head carries the [±specific] feature. In their analysis, DP should involve a [± hearer] point-of-view feature, since appropriate use of D requires taking into account the hearer's knowledge of discourse referents. Thus, children's early grammar contains 'theP' and NumP, but not DP. Their analysis is taken to be compatible with findings of the psychological literature on theory of mind, in that if children before four years of age cannot represent the beliefs of others, they would have problems taking into account the referential perspectives of the hearer, hence the absence of DP in early child language.[11]

## 2. Objectives of the present study

The Chinese DP contains as its constituents the determiner phrase, the numeral phrase, the classifier phrase, and the noun phrase. Chinese being a classifier language, the classifier is central to nominal structure in being syntactically required for enumeration, and semantically relevant to the determination of noun denotation. This paper explores early nominal structure in child Mandarin, focussing on whether the full-fledged nominal is present, and what kinds of syntax-semantics mappings can be observed, in early language, based on longitudinal data from two Mandarin-speaking children covering the period one and a half to two years three months of age. The following issues will be addressed:

9  The experiments of Schafer and de Villiers (2000) replicate the results of Karmiloff-Smith (1979) in showing that young children experience difficulty in using the indefinite article to refer to one of a plural set of objects of the same kind, as on the following task: "Three ducks and two dogs were walking across a bridge. One of the animals fell off the bridge and said 'Quack'. Guess which?" Studies carried out on Mandarin-speaking children have also found late acquisition of the distinction between definite vs. indefinite reference (Hickmann and Liang 1990).

10 Schafer and de Villiers (2000) found that children have no problem with questions that require reference to unique objects familiar to the child, as on the following task: "Adrienne got a pet hamster for her birthday and put it in a nice cage. It tried to escape so she quickly closed something. What did she close?"

11 Other studies exploring children's grasp of the semantics of reference, e.g. Pérez-Leroux (1998), have shown that Spanish-speaking children take time to acquire the use of a relative clause in the subjunctive mood to mark the non-specificity of the nominal modified by the relative clause. This use is correlated with children's performance on theory-of-mind tasks. The study of De Villiers and Roeper (1995) argue that children begin with NPs rather than DPs when representing complex nominals, but this perspective is tangential to the issue of whether early nominals are DPs.

First, when do numerals and classifiers appear in early child Mandarin? Since the numeral and the classifier have inherent semantic properties in addition to their respective grammatical functions, it is unclear whether numerals and classifiers are acquired in the same way as determiners and NPs, and whether the DP containing all four types of constituents are present in the earliest stages of syntactic development. When do children begin to use a full-fledged nominal structure containing the full range of constituents? Answers to these questions would shed light on the issue of continuity.

Secondly, we are interested in children's knowledge of the mapping between syntactic form and referentiality. It is well known that there are constraints on how syntactic form maps to referential meanings. Some nominal structures map to certain canonical meanings: for example, demonstratives and pronouns typically denote individuals and cannot be used as predicates. Some nominal structures such as numeral phrases may be interpreted as specific or non-specific, but are generally prohibited from taking on definite reference.[12] We are specifically interested in the nominal structures used by children to represent predicate nominals and arguments. Drawing an argument versus predicate nominal distinction is critical for our understanding of the early appearance of what looks like headless *de* nominals in child Mandarin, observed first by Packard (1987), and confirmed in our study.[13]

Third, we would like to find out whether the earliest uses of numeral phrases are specific or non-specific. As numeral phrases belong to a type of quantifier phrase,

---

12  Chen (1987, 2003) observed that numeral phrases in Mandarin may denote definite referents which are identifiable to both speaker and hearer in the discoursal context. The numeral phrases in his examples, however, can be analyzed as numeral phrases having a null specifier in the DP, and are therefore not genuine numeral phrases. The claim that numeral phrases generally do not denote definite reference remains a valid one. For example, one of his examples (Chen 1987:90), simplified here for the sake of illustration, is as below. The definite numeral phrase *sange keren*, '(the) three guests', can be analyzed as having a null DP specifier, on a par with *zhe sange keren* (this three-CL guest) or *menkou sange keren* (door-at three-CL guest), in which the null DP specifier may represent a demonstrative or a location. This point will become clear when we introduce the Mandarin DP structure in the next section.

(a)  Men yi dakai, jinlai yi nan liang nu sange qingnian, dou hen jingshen ...
     door once open, enter one male two female three-CL youth, all very spirited
     *sange keren* xiuxiu bizi, sihu bu xiguan zhe wuzi de yanwei he
     three-CL guest sniff nose, look-like not used-to this room NOM cigarette-smell and
     chou wazi wei.
     stinky-socks smell
     "The door opened, and there entered three young men, a man and two women, all very spirited. (The) three guests sniffed their nose, as if they were not used to the smell of cigarettes and stinky socks in the room.»

13  Headless *de* nominals are those such as (4a-b) and (6) with the modified noun left out, as will be discussed later. The particle *de* is glossed as NOM (=nominalizer) in this paper. It could mark a possessor-possessed relationship, attribution or a relative clause.

if they are first used not referentially, but non-referentially, this will disconfirm the hypothesis of Jackendoff (1983) which suggests that nominals are referential by default, and will lend support to the view of Hornstein (1984) which assumes that quantifiers carry the feature [+operator] by default. This hypothesis will predict that non-specific interpretations are readily available to children.

The paper is organized as follows. We first introduce the syntactic representation of the Mandarin DP, borrowing from the analyses of Cheng and Sybesma (1999) and Sio (2006). Then, the robust findings on the acquisition of the Mandarin nominal are reviewed. Next, we analyze the nominals in the longitudinal development of the two Mandarin-speaking children, looking at headless relatives, the NP structure of arguments and nominals, and the referentiality of numeral phrases. Finally, we give our conclusions, and propose our analysis of nominal structure in early Mandarin in light of the issue of continuity.

## 3. Nominal structure in Mandarin

Various analyses have been proposed for the Mandarin nominal, notably Tang (1990), Li (1998), Cheng and Sybesma (1999), Hsieh (2005) and Sio (2006). These proposals differ in whether they treat numerals and classifiers as heads, and whether they attempt to capture syntax-semantics mappings between nominal structure and referentiality. I will adopt the broad outlines of the analysis of Sio (2006) which developed out of that of Cheng and Sybesma (1999), primarily for its ability to explain systematic dialectal variation between Mandarin and Cantonese. As we will see, this syntactic representation will allow us to capture the facts of early nominal use in child Mandarin in a straightforward way.

Apart from proper names and pronouns, the Mandarin nominal may consist of a bare noun, which is unspecified for number or count/mass distinctions.[14] A bare noun such as *pingguo* 'apple' may denote one or more apples, pieces of apple, or apple substance, depending on the context. Sortal classifiers (or individual classifiers in traditional terminology) such as the general classifier *ge* are needed to individuate nouns (Chao 1968, Cheng and Sybesma 1999, Borer 2005). In Mandarin, when numerals are used for enumeration, classifiers are obligatory; on the other hand, when demonstratives are used for determination, the classifier is optional. Nominals that include both the demonstrative and the numeral will also require the presence of the classifier. These facts are illustrated in (1a-d).

---

14  I take nouns in Chinese to be unspecified for count/mass distinctions, a view that departs from Cheng and Sybesma (1998). See Huang (2009) and Huang and Lee (2009) for further discussion of this issue.

(1) a. pingguo
    'apple/apples'
 b. yi/liang *(ge) pingguo
    one/two CL apple
    'one apple/two apples'
 c. na (ge) pingguo
    that CL apple
    'the apple'
 d. na yi/liang ge pingguo
    that one/two CL apple
    'the apple/the two apples'

While the classifier is required in the presence of the numeral, the classifier may occur without an overt numeral, resulting in a unitary interpretation, as shown in (2a). However, the distribution of the 'classifier+noun' nominal is restricted to non-subject positions (2b). This restriction has to do with the fact that subjects tend to be definite in Chinese (Chao 1968, Li and Thompson 1981), and numeral phrases are generally prohibited from the subject position (Chen 1987), as seen in (2c).[15] Bare nouns can occur in subject as well as object position (2d); in subject position, bare nouns must be interpreted as definite, as shown in (2e).

(2) a. Zhuoshang you ge pingguo.
    table-on exist CL apple
    'There is an apple on the table.'
 b. *Ge pingguo fangzai zhuoshang.
    CL apple put-at table-on
    Intended: 'The apple is on the table.'
 c. *Liang ge pingguo fangzai zhuoshang.
    two CL apple put-at table-on
    Intended: '(The) two apples are on the table.'
 d. Zhuoshang you pingguo.
    table-on exist apple
    'There is (an) apple on the table. / There are apples on the table.'

---

15 Dialects differ on whether they tolerate 'classifier+noun' in subject position. In Cantonese, as opposed to Mandarin, the 'classifier+noun' nominal may occur in subject position with a definite reading (Cheung 1989, Cheng and Sybesma 1999). Whether numeral phrases can occur in subject position depends on a host of factors such as the vividness of the prenominal modifiers, root vs. non-root context, and modal licensing (see Fan 1985, Lee 1986, Li 1998, and Tsai 2001 for further discussion).

    e.    Pingguo fangzai zhuoshang.
         apple put-on table-on
         'The apple(s) are on the table.'

The nominal structure adopted in this study is given in (3), in which determiner, numeral, and classifier are treated as heads of functional categories. The topmost phrase is the Specificity phrase, SpP, whose head can bear the referential features [±specific] or [±definite].[16] An agreement relation must obtain between the specifier of the Specificity phrase and its head, so that if a proper name or a demonstrative or both occur in the specifier position, as in phrases such as (1d) or *Zhangsan na liang ge pingguo* (Zhangsan-that-two-CL-apple) 'the two apples of Zhangsan's', the head must select the [+definite] feature. If nothing occurs in the specifier position of the specificity phrase, the head of SpP can take on any of the referential features. If numerals are present, the features on the head of SpP will be [±specific] since by default numerals are incompatible with definiteness in the absence of demonstratives, proper names or pronouns.[17] In the case of bare nouns, following the analysis of Cheng and Sybesma (1999), the noun in the head of NP can move to the head of the Specificity phrase to pick up [±definite] features. In other words, the syntactic representation will allow bare nouns to be interpreted as definite or indefinite.

    To be able to account for the nominals in child Mandarin, one would also need to analyze nominals with prenominal modification, such as those in (4). Following Sio (2006), I will treat adjective phrases such as those in (4a) as adjuncts to NP. Possessive phrases such as those in (4b) are regarded as adjuncts to either SpP or NP, since one may have phrases such as (4c) and (4d). The difference between the two is a subtle one: when the possessive phrase occurs before the demonstrative-numeral-classifier, the reading is a restrictive or a contrastive one; when the possessive phrase occurs after the demonstrative-numeral-classifier, the reading seems to be an appositive one. Thus (4c) means something like 'the two apples that belong to Zhangsan' as distinguished from other sets containing two apples

---

16    The Specificity Phrase can be taken as the equivalent of DP. In Sio (2006), the Specificity Phrase is represented by SP. I use a different symbol to make the nature of the projection more transparent. I am giving an intuitive account of how the mapping between syntactic form and referential meaning is handled in the analysis of Sio (2006) and Cheng and Sybesma (1999). For a precise statement of the workings of the feature mechanism, the reader is referred to their works.

17    In the analysis of Cheng and Sybsema (1999), Mandarin differs from Cantonese in that Mandarin always requires a numeral to be present syntactically whenever there is an overt classifier. Thus, the 'classifier +noun' nominal in Mandarin is analyzed as a structure with an empty numeral. For this reason, such a nominal is considered to have only a non-specific interpretation, a claim that needs further empirical verification.

(3)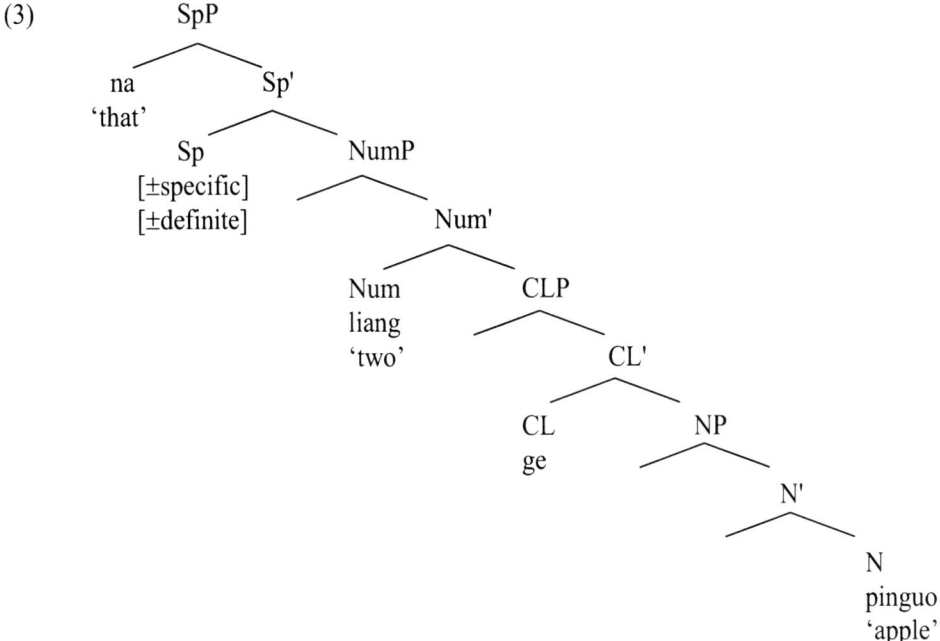

that may belong to other persons. On the other hand, (4d) is understood as 'the two apples of Zhangsan's' or 'those two apples, which belong to Zhangsan'.

(4) a. shifen xinxian de pingguo
very fresh NOM apple
'apple(s) that are very fresh'
b. Zhangsan de pingguo
Zhangsan NOM apple
'Zhangsan's apple(s)'
c. Zhangsan de na liang ge pingguo
Zhangsan NOM that two CL apple
'the two apples that belong to Zhangsan'
d. na liang ge Zhangsan de pingguo
that two CL Zhangsan NOM apple
'those two apples of Zhangsan's'

Other prenominal modifiers such as relative clauses can be treated in the same way as possessive phrases, that is, as adjuncts to SpP or NP, with more or less the same subtle semantic distinction. That is, when the relative clause occurs before the demonstrative-numeral-classifier, a restrictive reading is obtained, whereas if the relative clause occurs after the classifier, a non-restrictive reading results, illustrated in (5).[18] In (6), a relative clause modifies a noun in the absence of a classifier so that the cardinality of the set of referents denoted by the noun is unspecified. Such a nominal may be referential (as in (7)) or may function as a predicate nominal (as in (8)).

(5) a. mama mai de na liang ge pingguo
 mother buy NOM that two CL apple
 'the two apples that mother bought'
 b. na liang ge mama mai de pingguo
 that two CL mother buy NOM apple
 'those two apples, which mother bought'

(6) a. mama mai de (pingguo)
 mother buy NOM apple
 '(the) apple(s) mother bought'
 b. gei mama de (pingguo)
 give mother NOM apple
 '(the) apple(s) that (I) gave to mother'

(7) a. mama mai de pingguo zai nali
 mother buy NOM apple exist there
 'The apple(s) mother bought is/are there.'
 b. mama mai de zai nali
 mother buy NOM exist there
 'The thing(s) mother bought is/are there.'

(8) a. zhe shi mama mai de pingguo
 this be mother buy NOM apple
 'This is an apple that mother bought. / These are apples that mother bought.'
 b. zhe shi mama mai de
 this be mother buy NOM
 'This is what mother bought.'

---

18 The issue whether one should draw a distinction between restrictive and non-restrictive relative clauses is a much debated one, going back to the earlier observation of Chao (1968), later disputed by Teng (1987). This issue was further discussed in Huang (1982) and Del Gobbo (2003).

A word is in order about the nominals in which a relative clause modifies a noun, as in (6) and (7); if the noun is covert, the nominal is in essence a free relative, as in (7b). These nominals behave the same as bare nouns without prenominal modification.[19] If they occur in subject position, they must receive a definite interpretation, like bare nouns in (2e), regardless of whether the noun is overt. Thus, the nominals in (7a) and (7b) must be interpreted referentially as definite nominals. On the other hand, if these nominals occur as complements to the copula verb, as in (8), they are understood as predicate nominals, regardless of whether the noun is overt.[20] As predicate nominals, they have the status of NPs rather than Specificity phrases or DPs. This point will be relevant to our analysis of child Mandarin.

## 4. Earlier findings on nominal acquisition in Mandarin-speaking children

Three generalizations can be made based on earlier studies of nominal development in Mandarin-speaking children. These findings serve as a point of departure for the analysis of our child Mandarin data. First of all, it is clear that the earliest nominals of Mandarin-speaking children are dominated by bare nouns and null forms, with classifiers becoming productive only at a later stage. In the longitudinal study of Min (1994), one of her subjects (Mengmeng) was observed in detail from 1;3 to 2;8. During the period 1;3 to 1;8, around 60% or more of the nominals were bare nouns, and approximately 25% were null arguments (Min 1994:74). On the other hand, on average only 1% or less of the nominals in this period contained a classifier. The delayed onset of classifiers in nominal development has also been reported in the acquisition of Cantonese.[21]

---

19  In the semantic analysis of Chinese common nouns by Krifka (1995), bare nouns include those with prenominal modification.
20  Nouns modified by relative clauses can of course receive a referential reading in object position if they are not complements to the copula, as in:
    (a)  Wo zhaodao mama mai de pingguo.
    I find-asp mother buy NOM apple
    'I found the apple(s) that mother bought.'
21  In the earlier child Chinese literature, the most explicit demonstration of the delayed onset of classifiers compared to bare nouns can be found in Wong (1998), a study of noun phrase development in four Cantonese-speaking children. She defined the age of acquisition as the first of three consecutive sessions in which the child used the category in three different syntactic positions. By this stringent criterion of category acquisition, it was shown that bare nouns are acquired at 1;11, but classifiers are not acquired until after 2;0.

The second generalization about nominal acquisition in Mandarin based on earlier literature relates to the mapping between the syntactic form and their semantic interpretation, in particular with respect to the specific vs. non-specific distinction. It was observed by Min (1994) that the specific vs. non-specific distinction was acquired early by Mandarin-speaking children, and numeral phrases of the form 'numeral-classifier-noun' are first used for non-specific reference. In Min's taxonomy, specific reference is involved "when the speaker refers to particular individuals, which are distinct from all the other members of their class or of a group" and non-specific reference is involved "when there is no reference to particular individuals" (Min 1994: 18). It was found that 70% or more of the children's nominals involved specific reference, with the percentage of non-specific uses ranging from 1 to 10% in each of the periods studied. Only four types of nominals were used for non-specific reference by her subjects: bare-noun, numeral-classifier-noun, kinship term, and other-N, with bare noun being the most frequently used type.[22] However, the following nominal types were never used for non-specific reference: demonstrative-classifier-noun, posssessive NP, demonstrative pronoun, personal pronoun and null nominals. This clearly reflects early sensitivity to the mapping between nominal structure and referentiality.

The subject studied in greatest detail by Min (1994), Mengmeng, started using numeral-classifier-noun, bare-nouns and kinship terms for non-specific reference during the period 1;3-1;5. The child then started to use other-N (including mainly bare nouns with prenominal modification marked by the nominalizer *de*) for non-specific reference from 1;9-1;11 onwards. Specific reference encoded by the numeral-classifier-noun structure was said to be rare in early phases, occurring only in the period 2;0-2;8. Example (9) is an example of non-specific reference in the form of a bare noun with prenominal modification. Example (10) represents an instance of specific reference by one of her subjects JJ.

(9) (Mengmeng, at 2;2;27, was in the experimenter's lab and said that she would give her sweets to eat)
 CHI: deng wo hui jia
 wait I return home

---

[22] The category 'other-N' is described as follows: "Other nominals mainly consisted of DE-constructions for children under 2;0, and of a few relative clauses for children from 2;0-2;2 onwards" (Min 1994:76). It would be safe to interpret these as bare nouns with prenominal modification by adjective phrases, possessive phrases or relative clauses.

|     |     |
| --- | --- |
| CHI: | gei ni chi haochi de |
|     | give you eat good-eat-NOM |
|     | 'When I return home, I will give you tasty things to eat.' |

(10) JJ (2;9;11)
    CHI:     ta dai yige xiao houzi
                  he bring one-CL little monkey
                  'He comes with a little monkey.'

Non-specific uses of the numeral-classifier-noun are also reported by Chang-Smith (2005), who observed a monolingual Mandarin-speaking child at two-week intervals for 12 sessions, from 21 months (MLU 1.74) to 27 months (MLU 2.63). It was observed that numerals and classifiers were initially used without complements, interpreted by Chang-Smith as an indication that the functional heads of numeral and classifier are underspecified. Early non-specific indefinite uses of the numeral phrase by her subject BING, at 1;8;22, are documented, as shown in (11).

(11) a.    MOT:     ni you-mei-you gei wo qianqian? (The mum asked Bing to pay)
                              you have not have give me money
                              'Have you paid me?'
           BING:    shi kuai qian (He pretended to pay)
                              ten CL money
                              'Ten dollars.'
   b.    AUN:     ni chi ji-ge? (The aunt was referring to the jellies)
                              you eat how-many-CL
                              'How many pieces have you eaten?'
           BING:    liang ge
                              two CL
                              'Two pieces.'

The third generalization that can be gleaned from earlier Mandarin acquisition studies is the preponderance of headless nominals in early child Mandarin, first observed in a cross-sectional study of Packard (1987). He analyzed the natural speech utterances of 27 Mandarin-speaking children from Taiwan, consisting of a younger group with mean age 2;3 and an older group with mean age 2;9, yielding a total of around 400 utterances with the nominalizer *de*. Packard found that younger children preferred to use *de* nominals with the complement noun unexpressed, what he calls 'headless' structures, i.e. structures analogous to (4a-b) and (6) with the complement noun left out. In the *de* structures with the complement noun being overt, in what he calls 'headed' structures, there were significantly more nonverbal than verbal modifiers; in the 'headless' *de* structures, there were significantly more verbal than nonverbal modifiers.[23] Packard argues that the younger children's preference for 'headless' *de* forms cannot be ascribed to length limitations or pragmatic context. It is observed that the binding relationship between the head and the gap exists for verbal modifiers, but not for nonverbal modifiers. This accounts for why nominals with verbal modifiers would favor headless structures, whereas nominals with nonverbal modifiers favored headed *de* structures. As we will see, the early productivity of headless *de* nominals is a robust phenomenon in child Mandarin. While the binding account of Packard (1987) has some plausibility, his paper does not give detailed information about the contexts of use of these *de*-nominals. We will argue that the early *de*-nominals in child Mandarin with 'missing' complement nouns are typically predicate nominals, i.e. NPs, and not DPs, based on our longitudinal data.

## 5. Nominal structure and referentiality in early child Mandarin

### 5.1 Data and methodology

Our analysis of nominal structure in early child Mandarin is based on longitudinal data from two Mandarin-speaking children growing up in Changsha, a male child LSY covering the period 1;05;19-2;03;06, and a female child AJR covering the period 1;05;13-2;02;12, with 17 sessions of approximately hour-long observations for each child.[24] The beginning session for analysis was set at 1 year 5 months, as the lexical spurt of these children occurred around that time, and two-word combinations began to appear at roughly the same time (Zeng 2010). As our concern is focused on nominal structure in the earliest stage of syntactic development, we included data only up to shortly after two years of age. In our nominal analysis, the

---

23  In our current analysis, the modified noun is a complement to higher functional projections such as the head of the classifier phrase or the head of the specificity phrase. Thus they are strictly speaking not heads, but complements. However, for the sake of continuity, I will temporarily maintain Packard's terminology in our review of the literature.

24  The two subjects were each observed and taped with audio recorders and audiovisual cameras for a greater number of sessions, LSY from 10 months to 2 years 11 months, and AJR from 9 months to three years of age. Thirty six of the observation sessions of LSY were transcribed, spanning the period 1;00;19 to 2;03;06, and 38 of the observation sessions of AJR were transcribed, covering the period 1;02;22 to 2;02;12. Seventeen of these transcripts were used for each child in the present study, with one to two transcripts per month.

data are drawn from Hu (2007), who classified the nominal uses of the children into predicate nominals and arguments.

Hu (2007) adopted a number of criteria to determine whether a nominal is an argument or a predicate, based on linguistic context and the nonlinguistic situation. In multi-word utterances in which a verb is present, the linguistic context can often help decide on the status of the nominal. Thus, for instance, LSY at age 1;10;23 took a picture book from a book shelf, looked at it and uttered (12).

(12) CHI:  shi mama mai de
          be mother buy NOM
          '(This) is (a thing that) mother bought.'

In such an instance, the phrase word *mama mai de* 'what mother bought' is a nominal that can be analyzed as a headless relative serving as a predicate, while the word *mama* 'mother' in the phrase is an argument, being the subject of the verb *mai* 'buy'. Sometimes, in a multi-word utterance that lacks a verb, the argument relationship will need to be inferred. For example, our subject AJR at 1;10;02 is holding a biscuit, and gives it to her mother, uttering spontaneously *mama binggan* 'mother biscuit'. The context warrants the intended meaning 'mother (eat/have) biscuit', as the child seems to want the mother to eat the biscuit or have it. Thus, the two nominals *mama* and *binggan* are classified as arguments.

It is harder to determine whether a nominal occurring alone as an utterance should be classified as an argument or a predicate, and the nonlinguistic situation is critical for the classification. In single-word utterances, a noun phrase used by the child is considered an argument if it fits the argument slot of an immediately preceding adult question; it will be considered a predicate if it fits the predicate slot of an immediately preceding adult question. For example, at 1;08;12, an adult investigator is holding a toy spoon and asks AJR what it is. The child looks at it and gives the name of the object *shaozi* 'spoon'. Such a token, illustrated in (13), will be regarded as a predicate nominal.

(13) Adult:  Zhe shi shenme?
             this is what
             'What is this?'
     Child:  Shaozi
             spoon
             'Spoon.'

In some instances, the classification of the nominal will depend on rich interpretation of the situation and the child's linguistic history. If the child points to or gazes at a particular object whose existence or location is newly noticed by him/her, and uses the nominal to refer to the object, then such a nominal will be analyzed as an argument if the name of the object is already known to the child, as ascertained from the name's occurrence in two or more previous recording sessions, and if the ongoing activity does not appear to be an act of naming. The child in such a situation is assumed to be asserting the existence or appearance of the object rather than the name of the object, equivalent to saying 'There is an X here/over there.' For example, in the observation session at age 1;08;07, AJR sees a toy racket on the floor, picks it up and utters *paizi* 'racket'. The word *paizi* has been known to the child, as determined from the audiovisual recordings of the two preceding observation sessions, and the utterance is not produced as part of an activity of naming. Therefore, the single-word utterance *paizi* 'racket' is seen as an argument.

In other instances, if the child produces a nominal without any accompanying gestures, and the nominal fits the argument slot of a proposition that can be inferred from the context of the utterance, the nominal will be considered an argument. For example, the child LSY at age 1;08;16 takes up a pencil, and is going to draw on a piece of paper; she utters spontaneously the word *pingguo* 'apple'. Based on the nonlinguistic situation, one may assume that the child intends to draw an apple on the piece of paper. The nominal is thus classified as an argument.

Once a nominal is classified as an argument, we would need to ascertain whether it is specific or nonspecific. Generally, if the nominal is used to refer to a particular object or person in the immediate situation, the nominal will be considered as specific. For example, the child LSY at age 1;08;16 sees a basketball on the floor, picks it up and utters *qiu* 'ball'. He is not involved in a naming activity, and is already familiar with the name of the object (as determined from recordings of previous sessions), he is clearly using the nominal as an argument, and using it to refer to a particular object. Such a nominal use will be considered specific. By the same token, if the nominal used by the child refers to an object which can be uniquely determined by the context, and the referent is clearly a particular object rather than any one of a kind, the nominal will be considered as a specific one. If the child uses the nominal to refer to an object which cannot be uniquely identified from the context, the nominal will be considered as nonspecific. For instance, at age 1;07;16, AJR is standing in front of a big toy box containing many different kinds of toys. She looks into the box and utters *paizi* 'racket', which can be regarded as a nominal based on preceding observation sessions. Since in the situation, it is hard to identify which racket the child wants to get, the nominal is considered as nonspecific.[25]

The numbers of tokens of argument nominals of LSY and AJR are given in Tables 1 and 2, classified according to age and also the syntactic form of the nominal. The numbers of tokens of the multi-word predicate nominals of the two children are given in Tables 3 and 4, broken down also according to observation session as well as the internal structure of the nominal. With respect to the classification of syntactic form in Tables 1 and 2, 'N' refers to bare nouns; 'Dem locative N' refers to demonstrative locatives like *zheli* 'here' and *nali* 'there'; 'Dem pronoun' designates demonstrative pronouns such as *zhe* 'this' and *na* 'that'; 'NP-dem locative N' labels nominals such as *mama nali* 'mother-there'. As for the classifier-related structures, 'Dem' represents a demonstrative, 'Num' stands for numeral, 'CL' a classifier, and 'N' a noun. 'NP-N' groups together nominals that are equivalent to 'NP-*de*-N' with the marker *de* omitted, such as *baobao qiqiu* 'baby balloon'. 'Wh-NP' represents an interrogative phrase. In Tables 3 and 4 giving the data on predicate nominals, besides bare nouns, proper names, and classifier-containing structures, one also observes a variety of nominals marked by *de*, which could signal possession or association, or mark relative clause modification. 'ADJ-*de*-(N)' stands for a nominal with adjectival modification in which the noun may be left out, such as *hong de* 'red one'; 'NP-*de*-(N)' represents a possessive phrase such as *taiyang de guang* (sun-*de*-beam) 'the sun's beam'. The categories containing *de* and a verb are essentially different kinds of relative clause modification. 'V-NP-*de*-(N)' represents a case of subject relativization, as in *qie youzi de* (cut-grapefruit-NOM) '(the thing) that cuts grapefruit'; 'NP-V-*de*-(N)' represents an instance of object relativization, as in *baobao zuo de* (baby-sit-NOM) 'what baby sits on'; and in 'V-*de*-(N)', both arguments within the relative clause are covert, as in *chi de* (eat-NOM) '(the thing that one) eats'.

## 5.2 The delayed onset of classifier-related nominals

The figures in Tables 1 and 2 show that with respect to argument nominals, structures containing classifiers appear a few months later than the first nominals, which consisted predominantly of bare nouns, proper names and demonstrative locatives. These structures were evidenced from 1;05;19. As can be seen from Table 1, in

---

25  Clearly there are ambiguous instances in which the context does not allow us to decide on the status of the nominal based on the criteria adopted. For example, at age 1;07;16, LSY was drawing a wavy line on a piece of paper, and uttered spontaneously the word *he* ('river') upon the completion of his drawing. In such a situation, it is hard to decide whether the child was saying 'here was a river' or 'this is a river'. The ambiguous nominals are treated separately from the ones whose status is clear, and do not enter into the figures in the tables.

the case of LSY, the classifier-related structures did not become productive until 1;08;16, three months after the first observation session. The same picture is seen in the data of AJR in Table 2. Bare nouns and proper names were used in abundance from 1;05;13. However, classifier-related argument nominals did not surface until around 01;08, and were not produced a great deal before two years of age. Of the classifier-containing argument nominals, i.e. 'Dem-CL-(N)', 'Num-CL-(N)', 'CL-(N)', and 'Dem-Num-CL-(N)', the last category consisting of the full expansion of demonstrative, numeral and classifier is negligible, accounting for only 0.02% (10/551) for the entire period of observation in the case of LSY (Table 1) and 0% in the case of AJR, who did not produce any such structure.

If we turn to Tables 3 and 4 giving the uses of predicate nominals, we also observe a relative delay in the appearance of classifier-related structures. In the case of LSY, as seen from Table 3, the structures 'CL-(N)' and 'Num-CL-(N)' began to be used at 1;08;16, and continued to be used to a limited extent in subsequent sessions. In the case of AJR, classifier-related structures are not used at all as predicate nominals during the period of observation.

In contrast, with both children, predicate nominals primarily assume the form of bare nouns or bare nouns with prenominal modification marked by *de*, typically the headless *de* nominals.[26] Bare nouns (including N and 'NP-N') and *de* nominals containing a verb or adjective in the modifier (including the 'ADJ-*de*-(N)', 'V-NP-*de*-(N)', 'NP-V-*de*-(N)' and 'NP-V-N-*de*-N' types) constituted 38% (86/226) and 24% (55/226) of the predicate nominals in the data of LSY (Table 3) respectively. These two categories formed 39% (47/119) and 43% (51/119) of the predicate nominals in the data of AJR respectively (Table 4). Our data thus confirm the findings of Min (1994) for Mandarin and Wong (1998) for Cantonese in pointing to the relative delayed occurrence of classifier-containing nominals in comparison to bare nouns, proper names and demonstratives. As pointed out in our syntactic analysis of Mandarin nominals, nouns in Chinese are individuated by sortal classifiers, which are obligatory for the purpose of enumeration. It probably takes children time to acquire the syntax of individuation, as some number words must be in their command before they can learn the syntax of classifiers, that is, the fact that the presence of a numeral calls for the placement of a classifier.

---

26  Proper names would be considered predicates in contexts in which the child is asked to supply the name of a person or object.

Table 1. Argument nominals of various structures produced by LSY in each session (number of tokens).

| Age | N | Proper Name | Pronoun (incl. reflexives) | Dem Locative N (zheli 'here' nali 'there') | Dem Pronoun (zhe 'this' na 'that') | NP-Dem Locative N | Dem-CL-(N) | Num-CL-(N) | CL-(N) | Dem-Num-CL-(N) | NP-N | NP-de-(N) | Wh-NP |
|---|---|---|---|---|---|---|---|---|---|---|---|---|---|
| 1;05;19 | 19 | 16 | | 2 | | | | | | | | | |
| 1;06;00 | 25 | 18 | | 2 | 1 | | | | | | | | |
| 1;06;13 | 29 | 21 | | 15 | | | | | | | | | |
| 1;07;11 | 101 | 37 | 1 | 4 | 18 | | 1 | | | | 4 | | |
| 1;08;02 | 122 | 41 | 5 | 9 | 2 | | 1 | 1 | 1 | | | | |
| 1;08;16 | 135 | 43 | 4 | 11 | 15 | | 22 | 20 | 1 | | 3 | 1 | 1 |
| 1;08;30 | 69 | 47 | 2 | 10 | 4 | | 7 | 15 | 8 | 1 | | | |
| 1;09;12 | 75 | 31 | 2 | 17 | | | 20 | 13 | 2 | | 1 | | |
| 1;09;26 | 97 | 46 | 1 | 18 | 7 | | 14 | 16 | 5 | | 2 | 4 | 7 |
| 1;10;10 | 70 | 26 | | 3 | 6 | | 18 | 11 | 2 | | 21 | | |
| 1;10;23 | 53 | 18 | 1 | 5 | 1 | | 15 | 14 | 3 | 5 | 3 | | 1 |
| 1;11;06 | 52 | 17 | 1 | 8 | 2 | | 1 | 4 | | 1 | 1 | | |
| 1;11;29 | 99 | 23 | 4 | 9 | 2 | | 39 | 2 | 6 | | 4 | | 2 |
| 2;00;06 | 114 | 44 | 12 | 16 | 1 | 5 | 45 | 27 | 18 | 2 | 4 | 8 | |
| 2;01;04 | 129 | 56 | 25 | 19 | 1 | | 42 | 22 | 23 | | 3 | 8 | 3 |
| 2;02;02 | 62 | 35 | 16 | 7 | | | 10 | 15 | 13 | 1 | 2 | 2 | 3 |
| 2;03;06 | 90 | 25 | 43 | 28 | 9 | 2 | 34 | 20 | 10 | | 3 | 7 | 1 |
| Total=2909 | 1341 | 544 | 117 | 183 | 69 | 7 | 269 | 180 | 92 | 10 | 51 | 31 | 15 |

Table 2. Argument nominals of various structures produced by AJR.

| Age | N | Proper Name | Pronoun (incl. reflexives) | Dem Locative N (zheli 'here' nali 'there') | Dem Pronoun (zhe 'this' na 'that') | NP-Dem Locative N | Dem-N | Dem-CL-(N) | Num-CL-(N) | CL-(N) | NP- N | NP-de-(N) |
|---|---|---|---|---|---|---|---|---|---|---|---|---|
| 1;05;13 | 10 | 12 | | 1 | | | | | | | | |
| 1;06;03 | 19 | 8 | | 9 | | | | | | | | |
| 1;06;17 | 36 | 5 | | 2 | 1 | | | | | | | |
| 1;07;02 | 42 | 24 | 1 | 2 | | | | | | | | |
| 1;07;16 | 55 | 19 | 4 | 20 | | | | | 1 | | | |
| 1;08;07 | 85 | 45 | 3 | 13 | | | | 1 | | 2 | | |
| 1;08;12 | 48 | 11 | 1 | 6 | 2 | | | | | | | |
| 1;09;02 | 52 | 26 | 1 | 3 | | | | | 2 | 1 | | |
| 1;09;15 | 49 | 49 | 2 | 8 | | | | | 1 | 1 | 1 | 1 |
| 1;10;02 | 40 | 71 | 5 | 15 | | | | 2 | 2 | | 2 | |
| 1;10;23 | 61 | 82 | 4 | 10 | | | | | 4 | | 4 | |
| 1;11;08 | 86 | 96 | 21 | 19 | 3 | 1 | | 3 | 1 | 2 | 1 | 3 |
| 1;11;21 | 50 | 99 | 8 | 5 | | | 2 | 1 | | | 3 | 2 |
| 2;00;10 | 35 | 71 | 5 | 14 | | 7 | 1 | 8 | 7 | 2 | 2 | 1 |
| 2;01;09 | 69 | 25 | 13 | 17 | 2 | | | 4 | 3 | 2 | 2 | |
| 2;02;07 | 28 | 45 | 14 | 2 | 4 | | | | 1 | 3 | 2 | 2 |
| 2;02;12 | 69 | 40 | 13 | 3 | 9 | | | 5 | 2 | | 2 | 2 |
| Total=1927 | 834 | 728 | 95 | 149 | 21 | 8 | 3 | 24 | 24 | 11 | 19 | 11 |

Table 3. Predicate nominals in multi-word utterances of LSY in each session (number of tokens).

| Age | N | NP-N | Proper Name | ADJ-de-(N) | NP-de-(N) | V-NP-de-(N) | NP-V-de-(N) | V-de-(N) | Wh-NP | CL-(N) | Num-CL-(N) |
|---|---|---|---|---|---|---|---|---|---|---|---|
| 1;05;19 | | | | | | | | | | | |
| 1;06;00 | | | | | | | | | | | |
| 1;06;13 | | | | | | | | | | | |
| 1;07;11 | 1 | 7 | | | | | | | | | |
| 1;08;02 | 2 | 1 | | | | | | | | | |
| 1;08;16 | 9 | 3 | | | | | | | | 1 | 2 |
| 1;08;30 | 5 | | | 3 | | 2 | | | | 3 | 2 |
| 1;09;12 | 2 | 1 | 1 | | | | 1 | | 1 | 1 | |
| 1;09;26 | 8 | | 3 | | 2 | | | 1 | 3 | | 1 |
| 1;10;10 | 1 | 1 | 2 | 2 | 1 | | 1 | | 3 | | 1 |
| 1;10;23 | 2 | | 1 | 3 | 5 | 2 | 1 | 1 | 2 | | |
| 1;11;06 | 9 | 2 | | 6 | 4 | 4 | | | 2 | | |
| 1;11;29 | 9 | | 1 | | 2 | 2 | 1 | | 3 | | |
| 2;00;06 | 4 | | 3 | 2 | 1 | 1 | 1 | | 1 | | 2 |
| 2;01;04 | 6 | | | 5 | 6 | 2 | | 1 | 12 | | |
| 2;02;02 | 3 | | 1 | | 3 | | 3 | 1 | 1 | | |
| 2;03;06 | 10 | | 1 | 6 | 3 | 1 | 1 | | 2 | 1 | 1 |
| Total=226 | 71 | 15 | 13 | 27 | 27 | 14 | 9 | 5 | 30 | 6 | 9 |

Table 4. Predicate nominals in multi-word utterances of AJR in each session (number of tokens).

| Age | N | NP-N | Proper Name | ADJ-de- (N) | NP-de- (N) | V-NP-de- (N) | NP-V-de- (N) | NP-V-N-de- (N) | Wh-NP | CL-(N) | Num-CL-(N) |
|---|---|---|---|---|---|---|---|---|---|---|---|
| 1;05;13 | | | | | | | | | | | |
| 1;06;03 | | | | | | | | | | | |
| 1;06;17 | | | | | | | | | | | |
| 1;07;02 | | | | | | 2 | | | | | |
| 1;07;16 | | | | | | | | | | | |
| 1;08;07 | | 1 | | | | | | | | | |
| 1;08;12 | 2 | | | | | 4 | | | | | |
| 1;09;02 | | 1 | | | | | 1 | | | | |
| 1;09;15 | | 3 | | | | 1 | 2 | | | | |
| 1;10;02 | 1 | | | | | | 5 | | | | |
| 1;10;23 | | 5 | 2 | | 3 | | 6 | 3 | | | |
| 1;11;08 | 4 | | | | | 6 | | | | | |
| 1;11;21 | | 5 | 7 | | | 1 | 4 | | | | |
| 2;00;1 | 13 | | 3 | | | 1 | 2 | | | | |
| 2;01;09 | 2 | | | 2 | | 1 | 4 | | | | |
| 2;02;07 | | 3 | | | | 2 | 2 | | | | |
| 2;02;12 | 6 | 1 | 6 | | | 1 | 1 | | | | |
| Total=119 | 28 | 19 | 18 | 2 | 3 | 19 | 27 | 3 | | | |

## 5.3 Nominal structure and referentiality

The longitudinal data indicate that children from the earliest stage are sensitive to the mapping between syntactic form and referential meanings. It can be observed that certain types of nominal structures are never used as predicate nominals. Thus personal pronouns (including reflexives), demonstrative locatives, demonstrative pronouns, and demonstrative-(numeral)-classifier-(noun) structures are never used to express predicates. Some categories such as bare nouns and 'numeral-classifier-(noun)' structures can function as arguments as well as predicates. On the other hand, at least in the child language data, the *de*-nominals with a verb or adjective in the prenominal modifier, i.e. structures such as 'ADJ-*de*-(N)', 'V-NP-*de*-(N)', 'NP-V-*de*-(N)' and 'NP-V-N-*de*-N', are exclusively used to express predicates, and are generally not used as arguments, though in the adult language this option is available, as discussed earlier (cf. 7b).[27] The distribution of nominals in early child Mandarin reflects a strong sensitivity to the referential/ non-referential distinction, so that the nominal forms that are [+referential] are sharply separated from those that are [−referential].

To observe the specificity of the early nominals of the two subjects, we isolated the early numeral phrase structures, i.e. 'numeral-classifier-noun' and 'classifier-noun' structures, found in the two children from their first occurrences. As before, they are classified into predicate nominals and arguments, and the latter are further sub-classified into specific and non-specific tokens wherever possible. As shown in Table 5, the earliest uses of these two classifier-related structures in both Mandarin-speaking subjects were non-specific in reference. The non-specific use of numeral phrases preceded their specific use by one session in the case of LSY, and by two sessions in the case of AJR. The majority of the early [Num-CL-N] and [CL-N] nominals of LSY and AJR involved non-specific reference.

---

27 Diessel (2004) reports that the early relative clauses used by English-speaking children are often found in copula structures involving predicate nominals. Our data reflect the early availability of free relatives functioning as predicates, though we do not accept Diessel's conclusion that young children lack complex embedding structures.

*Table 5. The early [Num-CL-(N)] and [CL-(N)] nominals of LSY and AJR*

| Child | Age | Argument nominal[28] | | Predicate nominal |
|---|---|---|---|---|
| | | specific | non-specific | |
| LSY | 1;08;02 | 0 | 2 | 0 |
| | 1;08;16 | 8 | 12 | 3 |
| | 1;08;30 | 9 | 14 | 5 |
| AJR | 1;07;16 | 0 | 1 | 0 |
| | 1;08;07 | 0 | 2 | 0 |
| | 1;09;02 | 2 | 1 | 0 |
| | 1;09;15 | 1 | 1 | 0 |
| | 1;10;02 | 2 | 0 | 0 |
| | 1;10;23 | 0 | 2 | 0 |
| | 1;11;21 | 0 | 1 | 0 |
| | 2;00;10 | 3 | 6 | 0 |

(14) LSY 01;08;02
    MOT:    yao bu yao zai huan yi ge zhi?
                want not want again change one CL paper
                'Do you want to change for another (sheet of) paper?'
    MOT:    hao bu hao?
                good not good
                'Okay?'
    CHI:     hao
                good
                'Okay.'
    MOT:    mama shi shuo yao bu yao zenme &a?[29]
                mom be say want not want what-do SFP
                'Mom asks (you) want to do what?'

28  The number of argument nominals of the form 'Num-CL-(N)' and 'CL-(N)' may differ slightly from the figures reported in Tables 1-2, as not all instances can be clearly subcategorized into specific or non-specific.

29  In the child Mandarin transcription, a form prefixed by '&' indicates that the form is a romanization. Romanized forms are often used to represent sentence final particles and words produced by the child which may deviate from the adult pronunciation.

CHI:      huan ye zhi
              change CL paper
              '(To) change for another sheet of paper.'

(15) LSY 01;08;16
(The child takes the paper and the pencil and is ready to draw on the paper. He utters spontaneously)
CHI:      hua yi ge, hua yi ge pangxie!
              draw one CL, draw one CL crab
              'Draw a crab.'

(16) LSY 01;08;16
MOT:     tu dian shenme?
              rub-on-skin CL what
              'What would you like to rub on your skin?'
CHI:      tu dian yao you4you2.
              rub-on-skin CL medication-ointment
              '(I'd like to) rub some medical ointment.'

The examples in (14)-(16) illustrate the early non-specific uses of numeral phrases. In (14), the mother of LSY asks him whether he wants to change for another sheet of paper, and after a couple of exchange, the child expresses his wish to obtain a new sheet of paper. In (15), the child takes a sheet of paper and a pencil, and is about to draw on the sheet of paper. In (16), the child would like to rub some medical ointment on his skin. All these are instances in which the child does not have a particular object in his mind when producing the utterance. That is, these are examples of non-specific uses of numeral phrases.

    The examples in (17)-(18) exemplify the specific uses of numeral phrases in early child Mandarin. In (17), LSY is watching a particular picture on the screen, and remarks that an elephant is located near an elderly person. Likewise, in (18), he is watching a computer screen expecting an object which has been perceived earlier to reappear. He comments on his failure to see the particular elderly person that he anticipated.

(17) LSY 1;08;16
   (The child utters spontaneously, watching a picture on the computer screen)
   CHI:   zai qianmian, zhe lao yeye, yi zhi daxiang zai zheli
          at front this old grandpa, one CL elephant at here
          'Ahead, this old grandpa, here is an elephant.'

(18) LSY 1;08;16
   (The child utters spontaneously, watching a computer screen, expecting to see an elderly man that he had seen earlier)
   CHI:   yi ge lao yeye kan bu jian &la.
          one CL old grandpa see not seen SFP
          '(I can't see) an old grandpa.'

Our data show that contrary to what one might expect based on the assumption that referentiality is unmarked (cf. Jackendoff 1983), numeral phrases are not first used to denote specific referents. Rather, they are first used to mark non-specific reference before they are employed to denote specific referents. The earlier occurrence of non-specific uses of numeral phrases is nothing out of the ordinary considering the fact that number words are probably introduced to indicate numerosity. The facts replicate the earlier findings of Min (1994) and support the hypothesis of Hornstein (1984) that the default status of quantifier phrases is [+operator] reading, given that cardinal numeral phrases are a type of quantifier phrases. This finding also lends support to the idea that nominals with an empty numeral phrase are assigned a non-specific interpretation as a default reading (Cheng and Sybesma 1999).

## 5.4 The preponderance of 'headless' de nominals

As reported earlier, Mandarin-speaking children aged between two and three use nominals with modifiers marked by *de* productively (Packard 1987). Further, there seems to be a complementary distribution between the type of prenominal elements and the overtness of the noun which serves as complement to the higher functional projections (see the tree representation in (3)). If the prenominal element is nominal or substantive in nature, there is a strong tendency for the complement noun (or 'head noun' in traditional terminology) to be overtly expressed.[30] If, on the other

---

30  In our discussion of *de* nominals, we will abandon the terminology 'headed' or 'headless' as these terms are incompatible with our current analysis of Mandarin nominal structure. Our presentation of the data of Ji (2006) and Hu (2007) may therefore differ from theirs in terms of terminology, though the essence of the findings remains the same as theirs.

hand, the prenominal element is predicative in nature, then the complement noun tends to be covert, i.e. it tends to be dropped, resulting in the so-called 'headless' *de* nominals.

The observation of Packard (1987) based on cross-sectional investigation is confirmed by analyses of longitudinal data of Mandarin-speaking children. In a study of two Mandarin-speaking children growing up in Beijing[31], Ji (2006) found that there is an overwhelming tendency for *de*-nominals with modifiers containing verbs, adjectives or prepositions to appear with the complement noun dropped. On the other hand, *de*-nominals with modifiers containing nominal elements tend to occur in a structure with the complement noun overt. This essentially replicates the observation of Packard (1987). As shown in Table 6, for the child CY in the period under observation, when the prenominal element is of the type 'DP *de* NP', 81% of the *de*-nominals (91/112) appear with the complement noun overt. In ZTX, the corresponding figure is 64% (94/147). A total of 113 *de*-nominals with modifiers containing a verb, an adjective or a preposition can be found in the production of CY, and 200 in the production of ZTX. The percentage of these *de*-nominals that has covert complement nouns is 83% (94/113) for CY, and 73% (146/200) for ZTX, respectively.

*Table 6. De-nominals with overt and covert complement nouns (adapted from Ji 2006)*

| Child subject | CY (0;10;05- 2;04;31) | | ZTX (0;11;18-2;06;02) | |
|---|---|---|---|---|
| Nominal structure | modified noun overt | modified noun covert | modified noun overt | modified noun covert |
| [DP-*de*-N] | 91 | 21 | 94 | 53 |
| Subtotal | 112 | | 147 | |
| [(DP)-V-(DP)-*de*-N] | 14 | 71 | 37 | 100 |
| [AP-*de*-N] | 4 | 22 | 16 | 45 |
| [PP-*de*-N] | 1 | 1 | 0 | 1 |
| Subtotal | 113 | | 200 | |
| Total | 225 | | 346 | |

---

31   The child Mandarin data used in Ji (2006) are part of the Beijing Chinese Early Language Acquisition project, directed by Thomas Hun-tak Lee, Xiaolu Yang and Li Fang.

*Table 7. De nominals in predicate nominals of AJR and LSY (adapted from Hu 2007)*

| Child subject | LSY (1;05;19- 2;03;06) | | AJR (1;05;13-2;02;12) | |
|---|---|---|---|---|
| Nominal structure | modified noun overt | modified noun covert | modified noun overt | modified noun covert |
| NP-*de*-(N) | 10 | 17 | 21 | 81 |
| Subtotal | 27 | | 102 | |
| V-NP-*de*-(N) | 4 | 10 | 0 | 19 |
| NP-V-N-*de*-(N) | 0 | 9 | 0 | 27 |
| NP-V-N-*de*-(N) | 0 | 0 | 0 | 3 |
| V-*de*-(N) | 1 | 4 | 0 | 0 |
| ADJ-*de*-(N) | 0 | 27 | 0 | 2 |
| Subtotal | 55 | | 51 | |
| Total | 82 | | 153 | |

The data on *de*-nominals from our two Mandarin-speaking subjects LSY and AJR, given in Table 7, also confirm the patterns observed by Packard (1987) and Ji (2006). Our subcategorization of nominals according to their function provides us with a clearer window on the structure of *de*-nominals in early child Mandarin. As observed earlier, only *de*-nominals of the type 'NP-*de*-(N)' function as arguments (see Tables 1 and 2). The *de*-nominals with modifiers containing a verb or an adjective function exclusively as predicates. This is true of both children. Table 7 gives the numbers of *de*-nominals that function as predicates, classified according to whether the modified noun is overt or covert. One should note here while there is a tendency for *de*-nominals to have overt modified nouns when the prenominal modifier is nominal or substantive, the tendency is not strong. Thirty seven percent of *de*-nominals with nominal modifiers (10/27) have overt modified nouns for LSY, and 26% of such nominals have overt modified nouns (21/102) for AJR. On the other hand, virtually all of the *de*-nominals with verbal or adjectival modifiers contain covert modified nouns. The percentage of such *de*-nominals that has covert modified nouns is 91% (50/55) for LSY and 100% (51/51) for AJR. In view of the predicative function of these *de*-nominals, the covertness of the modified noun comes as no surprise, since the point of the predicate nominal having the structure of a free relative is often to subclassify a class of entities which is already named in the subject of the sentence, as in (19) (cf. Zhu 1978, Paris 1979). There is no need to repeat the subject noun within the structure of the nominal.

(19) Pingguo shi mama mai de
 apple be mother buy NOM
 'The apple is (something) mother bought.'/ 'The apple is what mother bought.'

# 6. Underspecifed nominal structures in early child Mandarin

In order to account for the patterns of findings from previous literature and from the present study, we propose that the child before two years of age goes through two stages of development, separated by a short span of two to three months. At the initial phase, the child represents the nominal with a structure such as (20), in which the Specificity phrase selects only NP. The head of the Specificity phrase can bear [+specific] as well as [-specific] features. Thus a bare noun such as *pingguo* 'apple' can occur in the head of Specificity phrase designating a particular object, or it can be used for non-specific reference in a context in which, for instance, the child says *yao pingguo* 'want apple'. If the noun functions as a predicate nominal, then one may simply consider the structure of such a nominal to be NP. One can regard demonstrative locatives, demonstrative pronouns and proper names as occupying the head of the Specificity phrase designating particular objects that the child has in mind. Such a representation seems to underlie the earliest nominals of our Mandarin-speaking children.

(20)　Nominal structure in early child Mandarin (Stage I)

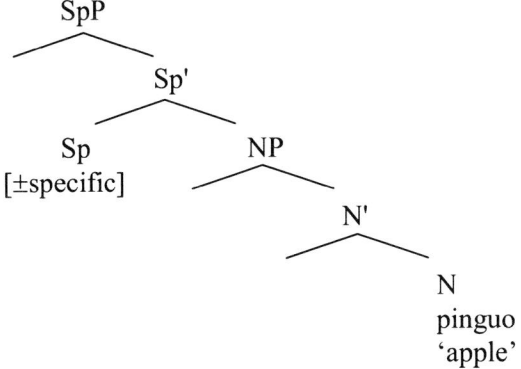

(21)   Nominal structure in early child Mandarin (Stage II)

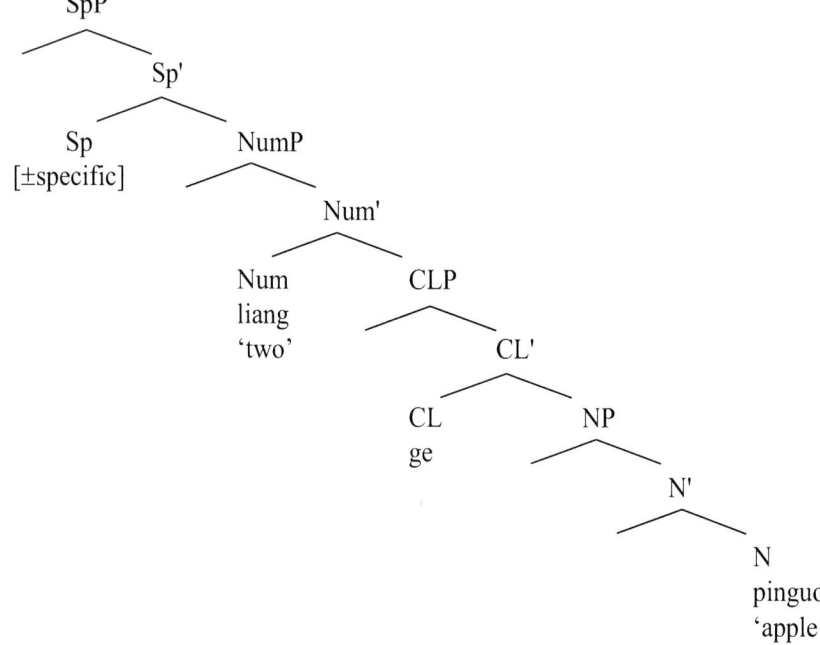

In a span of three months or longer, children begin to be aware that to individuate nouns, and to enumerate, one would need to invoke the category of classifiers. Numerals and classifiers develop hand in hand, introducing more complicated structures into the nominal, in particular the numeral phrase, as in (21). Here, too, the numeral phrase can be [+specific] or [-specific], though as we have observed, its default reading should be non-specific. If the referential feature on the head of the SpP is [-specific], as when the numeral phrase is used to refer to one of a set of objects of the same kind, or when the nominal is used predicatively, the head must not be filled with lexical material. On the other hand, if the feature on the head of SpP is [+specific], it may be left covert, or filled with a demonstrative such as *na* 'that' or *zhe* 'this'.

With respect to the preponderance of *de*-nominals, we should bear in mind that in our analysis, following Sio (2006), the prenominal modifiers in these structures, whether they be DP, or NP, or a CP (a relative clause), are treated as adjuncts. Some kind of economy principle seems to be at work, so that in the case of relative clauses (modifiers with a verb or adjective), the child projects only NPs, with the CP adjoined to NP, as these structures only function as predicates. On the other hand, if the modifiers are nominal in nature, they are adjoined to NP and function as predicates, or they may be located in the specifier or head of the Specificity phrase, and thus may be used referentially in argument positions.[32] Since these adjunction structures typically do not involve the numeral or the classifier, it seems that before two years of age, children adjoin only to the simplest type of Specificity phrase as indicated in (22). In the entire period under observation, up to the age of around 2;3, *de* structures with nominal or predicate modification that involve numerals and classifiers are not found, i.e. structures such as *wo yao de yi ben shu* (I-want-NOM-one-CL-book) 'a particular book that I want', or *san zhi mama mai de bi* (three-CL-mother-buy-NOM-pencil) 'three pencils that mother bought'.

(22)   Structure of *de*-nominal

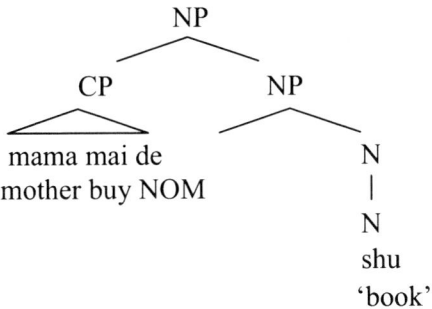

Our analysis of early nominal structure in Mandarin Chinese indicates while the full range of nominal structures may not be evidenced at the very beginning of nominal development, the child at two years of age has grasped the basic functional structure of nominals. Default syntax-semantics mapping principles compel the child to interpret certain structures only as arguments and others as arguments or predicates. These principles will also bias the child toward an initial non-specific interpretation of the numeral phrase. Principles of economy will gear the child toward projecting adjunction structures first on NPs before doing so on Specificity phrases.

The nominal structure in early child Mandarin is said to be underspecified in the same sense as Schaefer and de Villiers (2000), in that even with the more developed Stage II nominal structure in (21), the child is not fully capable of taking into account the hearer's perspective in using nominal structure and word order to mark definite/indefinite distinctions. One can hypothesize that for the first three

---

32   Both Ji (2006) and Hu (2007) have observed the prominence in early child Mandarin of nominals of the form 'NP-N' in which the marker *de* is dropped. This fact suggests that *de* poses a problem if the structure is to be used referentially. Thus either it is dropped or the *de* nominal tends to be used non-referentially as a predicate.

years of life, the young child has only a special kind of Specificity phrase that bears only [±specific] features but not [±definite] features. This marks the difference between a nominal structure such as (21) and the adult nominal structure in (3). Mastery of the latter will have to depend on acquisition of the related linguistic features that go into the signaling of information structures, as well as cognitive developments related to theory of mind, as pointed out by Schafer and de Villers (2000).

## 7. Conclusions

Based on longitudinal data from two Mandarin-speaking children covering the period 1 year 5 months to 2 years 3 months of age, each with 17 sessions of observations, we have reported a number of observations about nominal structure in early child Mandarin, examining the way syntactic form maps to semantic distinctions such as argument vs. predicate, and to referential distinctions such as specific vs. non-specific.

Both data sets show that nominals emerged first in the form of bare nouns, pronouns, proper names, and demonstratives, confirming the earlier studies of Min (1994) and Chang-Smith (2005). Classifier-bearing nominals developed at a later point, with a lag of two to three months, corroborating the earlier study of child Cantonese by Wong (1998). [Numeral-classifier-noun] and [classifier-noun] nominals were first used as either non-specific indefinites or as predicate nominals. Specific indefinite uses of these structures rapidly followed. This supports the hypothesis of Hornstein (1984) that the default status of quantifier phrases is [+operator] reading. It also lends support to the idea that nominals with an empty numeral phrase are assigned a default non-specific interpretation (Cheng and Sybesma 1999).

Children are aware of the mapping between nominal structure and semantic distinctions in the early stage. Some forms such as pronouns and demonstratives are never used as predicates, whereas other forms such as bare nouns and numeral phrases can function either as arguments or predicates. Some elaborate structures involving adjunction, such as the *de*-nominals modified by relative clauses, start out by playing the role of predicates rather than arguments.

Our data confirm the productivity of *de*-nominals in child Mandarin, and clarify the relationship between the nature of the modifier and the overtness of the modified noun. The *de*-nominals with predicate modifiers (i.e. relative clauses) occur overwhelmingly with covert modified nouns, with the so-called 'head noun' dropped, because they are predicates that have a classificatory function. This distribution suggests that children build adjunction structures in nominals initially on NPs rather than Specificity phrases, observing economy principles. NPs map to predicates, while the Specificity phrase carries referential features.

Adopting the spirit of the nominal structure proposed in Sio (2006), which posits a Specificity phrase in addition to a numeral phrase, a classifier phrase, and a noun phrase, we propose that children before two years of age have underspecified nominal structures. Initially, they begin with only the Specificity phrase and the NP. Further nominal specification is realized at a later stage (by two years of age) when the numeral and the classifier are integrated into the Specificity phrase. The relatively later acquisition of classifier-bearing structures probably stems from the difficulty in acquiring the individuation function of classifiers (Huang 2008), which is only clearly realized in the context of enumeration. It is further hypothesized that children before three years of age have Specificity phrases that lack features relating to hearer's referential knowledge, i.e. features that distinguish definite from indefinite reference.

# References

Borer, H. 2005. *Structuring sense*. Volume I: *In name only*. London: Oxford University Press.
Brown, R. 1973. *A first language*. Cambridge, MA: Harvard University Press.
Chang-Smith, M. 2005. *First language acquisition of functional categories in Mandarin nominal expressions: A longitudinal study of two Mandarin speaking children*. Doctoral dissertation, Australian National University.
Chao, Yuen-ren. 1968. *A grammar of spoken Chinese*. Berkeley: University of California Press.
Chen, Ping. 1987. Xi Hanyuzhong yu Mingcixing Chengfen Xiangguan de Sizu Gainian (On four sets of concepts related to nominal elements in Chinese). *Zhongguo Yuwen* (Chinese Language) 197, 81-92.
Chen, Ping. 2003. Indefinite determiner introducing definite referent: a special use of 'yi 'one' + classifier' in Chinese. *Lingua* 113, 1169-1184.
Cheng, L. and R. Sybesma. 1998. Yi-wan tang, yi-ge tang: classifiers and massifiers. *The Tsing Hua Journal of Chinese Studies* 28(3), 385-412.
Cheng, L. and R. Sybesma. 1999. Bare and not-so-bare nouns and the structure of NP. *Linguistic Inquiry* 30 (4), 509-542.
Cheung, Hung-nin S. 1989. *Yueyu Liangci Yongfa De Yanjiu* (A study of the uses of Cantonese classifiers), Di Erjie Guoji Hanxue Huiyi Lunwenji: Yuyan Wenzi Zu Xia Ce (Proceedings of the Second International Conference on Chinese Studies: Language and Writing Group, Vol B). Taipei: Academia Sinica, 753-774.
De Villiers, J. and T. Roeper. 1995. Barriers, binding, and acquisition of the DP-NP distinction. *Language Acquisition* 4(1&2), 73-104.
Del Gobbo, F. 2003. *Appositives at the interface*. Doctoral dissertation, University of California at Irvine.

Diessel, H. 2004. *The acquisition of complex sentences*. London: Cambridge University Press.

Fan, Jiyan. 1985. Wuding NP Shuyu Ju (Sentences with indefinite NP subjects). *Zhongguo Yuwen* (Chinese Language) 1985.5, 321-328.

Guilfoyle, E. and M. Noonan. 1992. Functional categories and language acquisition. *Canadian Journal of Linguistics* 37(2), 241-272.

Heim, I. 1982. *The semantics of definite and indefinite noun phrases*. Doctoral dissertation, University of Massachusetts at Amherst.

Hickmann, M. and J. Liang. 1990. Clause-structure variation in Chinese narrative discourse: a developmental analysis. *Linguistics* 28, 1167-1200.

Hoekstra, T and P. Jordens. 1994. From adjunct to head. In *Language acquisition studies in generative grammar: Papers in honor of Kenneth Wexler from the 1991 GLOW workshops*, eds. T. Hoekstra and B. Schwartz. Amsterdam: John Benjamins.

Hornstein, N. 1984. *Logic as grammar*. Cambridge, MA: MIT Press.

Hsieh, Miao-ling 2005. Two types of modifiers and parallelisms between DPs and TPs in Chinese. *Language and Linguistics* 6 (3), 397-429.

Hu, Yajuan. 2007. *The (non)-referential use of nominals in the early speech of Mandarin-speaking children*. MA thesis, Department of Linguistics, Hunan University.

Huang Aijun. 2009. *Count-mass distinction and the acquisition of Chinese classifiers*. MPhil thesis, Chinese University of Hong Kong.

Huang, Aijun and T. Lee. 2009. Quantification and individuation in the acquisition of Chinese classifiers. In *Proceedings of the Tenth Tokyo Conference on Psycholinguistics*, ed. Yukio Otsu. Tokyo: Hituzi Syobo.

Huang, C.T. James. 1982. *Logical relations in Chinese and the theory of grammar*. Doctoral dissertation, MIT.

Hyams, N. 1996. The underspecification of functional categories in early grammar. In *Generative perspectives on language acquisition: empirical findings, theoretical considerations and crosslinguistic comparisons*, ed. H. Clahsen. Amsterdam: John Benjamins.

Jackendoff, R. 1983. *Semantics and cognition*. Cambridge, MA: MIT Press.

Ji, Sunjing. 2006. *Children's acquisition of the nominal 'de' in Mandarin*. MA thesis, Tsinghua University, China.

Karmiloff-Smith, A. 1979. *A functional approach to child language*. London: Cambridge University Press.

Krifka, M. 1995. Common nouns: a contrastive analysis of Chinese and English. In *The generic book,* eds. G. Carlson and F. Pelletier. Chicago: University of Chicago Press.

Lebeaux, D. 1988. *Language acquisition and the form of grammar*. Doctoral dissertation, University of Massachusetts at Amherst.

Lee, T. H.-T. 1986. *Studies on quantification in Chinese*. Doctoral dissertation, University of California at Los Angeles.

Li, C. and S. Thompson. 1981. *Mandarin Chinese: a functional reference grammar*. Los Angeles: University of California Press.

Li, Y.-H. Audrey. 1998. Argument determiner phrases and number phrases. *Linguistic Inquiry* 29, 693-702.

Maratsos, M. 1976. *The use of definite and indefinite reference in young children*. London: Cambridge University Press.

Marinis, Theodoros. 2003. *The acquisition of the DP in Modern Greek*. Amsterdam: John Benjamins.

Min, Ruifang. 1994. *The acquisition of referring expressions by young Chinese children.* Doctoral dissertation, The Catholic University of Nijmegen.

Packard, J. 1987. The first language acquisition of prenominal modification with 'de' in Mandarin. *Journal of Chinese Linguistics* 16 (1), 31-53.

Paris, M.-C. 1979. *Nominalization in Mandarin Chinese.* Paris: Department de Recherches Linguistiques, Universite Paris VII.

Penner, Z. and J. Weissenborn. 1996. Strong continuity, parameter setting and the trigger hierarchy. In *Generative perspectives on language acquisition: empirical findings, theoretical considerations and crosslinguistic comparisons,* ed. H. Clahsen. Amsterdam: John Benjamins.

Pérez-Leroux, A. 1998. Specificity, acquisition of DPs and the development of a theory of mind. In *New perspectives on language acquisition,* ed. B. Hollebrandse. University of Massachusetts Occasional Papers. Amherst, MA: GSLA, University of Massachusetts.

Radford, A. 1988. Small children's small clauses. *Transactions of the Philological Society* 86(1), 1-43.

Radford, A. 1990. *Syntactic theory and the acquisition of English syntax.* Oxford: Blackwell.

Schafer, R. and J. de Villiers. 2000. What *a* and *the* can tell us about the emergence of DP. In *BUCLD 24 Proceedings,* ed. S. Catherine Howell et al, 609-620. Somerville, MA: Cascadilla Press.

Sio, Ut-Seong Joanna. 2006. *Modification and reference in the Chinese Nominal.* Doctoral dissertation, University of Leiden.

Tang, C.-C. Jane. 1990. A note on the DP analysis of the Chinese noun phrase. *Linguistics* 28, 337-354.

Teng, Shou-hsin. 1987. Relative clause in Chinese. In *Wang Li Memorial Volume: English volume,* ed. The Chinese Language Society of Hong Kong. Hong Kong: Joint Publishers.

Tsai, Wei-tien Dylan. 2001. On subject specificity and theory of syntax-semantics interface. *Journal of East Asian Linguistics* 10, 129-168.

Warden, D. 1981. Learning to identify referents. *British Journal of Psychology* 72, 93-99.

Wong, Sin Ping. 1998. *The acquisition of Cantonese noun phrases.* Doctoral dissertation, University of Hawaii.

Zeng, Tao. 2010. *The nature of word spurt--early lexical and semantic development of Mandarin-speaking children.* Doctoral dissertation, Guangdong Foreign Studies University.

Zhu, Dexi. 1978. De zi jiegou he panduanju (The *de*-construction and judgment sentences). *Zhongguo Yuwen* (Chinese Language) 1978(1-2).

Email: huntaklee@cuhk.edu.hk

# Post-Verbal Locative/Directional Phrases in Child Mandarin: A Longitudinal Study[1]

Miao-Ling Hsieh
*National Taiwan Normal University*

## 1. Introduction

A post-verbal *zai* phrase in Chinese may have a locative reading (Place) or a directional reading (Path):[2]

(1) a. Zhangsan zuo ***zai*** gongyuan li.  (locative/*directional)
 Zhangsan sit at park inside
 'Zhangsan sat inside the park.'
 b. Zhangsan tiao ***zai*** hu li.  (*locative/directional)
 Zhangsan jump in lake inside
 'Zhangsan jumped into the lake.'

*Zai* in (1a) denotes a static location, while that in (1b) denotes a goal. Despite this, the two examples in (1) are not ambiguous. A question that immediately arises is how the two different readings are derived and whether a child can distinguish them. This paper is thus concerned with the syntax and semantics of the post-verbal *zai* and how a child acquires it. The findings are briefly summarized as follows. First, whether a post-verbal *zai* phrase is allowed and what its interpretation is are subject to the constraints that different verb types have on a post-verbal *zai* phrase. Second, based on the longitudinal data of my child collected since he was about one year old up to 5;10, it will be shown that the acquisition of the post-verbal *zai* is not complete until he is around 5;10. A plausible analysis for his misuse of both the locative and directional post-verbal *zai* is that *zai* is taken

---

1 I would like to thank the National Science Council in Taiwan for the support of the collection and the analyses of the longitudinal data of my child from 2004 to 2010 ('Early Syntactic Development'). Many thanks also go to Chris Wilder and an external reviewer for their comments and suggestions.
2 Abbreviations used in this paper are given as follows: CL (classifier), BA (the object marker *ba*), BEI (the passive marker *bei*), De (the modification marker *de*), and PART (particle).

to be a verb independent from the preceding verb, instead of being analyzed as a preposition.

The rest of this paper proceeds as follows. Section 2 discusses the syntax and semantics of Place and Path in general. Section 3 focuses on the post-verbal *zai* phrase in Chinese. Section 4 discusses the acquisition of the post-verbal *zai*. Finally, Section 5 concludes the paper.

## 2. Syntax and Semantics of Place and Path

This section discusses general issues with respect to how Place and Path are syntactically encoded.

### 2.1 Verb-Framed Languages vs. Satellite-Framed Languages

According to Talmy (1985), two types of languages can be distinguished: verb-framed and satellite-framed languages. Compare the two examples in (2).

(2) a. He danced into the room.        English
     b. Il est entré dans la chambre (en dansant).    French
        he is entered in the room (dancing)
        'He entered the room (dancing).'

While the English example in (2a) is possible, the same meaning in French has to be expressed in a different way as in (2b). Specifically, Talmy points out that in English, a satellite language, verbs conflate manner and motion but do not encode path; paths are described by additional elements like PPs or particles, the so-called satellites. On the other hand, in French, a verb-framed language, verbs conflate motion and path semantics but any component of manner has to be expressed separately, for example, in a subordinate clause, or is left out entirely. Chinese, according to Talmy, is a satellite-framed language just like English. I assume the post-verbal *zai* is a preposition without further discussion. But before I go into the discussion of Chinese, first consider locative and directional PPs in English.

### 2.2 Locative and Directional PPs in English

English has locative PPs and directional PPs. Locative PPs (*in, on, within*) denote static locations, while directional PPs (*to, from, towards*) denote spatial goals (den Dikken 2006, Emonds 2000, Svenonius, to appear). The denotation of locative PPs can be treated as sets of Places (locations) in semantics, whereas directional PPs denote sets of Paths made up of Places (Jackendoff 1983, Zwarts 1997, 2005,

Zwarts & Winter 2000, among others).³ Despite this general distinction, *in* in (3a) can be either locative or directional, in contrast to its counterpart in (3b).

(3) a. Oscar jumped *in the lake*.           (locative/directional)
    b. Oscar swam *in the lake*.            (locative/*directional)

(3a) is ambiguous between a reading where Oscar jumped on a path which leads to a place inside the lake (directional) and a reading where Oscar did one or more jumps (up and down) in one location, namely inside the lake (locative). In contrast, (3b) can only have the locative reading where Oscar swam around in the lake, but not the directional reading where he, for example, swam from a river into the lake. A question arises as to whether they are indeed adpositions that are in principle (lexically) ambiguous between a directional and a locative reading and can thus license both Place and Path structures.

Thomas (2001, 2003) argues against such an analysis. Her experiment finds that the availability of the directional reading for prepositions such as *in* and *on* is restricted to verbs such as non-iterative *jump*, *throw* and *fall*. With manner of motion verbs (Levin 1993), i.e. motion verbs with a strong manner component like *crawl*, *walk* and *swim*, these prepositions only get a locative reading.

Similarly, discussing data from English, Dutch and German, Gehrke (2007) argues that these languages have no spatial prepositions that are lexically ambiguous between a locative and a directional reading. Rather, prepositions like *in*, *on*, *under* or *behind* always denote places and any meaning of directionality has to be licensed by other means. These means include additional directional prepositions, resultative verbs, certain movement operations, case and/or contextual or reference axes. In the following section, I will turn to the source of the two readings associated with the post-verbal *zai* in Chinese.

# 3. Syntax and semantics of post-verbal *zai* phrases in Chinese

In this section, the derivation of two different readings of the post-verbal *zai* is discussed.

---

3   Jackendoff (1983) makes a three-way distinction of path elements into source, goals and routes. Sources are paths with a definite starting-point, goals are paths with an ending-point but without a defined starting-point, and routes are paths that traverse via some ground or reference object but that have no defined starting- or ending-point. In this paper, I will mainly focus on goals.

## 3.1 Word order factor in Chinese

As shown above, the English PP in (3a) can have either a locative or directional reading, but this is not the case with post-verbal *zai* in Chinese. A post-verbal *zai* phrase with a non-iterative use of a verb such as *tiao* 'jump', *diu* 'throw', *luo* 'fall' and *da* 'hit' will only get a directional reading:

(4) Zhangsan tiao ***zai** hu li*.
 Zhangsan jump at lake inside
 'Zhangsan jumped into the lake.'

(5) Zhangsan ba na ben shu diu ***zai** zhuo shang*.
 Zhangsan BA that CL book throw at table top
 'Zhangsan threw the book onto the table.'

(6) Yezi luo ***zai** di shang*.
 leave fall at ground top
 'Leaves fell onto the ground.'

(7) Yushui da ***zai** chuanghu shang*.
 rain hit at window top
 'Raindrops hit at the window.'

A locative reading that specifies where an event takes place for this type of verbs can only be obtained by having a pre-verbal *zai* phrase:

(8) a. Zhangsan ***zai** hu shangmian* tiao.
 Zhangsan at lake top jump
 'Zhangsan jumped in the lake.'
 b. Zhangsan ***zai** zhuo shang* diu dongxi.
 Zhangsan at table top throw thing
 'Zhangsan was throwing things on the table.'

As for motion verbs with a strong manner component like *pa* 'crawl', *zou* 'walk' and *you* 'swim', the picture is not as clear. Consider the following examples.

(9) a. *Zhangsan pa *zai di shang*.
Zhangsan crawl at ground top
'Zhangsan crawled on the ground.'
b. *Zhangsan you *zai hu li*.
Zhangsan swim at lake inside
'Zhangsan swam in the lake.'

(10) a. Zhangsan zou *zai lu shang*.
Zhangsan walk at road top
'Zhangsan walked on the road.'
b. *Zhangsan zou *zai keting li*.
Zhangsan walk at living:room inside
'Zhangsan walked in the living room.'

Based on (9) and (10), it seems that both whether a post-verbal *zai* is allowed and what interpretation it receives are subject to other factors. In the following subsection, I will distinguish different verb types and discuss the constraints that different verb types have on the use of the post-verbal *zai*.

## 3.2 Constraints of different verb types

Based on the use of a post-verbal *zai* phrase, five types of verbs can be distinguished, presented in the following as Type A – Type E.

*Type A.* For this type of verbs, a post-verbal *zai* phrase is always locative. They include:

(11) a. verbs of posture/existence/placement, e.g. *zuo* 'sit', *zhu* 'live' and *fang* 'put'
b. some manner of motion verbs, e.g. *zou* 'walk' and iterative *fei* 'fly'

For the above two subtypes of verbs, both a pre-verbal *zai* and a post-verbal *zai* mark a static location where no path is implied. When occurring with the above verbs, a post-verbal *zai* does not mean any change of location from a previous location:

(12) a. Ni zuo *zai zheli*.
you sit at here
'You sit here.'
b. Ni *zai zheli* zuo.
you at here sit
'You sit here.'

(13) a. Zhangsan zou *zai lu shang*. (=(10a))
   Zhangsan walk at road top
   'Zhangsan walked on the road.'
 b. Zhangsan *zai lu shang* zou.
   Zhangsan at road top walk
   'Zhangsan walked on the road.'

(14) a. Ta kandao yi zhi laoying fei *zai tian shang*.
   he see one CL eagle fly at sky top
   'He saw an eagle fly in the sky.'
 b. Ta kanjian yi zhi laoying *zai tian shang* fei.
   he see one CL eagle at sky top fly
   'He saw an eagle fly in the sky.'

However, the place nouns used for the second subtype given in (11b) are not without restriction. While any *zai* phrase is acceptable in a pre-verbal position, a post-verbal *zai* phrase is more restricted. In contrast to the examples in (13a) and (14a), (15a) and (16a) do not seem to be acceptable.

(15) a. *Zhangsan zou *zai keting li*. (=(10b))
   Zhangsan walk at living:room inside
   'Zhangsan walked in the living room.'
 b. Zhangsan *zai keting li* zou.
   Zhangsan at living:room inside walk
   'Zhangsan walked in the living room.'

(16) a. *Ta kanjian you yi zhi laoying fei *zai feijichang*.
   he see have one CL eagle fly at airport
   'He saw an eagle fly in the airport.'
 b. Ta kanjian you yi zhi laoying *zai feijichang* fei.
   he see have one CL eagle at airport fly
   'He saw an eagle fly in the airport.'

The above contrast may be related to the notion of boundedness. *Keting* 'living room' and *feijichang* 'airport' are places that are spatially bounded, unlike *lu shang* 'road' and *tian shang* 'sky'. *Lu shang* and *tian shang* but not *keting* and *feijichang* are compatible with Type A verbs because the former describe an unbounded state due to unbounded space. More research will be needed for this analysis.

*Type B*. For this type of verbs, a post-verbal *zai* always gives a directional reading and only places that can be taken to be goals can occur with the post-verbal *zai*. The non-iterative use of verbs mentioned above, i.e. *tiao* 'jump', *diu* 'throw', and *luo* 'fall', belong to this type. They also include *pao* 'run', *qi* 'ride' and the non-iterative *fei* 'fly':

(17) a. Zhangsan pao ***zai*** *qianmian*.
    Zhangsan run at front
    'Zhangsan ran and ended up in the front.'
  b. *Zhangsan pao ***zai*** *gongyuan li*.
    Zhangsan run at park inside
    'Zhangsan ran in the park.'

(18) a. Zhangsan qi ***zai*** *ma shang*.
    Zhangsan ride at horse top
    'Zhagnsan mounted the horseback.'
  b. *Zhangsan qi ***zai*** *gongyuan li*.
    Zhangsan ride at park inside
    'Zhangsan rode in the park.'

(19) You yi zhi xiaoniao fei ***zai*** *chuangtai shang*.
    have one CL bird fly at windowsill top
    'A bird flew and landed on a windowsill.'

*Qianmian* 'front' in (17a) denotes a location that results from a change of location and *ma shang* 'horseback' in (18a) denotes a natural goal for mounting a horse, but *gongyuan li* 'park' does not imply a goal. As for (19), the windowsill can be considered to be a goal for the non-interative *fei* 'fly' and is thus acceptable to occur with the post-verbal *zai*.

*Type C*. Just like Type B, the post-verbal *zai* phrase that occurs with this type of verbs only allows a directional reading, but places that can be taken to be goals are more restricted compared to Type B verbs. The place noun either denotes the location of the participant of the action (cf. Tai 1975, Wang 1980) or the location which the activity reaches (Chen 1978 and Fan 1982). This verb type includes action verbs such *chi* 'eat', *kan* 'look', *na* 'take', *chuan* 'wear', *dai* 'wear' and *dai* 'bring'.

(20) a. Dongxi Zhangsan chi *zai zui li.*
 thing Zhangsan eat at mouth inside
 'Zhangsan ate it inside his mouth.'
 b. *Dongxi Zhangsan chi *zai keting li.*
 thing Zhangsan eat at living:room inside
 'Zhangsan ate it in the living room.'

(21) a. Zhe jian shi Zhangsan kan *zai yan li.*
 this CL matter Zhangsan see at eye inside
 'Zhangsan knew all about this matter.'
 b. *Dongxi Zhangsan kan *zai keting.*
 thing Zhangsan see at living:room
 'Zhangsan saw the thing in the living room.'

(22) a. Dongxi Zhangsan na *zai shou shang.*
 thing Zhangsan take at hand top
 'Zhangsan held the thing in his hand.'
 b. *Dongxi Zhangsan na *zai keting/shuo shang.*
 thing Zhangsan take at living:room/table top
 'Zhangsan took the thing to the living room/the table.'

Interestingly, for this type of verbs, the goal has to be an inalienable part of the body. The example in (22) is especially revealing because a place noun such as *keting* 'living room' or *shuo shang* 'table' cannot be considered to be a goal.

 *Type D.* For this type of verbs, no post-verbal *zai* phrase is allowed. This type includes directional verbs, e.g. *lai* 'come', some manner of motion verbs, e.g. *liu* 'flow', *tui* 'push' and *ban* 'move' and action verbs such as *he* 'drink'. Only *dao* 'to' can be used.

(23) a. *Zhangsan lai *zai zheli.*
 Zhangsan come at here
 'Zhangsan came here.'
 b. Zhangsan lai **dao** *zheli.*
 Zhangsan come to here
 'Zhangsan came here.'

(24) a. *Hua liu *zai he li*.
   flower flow at river inside
   'The flower flowed in the river.'
   b. Hua liu **dao** *he li*.
   flower flow to river inside
   'The flower flowed into the river.'

*Type E*. The last type of verbs are stative verbs, e.g. *tian* 'sweet' and *nan* 'difficult'. These only allow a post-verbal *zai* phrase, not a pre-verbal *zai* phrase.

(25) a. Zhangsan tian **zai** *xinli*.
   Zhangsan sweet at heart
   'Zhangsan felt sweet in his heart.'
   b. Shiqing nan **zai** *zheli*.
   matter difficult at here
   'The difficulty of the matter is in here.'

The post-verbal *zai* phrase marks a static location and does not give rise to a directional reading.

## 3.3 Post-verbal zai *is not ambiguous*

In the literature, while Tai (1975) and Wang (1980) claim that the post-verbal *zai* phrase denotes the location of the participant of the action, Chen (1978) and Fan (1982) argue that it denotes the location which the activity reaches. Liu (2009) argues against the above analyses. Consider (26).

(26) Wo yi xia da **zai** *chuanghu shang* le.
   I one CL hit at window top PART
   'I made a hit and it got the window.'

As pointed out by Liu (2009), the *zai* phrase in this example does not specify the location of any participant, contra to Tai (1975) and Wang (1980). It describes the location where the event of hitting reaches, supporting the analysis that the post-verbal *zai* phrase denotes the location which the activity reaches, as in Chen (1978) and Fan (1982).

On the other hand, Liu (2009) suggests that the following example is a problem for Chen (1978) and Fan (1982).

(27) Lian ni suan ***zai** limian*, yigong you ershi ge keren.
 including you count at inside altogether have twenty CL guest
 'Including you, there are altogether twenty guests.'

Liu claims that the *zai* phrase in (27) does not denote the location which the counting reaches. Instead, it denotes the location of the participant.

Liu (2009) argues that a post-verbal *zai* phrase serves different aspectual functions according to the aspectual properties of the verbs to which it is attached. For telic verbs, it provides a locative boundary to the events that may or may not coincide with the temporary boundary inherent in the verbs; for atelic dynamic verbs, it adds a locative boundary to the events and turns the predicate into a telic predicate; finally for stative verbs, it provides no boundary to the events. That the addition of a prepositional phrase can make the event telic by adding a spatial endpoint is appealing, but it is not clear why a dynamic verb such *fei* 'fly' sometimes gets an atelic reading as in *fei zai tian shang* 'flew in the sky' in (14a) and a telic reading as in *fei zai chuantai shang* 'flew and landed on the windowsill' in (19).

Based on the above discussion of the constraints that different verb types have on the post-verbal *zai* phrase in the previous section, I take the position that the post-verbal *zai* phrase is basically directional unless a locative reading is allowed by the verb it occurs with. Moreover, the occurrence of a directional *zai* is restricted. Only certain place nouns can be taken to be goals and occur with the post-verbal *zai*. With this mind, now let us go back to the examples in (26) and (27). The difference between (26) and (27) comes from the verb type: *da* 'hit' in (26) belongs to Type B and *suan* 'count' in (27) belongs to Type C. The post-verbal *zai* phrase in (27) is allowed because the participant is part of the understood domain at the end of counting, just like the body part connection mentioned above.

If my analysis is correct, the acquisition of the post-verbal *zai* then means children have to learn whether a verb allows a locative *zai* post-verbally and what the constraint the verb has on the place noun to yield a directional reading. I now turn to the acquisition of the post-verbal *zai*.

## 4. Acquisition of post-verbal *zai*

In this section, I will first review previous studies of the acquisition of the post-verbal *zai* and then discuss the longitudinal data I have collected.

## 4.1 Previous Studies

### 4.1.1 The locative usage appears earlier than the directional usage

From the data in Hsu (1996), the locative usage of a post-verbal *zai* phrase appears before a directional one. Moreover, a post-verbal *zai* appears before *dao* 'to' (Hsu 1996: 94):

(28) Zhu ***zai*** *fangjian li*. (1;8)
 live at room inside
 'live in the room'

(29) Dao ***zai*** *shui li*. (1;9)
 pour at water inside
 'pour into the water'

(30) Tou ***dao*** *youtong limian*. (1;10)
 drop to mail:box inside
 'drop into a mail box'

### 4.1.2 *Zai* is used instead of *dao*

A non-adult error found in Hsu (1996:98) is given as follows:

(31) Wo dai ta ***zai*** *mianbei li* wan. (3;11)
 I bring he at quilt inside play
 'I bring him to play inside the quilt.'

In adult grammar, *zai* in (31) should be replaced by *dao* because *dai* belongs to Type C and *mianbei li* 'inside the quilt', not a body part, cannot be considered to be a goal for this type of verb.

From the longitudinal language samples studied (taken from Cheung 1995), Yao (2009) also finds instances where *dao* is replaced by *zai*:

(32) Chou 2;4
 En, bei tou ***zai*** *zheli*.
 PART BEI steal at here
 'En, (it) is stolen in here.'

(33) Chou 2;5
    EXA:    Women qu zhao xiao xiao hanbao.
              we go find small small hamburger
              'We go to find the small hamburger.'
    CHI:    Xiao xiao hanbao **zai** <na>[//]nali qu le?
              small small hamburger at where go PART
              'Where is the small hamburger?'
    EXA:    Diao dao nali qu le?
              fall to wherego PART
              'Where did it fall?'
    CHI:    **Zai** zheli qu.
              at here go
              'In here.'

(34) Chou 3;0
    CHI:    <Wo wo wo>[/] Wo yao jie <hen yuan>[/] hen yuan.
              I I I I want catch very far very far
              'I want to catch (it) far away.'
    EXA:    Hao.
              OK
              'OK.'
    EXA:    Hao lihai.
              so good
              '(You are) so good.'
    CHI:    Name yuan a.
              so far PART
              '(It is) so far away.'
    CHI:    <Da da>[/] da **zai** na ge dianpao.
              hit hit hit at that CL bulb
              'Hit in that bulb.'
    EXA:    Da diandengpao.
              hit electric:bulb
              'Hit the electric bulb.'
    EXA:    Diandengpao hui podiao o.
              electric:bulb will break PART
              'The electric bulb will be broken.'

(35) Zhen 3;2
   Tui! Ranhou tui *zai* zhe bian.
   push then push at this side
   'Push! Then push to this side.'

(36) Chou 3;2
   Ban *zai* zheli.
   move at here
   'Move in here.'

According to Yao, in all of the above cases, *zai* should be replaced by *dao*. The data above will be discussed together with my data below.

## 4.2 Findings in this study
### 4.2.1 Data
The majority of the data in this study are the naturalistic data of my son, Sean, born on Oct. 31, 2003. They were collected from when he was one year old up to 5;10. In addition to videotaping my conversations with him regularly, I also kept a diary about his language development.

### 4.2.2 The appearance of *zai*
By the age of two, the child has all the uses of *zai*.

(37) a. ***Zai*** zhe bian. (2;0) (*Zai* as a main verb)
       at this side
       '(I'm) here.'
   b. ***Zai*** zhuzhu. (2;0) (*Zai* as a progressive marker)
       at cook
       '(I'm) cooking.'
   c. ***Zai*** zheli zhuzhu. (2;0) (A pre-verbal *zai* denoting a static location)
       at here cook
       '(I'm) cooking.'
   d. Gai ***zai*** zhe ge. (2;0) (A post-verbal *zai* denoting a goal)
       cover in this CL
       'I covered (it) on it.'
       cf.  gai *zai* zhe ge *shangmian*
            cover at this CL top

In adult grammar, to specify a location, a localizer like *shangmian* indicated in (37d) has to be used. Similarly, it is possible that a localizer is also missing in Yao's example in (34). If this is the case, then the use of a *zai* phrase is acceptable, because it refers to the endpoint of the hitting event.

*4.2.3 The appearance of* dao

The use of *dao* for marking direction appears much later than the occurrence of *dao* as a resultative complement denoting the success of achieving an action.

(38) a. Kan-***dao***. (1;10)
   see-arrive
   '(I) saw (it).'
 b. Zou zou ***dao*** zhe bian zhe bian. (2;7)
   walk walk to this side this side
   'Walk to this side.'

*4.2.4 Post-Verbal Locative* zai

The following data show that the child mistakenly takes the post-verbal *zai* to be locative, not sensitive to the verb type.

(39) Muotuoche na-chulai, wo yao qi ***zai*** waimian.[4] (2;9)
   motorcycle take-out I want ride at outside
   'Bring the motorcycle out. I want to ride it outside.'
   cf. ... ***zai*** waimian qi.
      at outside ride

(40) Wan ***zai*** zheli. (2;10)
   play in here
   '(I want to) play in here.'
   cf. ***zai*** zheli wan
      at here play

(41) Wo xiangyao shua ya ***zai*** chuang shang. (3;10)
   I want brush tooth in bed top
   'I want to brush in bed.'
   cf. ....***zai*** chuang shang shua ya
      at bed top brush tooth

4  In (39), the child didn't mean he would like to ride the motorcycle from the bedroom to the outside, because the motorcycle was inside of the bedroom and the child was not in the bedroom.

A related example found in Yao (2009) is the one given in (32). In adult grammar, action verbs such as *tou* 'steal', *wan* 'play' and *shu ya* 'brush teeth' do not allow a post-verbal *zai* at all. As far as *qi* 'ride' in (39) is concerned, a post-verbal *zai* phrase is possible only when the verb is understood to mean 'mounting a horse', as it belongs to Type B. *Waimian* in (39) cannot occur with the post-verbal *zai* because it cannot be a place where mounting a horse ends.

Despite the above errors, the fact that the child does not make the same kind of error after 3;10 shows that the child has acquired by then the knowledge that a post-verbal locative *zai* is only possible for certain verbs.

### 4.2.5 Post-verbal Directional zai

The following data show that the child used *zai* in places where *dao* should be used. There are quite a few examples in this category and many of them involve the same verbs with the same or different place nouns. Here I only quote the first instance of the child's non-adult use of the directional *zai* appearing in 2;8 and the last instance of such a use when the same verb and the same place noun are used.

(42) Fang **zai** limian qu. (2;8)
  Put at inside go
  'Put (it) inside.'
  cf. fang **dao** limian qu
    put arrive inside go

(43) Meiyou he **zai** limian le, you shui le. (2;9)
  not drink at inside PART have water PART
  '(I) won't drink (the water) and as a result hit the bottom (of the bottle). It has water already.'
  cf. ... he **dao** limian...
    drink to inside

(44) Qiuqiu yao  na  **zai**  waimian. (2;9)
  Qiuqiu want  take  at  outside
  '(I want you to) take (the pacifier) outside.'
  cf. ...na **dao** waimian
    take to outside

(45) Na baozhi *zai dongxi xiamian*. (3;1)
 take newspaper at thing below
 'Take the newspaper to put it under the thing.'
 cf. ...**fang** *zai dongxi xiamian*
  put at thing below

(46) Ni na *zai qianmian*, wo cai nadedao. (3;1)
 you take at front I then can:reach
 'You take it to the front, so I can reach it.'
 cf. ...na *dao qianmian*...
  take to front

(47) Shuishui liu *zai zheli*. (3;1)
 water flow at here
 'The water flowed here.'
 cf. ...liu *dao zheli*
  flow to here

(48) Fei *zai shangmian qu* le, wo nabudao. (3;1)
 fly at top away PART I cannot:take
 'Fly up there. I cannot reach it.'
 cf. fei *dao shangmian qu* le...
  fly to top go PART

(49) Qi *zai na bian qu* cai bu hui tiedao. (3;1)
 ride at that side go only not will fall
 'Ride (it) over there, or you will fall.'
 cf. ...qi *dao na bian*...
  ride to that side

(50) Zhe shi wo yao dai *zai jia li* de. (3;8)
 this be I want bring at home inside DE
 'This is what I want to bring home.'
 cf ...dai *dao jia li*
  bring to home inside

(51) Zou ***zai*** *zhe bian qu.* (4;6)
    walk at this side go
    'Walk toward this side.'
    cf.  zou ***dao*** zhe bian qu
         walk arrive this side go

(52) Wo gen Jiejie qi jiaotache qi ***zai nali****, nali you hua longzhou.* (4;7)
    I with Sister ride bike ride at there there have row dragon:boat
    'I rode with Sister there. There was a dragon boat race.'
    cf.  …qi ***dao*** *nali…*
         ride to there

(53) Child:   Mommy, Ni ***zai nali*** *qu le.* (4;8)   (cf. …***dao*** *nali qu…*)
              Mommy you at where go PART              to where go
    Mother:  Ni shuo shenme?
              you say what
              'What did you say?'
    Child:   Ni ***dao*** *nali qu le.*
              you to where go PART
              'Where did you go?'

(54) Ba ta tu koushui ***zai limian*** *qu.* (5;1)
    BA he spit saliva at inside go
    'Spit the saliva into it (the bottle).'
    cf.  …tiu ***dao*** *limian qu*
         throw to inside go

(55) Wo shi na ***zai ni fangjian li****, wo queding.* (5;8)
    I be take at you room inside I sure
    'I took it to your room. I'm sure.'
    cf.  …na ***dao*** *fangjian li*
         take to room inside

In the above examples, there are two subtypes of mistakes. First, the child was mistaken in distinguishing different verb types and wrongly accepted a *zai* phrase. For example, the verb *na* 'take' is a Type C verb and *qi* 'ride' is a Type B verb. The examples in (44), (45), (46), (52) and (55) are thus all unacceptable because their post-verbal *zai* phrases do not meet the requirement to be their goals. Similarly, *he* 'drink' in (43), *liu* in (47), *dai* 'bring' in (50), *tui* 'push' in Yao's (35) and *ban* 'move' in Yao's (36) are Type D verbs, which do not allow a post-verbal *zai* phrase at all. Second, the child mistakenly used *zai* with the directional particle *qu*, which is never possible for an adult. The relevant examples are in (42), (48), (49), (51), (53) and (54).

From the above data, it is clear that the child hasn't mastered the post-verbal *zai* up to the age of 5;8. What is then the child's assumption about the post-verbal *zai*?

The example in (53), just like (33) found in Yao (2009), seems to suggest that *zai* does not depend on a verb for the directional reading. It may be claimed that the directional reading in this example is related to the directional particle *qu* 'away', but *qu* does not seem to be required in all the other examples where the directional meaning is intended. It then follows that the source of the directional reading is *zai* itself. It may then be concluded that the child takes *zai* to be directional without considering the verb type, at least from 2;8 on.

*4.2.6 Other errors with a post-verbal zai*

The following examples show other cases in which the child overuses a post-verbal *zai* phrase.

(56) Guo **zai** qiao shang. (3;8) (cf. **guo qiao**)
 cross at bridge top     cross bridge
 'Cross the bridge.'

(57) Wo de yizhi   kan **zai** na bian. (4;6) (cf…**kan (xiang) na bian**)
 I DE all:the:time look at that side     look toward that side
 'My head has been looking toward that side.'

(58) Child:    Buyao mo **zai** wo zheli. (5;10) (cf…**mo wo zheli**)
         not touch at I here            touch I here
         'Don't touch me.'
  Mother: Ni ganggang shuo shenme? Ni shuo shenme buyao mo…
         you just:now say what      you say what not touch
         'What did you just say? You said, 'Do not touch…''
  Child:  Buyao mo wo.
         not touch I
         'Don't touch me.'

In (56) and (57), *zai* is used with a verb that requires a place noun to serve as a route. In adult grammar, *zai* cannot be used to mark a route. In the case of *guo*, the route can serve as a direct object, while in the case of *kan* 'see', *xiang* 'toward' is used. Finally in (58), *wo zheli* 'here' has to serve as a direct object for *mo* 'touch'. It is after 5;10 that the child no longer made errors with respect to the post-verbal *zai*.

## 5. Concluding remarks

Unlike in English and other languages where a PP can be either locative or directional with respect to some verbs, a post-verbal *zai* in Chinese is never ambiguous between a locative meaning and a directional meaning. The challenge for children learning Mandarin is to acquire the knowledge that a post-verbal *zai* phrase is locative with respect to some verbs and it is directional only when it can be interpreted to be a goal for the verb it occurs with. The longitudinal data studied show that the child mistakenly took the post-verbal *zai* to be locative in an early stage (up to 3;10) and allowed a non-adult directional reading (up to 5;8). Some other errors appeared when the child was between 3;8 to 5;10. The result is schematized below.

(59)  errors with the locative *zai*     2;9      3;10
                                          |----------|

       errors with the directional *zai*  2;8                               5;8
                                          |-----------------------------|

       other errors with the post-verbal *zai*    3;8                  5;10
                                                  |----------------------|

The findings show that the child first acquires the knowledge that only a special class of verbs allow the post-verbal *zai* to be locative and then he learns that whether the post-verbal *zai* phase can be directional is subject to different verb types. It seems to be the case that the child takes the post-verbal *zai* to be independent from its preceding verb. A possible analysis for the persistence of using *zai* instead of the correct *dao* is that the child takes it to be a verb rather than a preposition depending on the preceding verb. More research will be needed for this analysis.

## References

Chen, Chung-yu. 1978. Aspectual features of the verb and the relative positions of the locatives. *Journal of Chinese Linguistics* 6. 76-103.

Cheung, Hintat. 1995. Pingjun yuju changdu (MLU) zai Zhongwen de yingyong [The Application of MLU in Chinese]. NSC report.
den Dikken, M. 2006. On the functional structure of locative and directional PPs. Ms., CUNY Graduate Center.
Emonds, J. E. 2000. *Lexicon and grammar: The English syntacticon*. Mouton, Berlin.
Fan, Jiyan. 1982. Lun jieci duanyu *zai* + chusuo. [On the prepositional phrase *zai* + location]. *Yuyan yanjiu* 3. 71-86.
Gehrke, B. 2007. On directional readings of locative prepositions. *Proceedings of ConSOLE XIV*, 99-120.
Hsu, Joseph H. 1996. *A study of the stages of development and acquisition of Mandarin Chinese by children in Taiwan*. Taipei: Crane Publishing.
Jackendoff, R. 1983. *Semantics and cognition*. Cambridge: MIT Press.
Levin, B. 1993. *Verb classes and alternations. A preliminary investigation*. Chicago/London: The Diversity of Chicago Press.
Liu, Feng-hsi. 2009. Aspect and the post-verbal *zai* phrase in Mandarin Chinese. In Janet Zhiqun Xing (ed.), *Studies of Chinese linguistics: Functional approaches*, 103-129. Hong Kong: Hong Kong University Press.
Svenonius, P. To appear. Spatial P in English. In G. Cinque & L. Rizzi (eds.), *The cartography of syntactic structures*, vol. 6. Oxford University Press.
Tai, James H.-Y. 1975. On two functions of place adverbials in Mandarin Chinese. *Journal of Chinese Linguistics* 3. 154-179.
Talmy, L. 1985. Lexicalization patterns: semantic structure in lexical forms. In T. Shopen (ed.), *Language Typology and Syntactic Description III: Grammatical Categories and the Lexicon*, 5-149. Cambridge: Cambridge University Press.
Thomas, E. 2001. On the expression of directional movement in English. *Essex Graduate Student Papers in Language and Linguistics IV*, 87-104.
Thomas, E. 2003. Manner-Specificity as a factor in the acceptance of *in* and *on* in directional contexts. *Essex Graduate Student Papers in Language and Linguistics V*, 117-146.
Wang, Huan. 1980. Xai shuoshuo *zai* [More on *zai*]. *Yuyan jiaoxue yu yanjiu* 3. 25-29.
Yao, Yu-Fen. 2009. The early development of *zai4* in Mandarin-Speaking children. M.A. Thesis. National Taiwan University.
Zwarts, J. 1997. Vectors as relative positions: A compositional semantics of modified PPs. *Journal of Semantics* 14. 57-86.
Zwarts, J. 2005. Prepositional aspect and the algebra of paths. *Linguistics and Philosophy* 38.6. 739-779.
Zwarts, J. & Y. Winter. 2000. Vector space semantics: A model-theoretic analysis of locative prepositions. *Journal of Logic, Language and Information* 9(2). 168-211.

Email: miaolinghsieh@yahoo.com.tw

# Temporal reference of bare verbs in Mandarin child language

Yi-ching Su
*National Tsing Hua University (Taiwan)*

## 1. Introduction

This paper reports preliminary findings of an investigation into bare verbs in Mandarin child language. This topic is interesting in the context of recent research into the occurrence of non-finite forms in children's utterances around the ages of two to three years, including the use of bare verbs lacking tense and agreement markers in children acquiring English, the "root infinitive" phenomenon in languages like Dutch, German, French or Swedish, the use of bare perfective forms in Greek, and so on. Unlike these languages, adult Mandarin lacks tense and agreement, and it is controversial whether Mandarin has the finite vs. nonfinite clause distinction. Furthermore, sentences with bare verbs are grammatical in adult Mandarin. The question arises whether and to what extent Mandarin-acquiring children aged between 2 and 3 pass through a stage corresponding to the "root infinitive" stage, and what properties sentences with bare verbs have in child Mandarin.

Section 2 reviews previous research into the phenomenon of bare or nonfinite verbs in children's production in English and other languages, leading up to Hyams' (2006) proposal that the interpretation of non-finite clauses is determined by aspectual properties. Section 3 then presents the aims, methods and preliminary results of our investigation of Mandarin child language.

## 2. Previous research

It has been observed since the earliest documentation of the spontaneous speech of English-acquiring children that the tense- or agreement-bearing elements tend to be omitted in children's utterances when they are at the age of two to three, as shown in the following examples (cited from Guasti 2002).

(1) a. Papa have it. (Eve, 1;6)
  b. Cromer wear glasses. (Eve, 2;0)
  c. Marie go. (Sarah, 2;3)
  d. Mumma ride horsie. (Sarah, 2;6)

(2) a. Eve gone [has]. (Eve, 1;6)
  b. Kitty hiding [is]. (Sarah, 2;3)

(3) a. That my briefcase [is]. (Eve, 1;9)
  b. You nice [are]. (Sarah, 2;7)

(4) a. Fraser not see him. (Eve, 2;0)
  b. He no bit ya. (Sarah, 3;0)
  c. Where ball go? (Adam, 2;3)

For the sentences in (1), the inflectional morpheme is dropped, leaving a bare verb, and in the sentences in (2) to (4), the copula or the auxiliary bearing tense or agreement are missing in children's utterances.

To account for children's non-adult pattern of utterances, Radford (1990) proposed the Small Clause Hypothesis, which states that children's early clauses lack the corresponding inflectional category IP. Since Radford's discussion was mainly based on English, when cross-linguistic patterns are taken into consideration, this hypothesis soon raised some criticisms due to three major problems. Firstly, when finite forms are used by children, agreement is almost always correct. From reported studies, error rates of subject verb agreement range only from 0.5% to 4%. If children do not have adult-like representations of inflectional category, they would not be likely to reach such high accuracy. Secondly, children acquiring languages such as Dutch, German, French, and Swedish tend to use the infinitive form optionally in a finite context as in (5) instead of the bare verb as in English, and it is hence referred to as the "optional infinitive" (OI) or "root infinitive" (RI) phenomenon. This casts serious doubt on the idea that children at this age completely lack knowledge of the IP structure.

(5) a. Papa schoenen wassen (Dutch, Weverink 1989)
    Daddy shoes wash-INF
  b. Michel dormir (French, Pierce 1992)
    Michel sleep-INF
  c. Thorstn das haben (German, Poeppel & Wexler 1993)
    Thorsten that have-INF

d. Jag också hoppa där å där (Swedish, Santelmann 1995)
   I also hop-INF there and there

Thirdly, some languages such as Italian, Spanish, and Catalan do not exhibit an obvious stage similar to what was found in the child languages of English, Dutch, German, etc., and even if they do, the period is substantially short, ending around the age of two.

It is even more unlikely that children lack the adult-like syntactic representation of IP if we consider the systematic patterning of finite and non-finite clauses in the child languages with an RI stage. For instance, in French, Pierce (1992) found that finite verbs appear to the left of the negative adverb pas, while infinitives appear to its right, as displayed in Table 1.

*Table 1. Finiteness and position of negation in French (Pierce 1992)*

|  | Finite | Non-finite |
| --- | --- | --- |
| Verb Neg | 173 | 2 |
| Neg Verb | 9 | 122 |

Poeppel & Wexler (1993) also illustrated a similar finding in German, namely, finite verbs tend to appear in the V2 position, whereas infinitives appear in the final position, as shown in Table 2.

*Table 2. Finiteness and position of verbs in German (Poeppel & Wexler 1993)*

|  | Finite | Non-finite |
| --- | --- | --- |
| V2 | 197 | 6 |
| Verb-final | 11 | 37 |

Based on the systematic positioning of finite vs. non-finite verb forms in French and V2 languages, a possible explanation is the Null Modal Hypothesis (e.g., Boser et al. 1992; Krämer 1993), which states that the structure of RI utterances contains a non-overt modal verb, and that modal verbs select eventive predicates. This hypothesis captures the observation that RI utterances are restricted to event-denoting predicates (the Eventivity Constraint). As reported in French, Dutch, and Russian child languages, over 90% of children's non-finite utterances come with eventive verbs, and stative verbs are almost exclusively finite. A relevant property for postulating a null modal in these RI languages is that RI utterances typically have a modal interpretation.

Although it has considerable appeal, the Null Modal Hypothesis still faces empirical problems as it is not able to capture the morphosyntactic distinctions between children's finite and non-finite utterances. Specifically, it was observed that children acquiring V2 languages adhere to the restriction of topicalization in finite sentences, but not in non-finite utterances, as reported in Poeppel & Wexler (1993), Haegeman (1994), and Platzack (1992) for German, Dutch, and Swedish, respectively. Table 3 illustrates that in the child utterances of these V2 languages, non-subject initial non-finite utterances are virtually absent, i.e., non-finite utterances with objects or adverbs as topics do not occur, but topicalization of non-subjects in finite clauses is a robust phenomenon.

*Table 3. Number of subject initial and non-subject initial non-finite clauses and finite clauses*

|  | Subject initial | | Non-subject initial | |
|---|---|---|---|---|
|  | Finite | Non-finite | Finite | Non-finite |
| German | 130 | 24 | 50 | 0 |
| Dutch | 1223 | 101 | 1346 | 5 |
| Swedish | 145 | 147 | 61 | 1 |

In addition, in Dutch, German, Swedish, and French, non-finite *wh*-questions are virtually absent, as shown in Table 4 (cited from Hoekstra & Hyams 1998).

*Table 4. Percentage of finite and non-finite verbs in all clauses and in wh-**questions***

|  | All clauses | | *Wh*-questions | |
|---|---|---|---|---|
|  | Finite | Non-finite | Finite | Non-finite |
| Dutch | 3768 (86%) | 721 (16%) | 88 (97%) | 2 (3%) |
| German | -- | -- | 306 (99.6%) | 1 (0.4%) |
| Swedish | -- | -- | 675 (99.6%) | 5 (0.4%) |
| French | 921 (83%) | 195 (17%) | 114 (100%) | 0 (0%) |

Furthermore, in various languages that have been studied the vast majority of non-finite utterances occur with null subjects, as shown in Table 5 (cited from Hoekstra & Hyams 1998).

*Table 5. Percentage of null and overt subjects in finite and non-finite clauses*

| Language | Child | Finite verbs | | | Non-finite verbs | | |
|---|---|---|---|---|---|---|---|
| | | Overt | Null | Total | Overt | Null | Total |
| Flemish | Maarten 1;11 | 75% | 25% | 92 | 11% | 89% | 100 |
| German | Simone 1;8-4;1 | 80% | 20% | 3636 | 11% | 89% | 2477 |
| German | Andreas | 92% | 8% | 220 | 32% | 68% | 68 |
| French | Nathalie 1;9-2;3 | 70% | 30% | 299 | 27% | 73% | 180 |
| French | Philippe 2;1-2;6 | 74% | 26% | 705 | 7% | 93% | 164 |
| Dutch | Hein 2;3-3;1 | 68% | 32% | 3768 | 15% | 85% | 721 |

According to the Null Modal Hypothesis, RI utterances are covert finite clauses with a null modal which should pattern like overt finite clauses, and hence the above distinctions between finite and non-finite RI utterances would not be predicted.

To account for the cross-linguistic variation, Wexler (1994) proposed the Tense Omission Model, which postulates that an optional infinitive clause arises when the child leaves the tense feature underspecified in a given clausal representation. Adopting the idea of constraint interaction from Optimality Theory, the Tense Omission Model assumes the interaction of the following three constraints for children's optional infinitive utterances.

(6) a. *Tense Constraint*: A main clause must include a specification of tense.
 b. *Checking Constraint*: Both Agr and T have a D-feature, which must be eliminated by being checked against the D-feature of a DP subject that raises to Spec TP and Spec AgrP.
 c. *Uniqueness Constraint*: A subject can check the uninterpretable feature of either T or Agr, but not both.

The outcome of the constraint interaction is determined by the requirement to minimize violations. That is to say, given two representations, the grammar will choose the one that violates as few grammatical constraints as possible, but if two representations violate the same number of constraints, then either one may be chosen. In child grammars, since a finite clause violates the Uniqueness Constraint, but a non-finite clause violates the Tense Constraint, either one may be chosen. In adult grammars, due to the effect of maturation, the Uniqueness Constraint no longer has any effect, and hence adult utterances are always finite. As for why null subject languages like Italian, Spanish, and Catalan have a substantially short RI stage, Wexler (1994) argued that since Agr in pro-drop languages licenses a null subject, it does not have an uninterpretable D-feature to be checked, and hence the DP subjects only need to be raised to Spec TP to check the D-feature of T.

Although the Tense Omission Model can account for most of the characteristics found in RI languages, it runs into problems in construing the incompatibility of non-finite clauses with clitic and weak pronouns and the lack of infinitives in *wh*-questions. It is observed that in French and Dutch child languages, when clitic or weak pronouns are employed, the sentences are exclusively finite. If RI utterances result from the underspecification of the tense feature in child grammars, they should be found also in utterances with clitic or weak pronouns as well as in *wh*-questions. Similar problems apply to other variants of the Underspecification Accounts, including Hyams (1996), which argued that the number feature is unspecified, and Liceras, Bel, & Perales (2006), which proposed that whether the person feature is unspecified and whether there is a distinct infinitive marker in the language determine if a language has an RI stage and how long it lasts.

Another important account for the RI phenomenon is the Truncation Model, proposed by Rizzi (1994), which postulates that the Axiom on Clausal Representation is always operative in adults' grammar, but it applies optionally in children's grammar, i.e., RI clauses are structures truncated below TP. According to the Truncation Model, the Axiom on Clausal Representation states that CP is the root of all clauses, regardless of finite or infinitive. The Truncation Model can explain not only the morphosyntactic distinctions of the distributions for children's finite and non-finite utterances, but also the incompatibility of non-finite clauses with clitic and weak pronouns, as well as the lack of infinitives in *wh*-questions. Moreover, it can also account for why null subjects match with the development of RIs. As for why null subject languages like Italian, Spanish, and Catalan do not exhibit an extended RI stage, Rizzi (1994) proposed that in pro-drop languages, even infinitives must raise to TP and AgrP, and hence there are no RIs in these languages.

For those languages that do not demonstrate an extended RI stage, Salustri & Hyams (2002) proposed that in the null subject languages like Italian, Catalan, and Spanish, there is an analogue RI stage in which imperatives have higher percentages than in the adult language. However, a recent study by Pratt & Grinstead (2007) demonstrated that Spanish-acquiring children also have a parallel RI stage in which the third person singular present form with null subjects is overgeneralized to non-third person singular subjects, and this has not been found in the past because previous studies did not examine whether the verb inflections match with the intended subjects in the contexts for the utterances with null subjects. In addition, although Sano (1995) showed that Japanese-acquiring children also did not display an obvious RI stage, Murasugi & Fuji (2008) argued that the facts that Korean-acquiring children overuse the default mood marker –e (Kim & Phillips 1998), and that Japanese-acquiring children overgeneralize the past tense verb form (Murasugi, Fuji, & Hashimoto 2007), suggest that there is a parallel RI stage in these two languages.

In addition to the non-adult form of utterances found in 2-year-olds' spontaneous speech, it has also been observed that with overwhelming frequency, RIs have modal interpretations (i.e., the Modal Reference Effect). It was often found that children's non-finite clauses (e.g., RIs and English bare verbs) usually have an interpretation that is different from their finite counterparts. Take Dutch child language as an example. Wijnen (1997) reported that Dutch RIs often have a modal interpretation expressing volition, direction, or intention (about 73%-86% of the time), as illustrated in the following examples.

(7)  a.  Child:    Papa bouwen
              daddy build-INF
         Father:   Geef jij de blokjes maar aan dan
              'well, hand me the blocks then'
     b.  Child:    Drike(n)!
              Drink-INF
         Father:   Wil je de kamer drinden?
              'Do you want to have a drink in that room?'

On the other hand, English bare verbs can have ongoing meaning (as in (8a), about 72% of the time), in contrast to adult or child finite present tense clauses (8b), which denote only habitual but not ongoing events (Torrence & Hyams 2004).

(8) a. Mother: What's she doing with the tiger now?
    Child: Play # play ball with him. (Nina, file 39)
  b. She plays with him every day / *now

In addition, sometimes English bare verbs can also have a temporal interpretation denoting past events, as shown below.

(9) a. Child: He fall down (Sarah, file 40)
       Mother: He did?
    b. Child: He lose it (Sarah, file 40)

Moreover, identical forms in different languages can have very different interpretive properties. Although Dutch RIs usually have a modal interpretation, Russian RIs most often have a temporal meaning, denoting ongoing or past events (about 74% of the time, e.g., Brun et al. 1999), as demonstrated in (10).

(10) a. Mama maslo kupit'                    (past)
        mommy butter buy-INF
        'Mommy has bought the butter'
     b. Kupat'sya                            (present)
        bath-INF
        '(He) is bathing'
     c. Rubaška snimat                       (modal/future)
        shirt take-off-INF
        '(I will/want to) take off the shirt'

For languages that do not have an infinitive morpheme such as Greek, children may employ another verb form that is not grammatical in adult grammar instead of the infinitive in finite sentences during the corresponding RI stage. For instance, Greek-acquiring children have been found to use the non-adult 'bare perfective', i.e., the perfective form of a verb that does not come with past tense morphology or a modal particle, and the 'bare perfective' form is overwhelmingly modal in meaning (almost 100% of the time, see e.g. Stephany 1995). The following examples display the phenomenon.

(11) a. Pio vavási
Spiros read-PRF.3SG
'Spiro is going to / wants to read'
b. Pári γugunáki?
Take-PRF.3SG the piggy
'May she take the piggy?'
c. Xalási toa
break-PRF.3SG
'It is going to break'

The cross-linguistic differences in the interpretations of non-finite sentences in child languages discussed above are summarized in Table 6 (cited from Hyams 2006).

*Table 6. Temporal and modal characteristics of non-finite clauses in child language*

|  | Present | Past | Modal/Future |
|---|---|---|---|
| English | 65% | 25% | 8% |
| Russian | 26% | 48% | 26% |
| Greek | n.s. | n.s. | Approx. 100% |
| Dutch | 10-26% | 1-3% | 73-86% |

*n.s. non-significant, <10% across children

Hyams (2006) proposed that the interpretation of all non-finite clauses, including RIs, English bare verbs and others, is determined by the aspectual properties of the predicates. To be more specific, she argued that the temporal interpretation of non-finite verbs depends on (i) universal principles of aspectual interpretation, especially the Punctuality Constraint proposed in Giorgi and Pianesi (1997), and (ii) the particular aspectual properties of the target language. Take English as an example. The temporal reference of the bare verb in child English is strongly contingent on the telicity of the predicate, i.e., children typically describe past events with telic verbs while present tense interpretation is almost always expressed with atelic verbs, as illustrated in Table 7.

*Table 7. Temporal reference and (a)telicity of English bare verbs*

| Interpretation | Telic | Atelic |
| --- | --- | --- |
| Past | 48 (94%) | 9 (6%) |
| Present | 16 (15%) | 88 (85%) |

In Russian, since all verbs are marked for grammatical aspect, either perfective or imperfective, RIs' perfectivity correlates with temporal reference, i.e., verbs that occur in past tense contexts are overwhelmingly perfective while verbs that occur in present contexts are imperfective, as displayed in Table 8.

*Table 8. Temporal reference and (im)perfectivity in Russian RIs*

| Interpretation | Perfective | Imperfective |
| --- | --- | --- |
| Past | 67 (94.6%) | 4 (5.4%) |
| Present | 2 (1.7%) | 36 (98.3%) |
| Future / Modal | 40 (53%) | 36 (47%) |

To account for the cross-linguistic variation in the interpretations of RI utterances, Hyams (2006) based her framework on Giorgi & Pianesi (1997, 2001), who proposed a theory of aspect in terms of the topological property of event closure or terminativity. In this theory, imperfective verbs denote non-closed or open events, whereas perfective verbs denote closed events, as schematized in (12).

(12) a.  Perfective  → completed / closed event   […..e…..]
     b.  Imperfective → ongoing / open event       ……e…..

Besides, in this system, the closure of an event can be obtained in two ways—(i) perfective aspect, or (ii) telicity (i.e. the introduction of second event variable, $e_2$, representing the telos, as with achievement predicates, e.g., reach the top). Closure by telicity is schematized as in (13).

(13) [.....e1.....]e2     closed/telic     e1 = process; e2 = telos

In Giorgi & Pianesi's theory, the Punctuality Constraint in (14) plays the role of a universal constraint on the temporal anchoring of closed events.

(14) *The Punctuality Constraint* (PC)
   A closed event cannot be simultaneous with the utterance event/time (=UT)

The Punctuality Constraint blocks perfective verbs (which denote closed events) from having ongoing reference, as illustrated in the following Russian and Greek contrasts.

(15) a. *Misha pročitaet knigu sejčas     (Russian)
        Misha reads-PERF book now
    b. Misha čitaet knigu sejčas
        Misha reads-IMPF book now
    c. *O Giorgos diavási to vivlia     (Greek)
        the George read-PERF the book
    d. O Giorgio diavázi to vivlia
        the George read-IMPF the book
        'George reads the book.'

Central to Hyams' (2006) framework are the Closed Event Hypothesis, the Temporal Anchoring Requirement, and the Default Anchoring Requirement, as stated below.

(16) *The Closed Event Hypothesis*
   In the early grammar temporal reference is assigned to a non-finite clause according to the topological property of closure.

(17) *Temporal Anchoring Requirement* (TAR)
   Events must be temporally interpreted, that is, they must be ordered with respect to a reference time (UT).

(18) *Default Anchoring Requirement* (DAR)
In the absence of a tense specification, the event time coincides with the utterance time (UT = ET).

Based on the three assumptions in (16) to (18) and the Punctuality Constraint, a restricted set of temporal options in the early grammar can be derived, as schematized in (19).

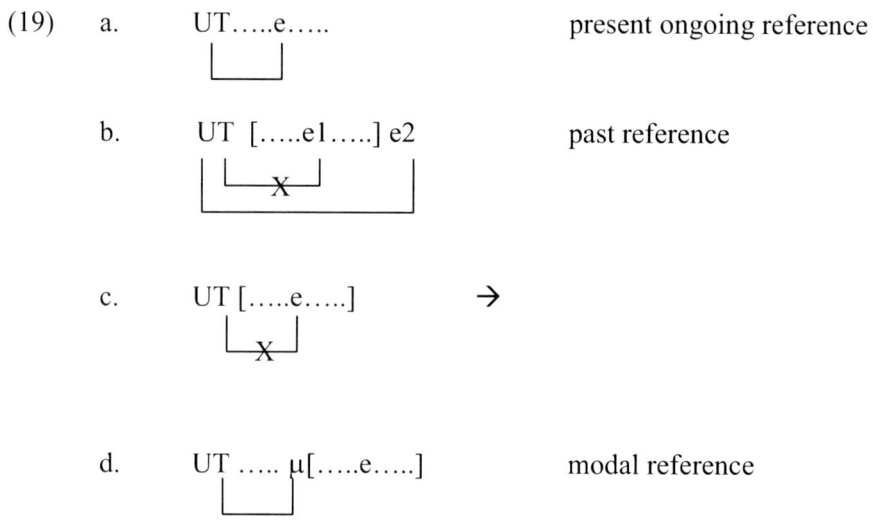

(19)  a.   UT.....e.....                    present ongoing reference

b.   UT [.....e1.....] e2              past reference

c.   UT [.....e.....]        →

d.   UT ..... μ[.....e.....]           modal reference

Since an open event consists of an unbounded single event as in (19a), according to the Default Anchoring Requirement, the event variable is linked to the utterance time, and hence the event is construed as ongoing. For a telic predicate, the event is closed by a second event variable e2 as in (13), and the process e1 is not accessible to the utterance time due to the Punctuality Constraint. As the Default Anchoring Requirement wants an anchoring to the utterance time, the Punctuality Constraint and Default Anchoring Requirement impose conflicting requirements. The conflict is resolved by having the utterance time linked to the second event variable as in (19b), thus deriving the past reading as the processual part of the event e1 is prior to the telos e2. For perfective predicates, their closure comes without a second event variable, and the Punctuality Constraint blocks the utterance time from linking it to the event, as shown in (19c). In this case the Default Anchoring Requirement is satisfied by the insertion of a null modal which is non-finite, as schematized in (19d). This naturally explains the contrast of interpretations for English telic and atelic predicates, why Russian imperfectives have the present reading, and why Greek bare perfectives have exclusively the modal interpretation, as displayed in Table 9.

*Table 9. Possible event / temporal structures of non-finite verbs in different child languages*

| Temporal Schema | Reference | English | Russian RI | Greek bare perfective | Dutch RI |
|---|---|---|---|---|---|
| A | Present | atelic | imperfective | --- | |
| B | Past | telic | perfective | --- | --- |
| C → D | Modal | --- | perfective | | --- |
| D | Modal | --- | | | |

As for why perfective verbs in Russian allow either the past reading or the modal reading, Hyams (2006) assumed that this is due to the fact that perfective verbs in Russian are of two types—those that introduce a second event variable and those that denote simple closed events. The former gives rise to a past interpretation, and the latter, according to (19c), has a modal reading.

The pattern in Dutch is peculiar as Dutch RIs sometimes refer to present events, but most often they have modal reference. Hyams (2006) attributed the pattern in Dutch to the fact that Dutch verbs are aspectually neutral, so the simple present can denote either an ongoing or habitual event, the simple past is neutral between a perfective and imperfective reading, and the infinitive is neutral between a closed or open reading, as demonstrated in the examples below.

(20) a. Jan eet een appel
        'John eats/is eating an apple.'
     b. Jan at een appel
        'John ate/was eating an apple.'
     c. Ik zag Jan de straat ovesteken toen hij door auto aangereden werd
        'I saw John cross/crossing the street when he was hit by a car.'

According to Hyams (2006), since the Dutch verb is neither overtly nor covertly marked for perfectivity, the absence of an event closure means the schema in (19a) is possible, giving rise to RIs with present ongoing interpretation. Besides, since the Dutch verb is aspectually neutral, there is no event closure, and hence no past tense reference will be obtained. Finally, since there is no closure in the event structure of the Dutch verb, there should be no source for the modal interpretation. However, as Dutch RIs predominantly have the modal reading, Hyams (2006) postulated that the null modal option as in (19d) is not necessarily a last resort, but is rather an option that is freely available as a way to satisfy the Default Anchoring Requirement.

## 3. The investigation of Mandarin

Without overt tense or agreement marking, it has been controversial whether Mandarin has the distinction of finite vs. non-finite clauses. Although some tests have been proposed, e.g., the occurrence of aspectual markers and modals as finite, the obligatory nullness of the subject for non-finite clauses (Huang 1982, 1984, 1987, 1989), and the cooccurrence constraint and the licensing of negative polarity items (Li 1985, 1990), they do not really make a reliable distinction between finiteness and non-finiteness as counter-examples can easily been found (Hu, Pan, & Xu 2001). Furthermore, Mandarin sentences with bare verbs, i.e., sentences without a time adverb or an aspect marker, can be easily construed as present tense sentences or past tense sentences even without resort to the context of the utterance, as the examples shown below (cited from Lin 2002b).

(21) Covert present tense
    a.    Ta hen congming
          he very clever
          'He is very clever.'
    b.    Wo xiangxin ni
          I believe you
          'I believe you.'

(22) Covert past tense
    a.    Ta song wo yi ben shu
          he give me one CL book
          'He gave me a book.'
    b.    Ta ma wo bendan
          he call me idiot
          'He called me an idiot.'

Lin (2002b) argued that the Mandarin covert present tense must select a homogeneous situation as its complement (e.g., stative adjectives and verbs), whereas the covert past tense must select a heterogeneous situation as its complement (e.g., resultative compound verbs like *dapuo* 'break'), and a covert tense is never interpreted as a future tense. Lin (2002a) further illustrated that in Mandarin, without an aspect or an adverb, a stative verb can have a present tense reference, and an achievement verb a past tense reference.

## 3.1 Aims

Given that sentences with bare verbs are also grammatical in adult Mandarin, whether there is any corresponding stage of RI in child Mandarin is unclear, and if there is, what characteristics are manifested in Mandarin-acquiring 2-year-olds' utterances is certainly still unknown. Therefore, this study aims to examine whether bare sentences, i.e., sentences with bare verbs, in the spontaneous speech of Mandarin-acquiring children at the age between 2 and 3 exhibit the following properties found in languages with or without an RI stage.

(i) Since bare sentences are also found in the utterances of Mandarin-speaking adults given appropriate contexts, but in adult Mandarin, bare sentences do not allow future event reference or modal interpretations, the first question to be asked is whether bare sentences in child Mandarin show exactly the same properties of temporal reference as in the adult grammar?

(ii) As a null-subject language without rich inflectional morphology, does child Mandarin also show high percentages of imperatives as in languages with a short RI stage such as Italian, Spanish, and Catalan, or does it pattern more similarly to languages with an extended RI stage such as English, Dutch, and German?

(iii) It has been observed that children's root infinitive utterances are predominantly restricted to eventive verbs, and hence the third question is whether child Mandarin also shows the contrast of eventive vs. non-eventive in bare sentences found in languages with an RI stage?

(iv) Does child Mandarin show any correlation between temporal reference and (a)telicity of predicates of the type found in languages with an RI stage, whereby telic predicates tend to have past tense reference, whereas atelic predicates mostly have an ongoing present reference or modal interpretation?

(v) It has been reported that children's root infinitive utterances tend to occur with null subjects, and so the fifth question to be probed is whether bare sentences in child Mandarin come mostly with null or overt subjects?

## 3.2 Methods

As a preliminary pilot study, we examined the spontaneous speech of one of the children in the Tsing Hua Mandarin Child Language Corpus between the ages of 1;11 and 2;4, with MLU from 1 to 2.4 (following the criteria of Cheung 1998). The basis for choosing the child was that the recordings were made by the child's mother, and hence contained more varieties of utterance types and reflected more naturally the interaction between a child and the major care-taker.

We first coded the child's utterances based on the criterion that they are spontaneous utterances with eventive or stative predicates, i.e., excluding repetitions, answers of questions, and utterances with unclear contexts. The total number of utterances obtained was 741, and the total number of bare sentences (i.e., excluding utterances with aspect markers or modal verbs) was 625 (84.3%). Among the bare sentences, there were 43 imperative sentences (7%)—a percentage more similar to what was found in German and Icelandic than in Italian, Catalan, and Spanish. The number of bare sentences with non-eventive predicates was 126 (20%), whereas it was 499 (80%) with eventive predicates.

We then examined the temporal reference of the child's bare sentences, and found that they can not only have past tense reference and present tense reference as in adult Mandarin, but also the non-adult modal interpretation, as illustrated in the following examples.

(23) Temporal reference of bare sentences
    a.    *Past*
           Child:        yi-ge ayi shoushang
                          a-CL aunt hurt
                          'An aunt got hurt.' (2;4)
           Mother:     dui, shangci you yi-ge ayi shoushang, dui-bu-dui
                          yes, last time have a-CL aunt hurt yes-not-yes
                          'Yes, last time there was an aunt got hurt.'
    b.    *Present*
           Child:        ama shuijiao, agong shuijiao
                          grandmother sleep grandfather sleep
                          'Grandmother is sleeping. Grandfather is sleeping.' (2;4)
           Mother:     agong zai shuijiao o
                          grandfather ASP sleep PAR
                          'Is grandfather sleeping?'
           Child:        en
                          Yes

c. *Modal*
   Child:      ziji zhuang
               self assemble
               'I assemble it myself.' (1;11)
   Mother:    o, ni yao ziji zhuang o
               o you want self assemble PAR
               'Do you want to assemble it yourself?'

Table 10 shows a cross-linguistic comparison of temporal reference for English bare verbs and Dutch RIs as reported in Hoekstra & Hyams (1998) and bare sentences in child Mandarin in our pilot study. As can be observed in this table, this Mandarin-acquiring child's bare sentences pattern more like the Dutch RIs in that they predominantly have a modal interpretation. Recall that the modal / future reading for bare sentences is not possible in adult Mandarin.

*Table 10. Temporal reference of RIs in Dutch and bare sentences in English and Mandarin*

|  | Past | Present | Future/modal | Total |
|---|---|---|---|---|
| Mandarin | 98 (15.7%) | 172 (27.5%) | 355 (56.8%) | 625 |
| English | 59 (22.3%) | 171 (64.8%) | 34 (12.9%) | 264 |
| Dutch | 64 (3%) | 194 (10%) | 1625 (86%) | 1883 |

Next we analyzed if there exists any correlation between temporal reference and the (a)telicity of predicates. The results are shown in Table 11. It is clear from this table that a telic predicate almost always has a past tense reference, whereas an atelic predicate can have either a present tense reference or a modal reading.

*Table 11. Temporal reference and (a)telicity of bare sentences (1;11-2;4)*

|  | Telic | Atelic | Total |
|---|---|---|---|
| Past | 84 (85.7%) | 14 (14.3%) | 98 |
| Present | 0 | 172 (100%) | 172 |
| Future/modal | 39 (11%) | 316 (89%) | 355 |

Finally, we counted the number of overt subjects for the child's bare sentences. The figures are given in Table 12 and Table 13. As shown in Table 12, the use of overt subject increases gradually as the child grows, and Table 13 exhibits an interesting pattern, i.e., overt subjects mainly come with bare sentences with either past or present tense reference rather than those with a modal interpretation.

*Table 12. Overt subjects in bare sentences for the three periods*

|  | Number of Overt Subject | % |
|---|---|---|
| 1;11-2;0 | 14 / 80 | 17.5% |
| 2;1-2;2 | 39 / 134 | 29% |
| 2;3-2;4 | 202 / 368 | 54.9% |
| Total | 256 / 582 | 43.8% |

*Table 13. Overt subjects in bare sentences for the three temporal references*

|  | Number of Overt Subject | % |
|---|---|---|
| Past | 54 / 98 | 55% |
| Present | 121 / 172 | 70% |
| Modal | 81 / 312 | 26% |
| Total | 256 / 582 | 44% |

## 3.3 Concluding Remarks

To sum up, our pilot study demonstrates the following preliminary findings:

- There appears to be an analogue stage of RI in Mandarin child language in which children produce predominantly bare sentences with modal interpretations.
- Unlike null subject languages with rich morphology, imperatives do not prevail in Mandarin child language.
- Like RI languages such as Dutch, child Mandarin also exhibits the contrast between eventive vs. stative predicates (i.e., the Eventivity Constraint).
- There is a correlation between temporal reference and the (a)telicity of predicates, i.e., telic predicates almost always have past tense reference, whereas atelic predicates mostly have a modal interpretation or sometimes past tense reference.
- There appear to be developmental stages in which bare sentences with a modal reading predominantly have null subjects, but the percentages of overt subjects for those with past or present tense reference increase dramatically as the child grows older.

However, some questions remain for further investigation in this study, as illustrated below.

- Will the use of bare sentences with a modal reading decrease and eventually disappear when the child turns 3, as found in those RI languages?
- Are the overt subjects for bare sentences with present and past tense reference an effect of the covert tense in child Mandarin?
- Does the use of overt or null subjects in adult Mandarin show any correlation with the temporal reference of the predicates?
- Do children other than the one examined in our pilot study show similar developmental patterns? Specifically, since the data used in the pilot study were the interactions between the child and the major care-taker, it will be necessary to examine other children's spontaneous speech in the corpus in which the interactions were between the child and someone outside the family (i.e., the investigator or research assistants).
- Since atelic predicates in child Mandarin mainly have modal readings or sometimes present tense references, similar to Dutch RIs, does this suggest that Mandarin atelic predicates are aspectually neutral, as in Dutch? Or does the similar pattern of temporal reference for atelic predicates in the two languages in fact result from different factors?

# References

Boser, Katharina, Barbara Lust, Lynn M. Santelmann, & John Whitman. 1992. The syntax of CP and V-2 in early German child grammar: The Strong Continuity Hypothesis. *Proceedings of the North Eastern Linguistics Association*, 22, 51-66.

Brun, Dina, Sergey Avrutin, & Maria Babyonyshev. 1999. Aspect and its temporal interpretation during the optional infinitive stage in Russian. *BUCLD*, 23, 120-131.

Cheung, Hintat. 1998. Ping jun yu ju chang du zai zhong wen de yun yong [The application of MLU in Chinese]. *The Journal of Speech-Language-Hearing Association*, 13, 36-48.

Giorgi, Alessandra, & Fabio Pianesi. 1997. *Tense and Aspect: From Semantics to Morphosyntax*. Oxford: Oxford University Press.

Giorgi, Alessandra, & Fabio Pianesi. 2001. Ways of terminating. In G. Chierchia, and M. T. Guasti (eds.) *Semantic Interfaces*. CSLI. 211-277.

Guasti, Maria T. 2002. *Language Acquisition: The Growth of Grammar*. Cambridge, MA: The MIT Press.

Haegeman, Lilian. 1994. Root infinitives, tense and truncated structures. *Language Acquisition*, 4(3), 205-255.

Hoekstra, Teun, & Nina Hyams. 1998. Aspects of root infinitives. *Lingua*, 106. 81-112.

Hu, Jianhua, Haihua Pan, & Liejiong Xu. 2001. Is there a finite vs. nonfinite distinction in Chinese? *Linguistics*, 39(6), 1117-1148.

Huang, C.-T. James. 1982. *Logical Relations in Chinese and the Theory of Grammar*. Ph.D. Dissertation, MIT.

Huang, C.-T. James. 1984. On the distribution and reference of empty pronouns. *Linguistic Inquiry*, 15, 531-574.

Huang, C.-T. James. 1987. Remarks on empty categories. *Linguistic Inquiry*, 18, 321-337.

Huang, C.-T. James. 1989. Pro-drop in Chinese: A generalized control theory. In O. Jaeggli and K. Safir (eds.) *The Null Subject Parameter*, 185-214. Dordrecht: Kluwer.

Hyams, Nina. 1996. The underspecification of functional categories in early grammar. In H. Clahsen (ed.) *Generative Perspectives on Language Acquisition*, 91-128. Amsterdam: Benjamins.

Hyams, Nina. 2006. Aspect matters. In K. U. Deen, J. Nomura, B. Schulz, & B. Schwartz (eds.) *Proceedings of the Inaugural Conference on Generative Approaches to Language Acquisition – North America (GALANA)*. University of Connecticut Occasional Papers in Linguistics 4, 1-18.

Kim, Meesook, & Colin Phillips. 1998. Complex verb constructions in child Korean overt markers of covert functional structure. *BUCLD*, 22, 430-441.

Krämer, Irene. 1993. The licensing of subjects in early child language. *MITWPL*, 19, 197-212.

Li, Y.-H. Audrey. 1985. *Abstract Case in Chinese*. Ph.D. Dissertation, University of Southern California.

Li, Y.-H. Audrey. 1990. *Order and Constituency in Mandarin Chinese*. Dordrecht: Kluwer.

Liceras, Juana, Aurora Bel, & Susana Perales. 2006. 'Living with optionality': Root infinitives, bare forms and inflected forms in child null subject languages. In N. Sagarra & A. Toribio (eds.), *Selected Proceedings of the 9th Hispanic Linguistics Symposium*. Somerville, Mass.: Cascadilla. 203-216.

Lin, Jo-wang. 2002a. On temporal reference in modern Chinese. *Language and Linguistics*, 3 (1), 1-25.

Lin, Jo-wang. 2002b. Selectional restrictions of tenses and temporal reference of Chinese bare sentences. *Lingua*, 113, 271-302.
Murasugi, Keiko, Chisato Fuji, & Tomoko Hashimoto. 2007. What acquired later in an agglutinative language. Paper presented in GLOW in Asia VI, Chinese University of Hong Kong.
Murasugi, Keiko, & Chisato Fuji. 2008. Root infinitives: The parallel routes the Japanese- and Korean-speaking children step in. Paper presented in the 18th Japanese/Korean Linguistics Conference.
Pierce, Amy E. 1992. *Language Acquisition and Syntactic Theory: A Comparative Analysis of French and English Child Grammars*. Dordrecht: Kluwer.
Platzack, Christer. 1992. Functional categories and early Swedish. In J. Meisel (ed.) *The Acquisition of Verb Placement: Functional Categories and V2 Phenomena in Language Acquisition*, 63-82. Dordrecht: Kluwer.
Poeppel, David, & Ken Wexler. 1993. The full competence hypothesis of clause structure in early German. *Language*, 69, 1-33.
Pratt, Amy, & John Grinstead. 2007. Optional infinitives in child Spanish. In *the Proceedings of the 2nd Conference on Generative Approaches to Language Acquisition North America (GALANA)*.
Radford, Andrew. 1990. *Syntactic Theory and the Acquisition of English Syntax*. Oxford: Blackwell.
Rizzi, Luigi. 1994. Some notes on linguistic theory and language development: The case of root infinitives. *Language Acquisition*, 3, 371-393.
Salustri, Manola, & Nina Hyams. 2002. Is there an analogue to the RI stage in the null subject languages? In *the Proceedings of the BU Conference on Language Development 27*.
Sano, Tetsuya. 1995. *Roots in Language Acquisition: A Comparative Study of Japanese and European Languages*. Ph.D. Dissertation, UCLA.
Santelmann, Lynn M. 1995. *The Acquisition of Verb Second Grammar in Child Swedish*. Ph.D. Dissertation, Cornell University.
Stephany, Ursula. 1995. The acquisition of Greek. In D. Slobin (ed.) *The Crosslinguistic Study of Language Acquisition*, vol. 4. New Jersey: Lawrence Erlbaum Associates.
Torrence, Harold, & Nina Hyams. 2004. On the role of aspect in determining finiteness and temporal interpretation in early grammar. In J. van Kampen & S. Baauw (eds.), *Proceedings of GALA 2003*. Utrecht, The Netherlands: LOT. 481–491.
Weverink, M. 1989. *The Subject in Relation to Inflection in Child Language*. MA Thesis, University of Utrecht.
Wexler, Ken. 1994. Optional infinitives, verb movement and the economy of derivation in child grammar. In D. Lightfoot and N. Hornstein (eds.) *Verb Movement*. Cambridge: Cambridge University Press. 305-382.
Wijnen, Frank. 1997. Temporal reference and eventivity in root infinitives. *MIT Occasional Papers in Linguistics*, Vol. 12. 1-25.

Email: ycsu@mx.nthu.edu.tw

# Pro-drop in Mandarin–Norwegian Bilinguals

Fufen Jin, Kristin M. Eide & Tor A. Åfarli
*Norwegian University of Science and Technology (NTNU)*

## 1. Introduction

One of the major concerns of bilingual first language acquisition (BFLA) is whether or not bilingual acquisition is the same as monolingual acquisition. In the literature, there are two competing positions regarding the nature of bilingual development: autonomous vs. interdependent. The autonomous development hypothesis assumes that the two grammatical systems develop independently of each other. As a result, both languages in bilingual acquisition develop in the same fashion as for monolingual acquisition (see e.g. De Houwer 1990, Chang-Smith 2005, 2010). The interdependent development hypothesis, on the other hand, assumes that there is systematic influence of the grammar of one language on the grammar of the other language during acquisition. Consequently, the course and developmental patterns of bilingual acquisition can be different from those of monolingual acquisition (see e.g. Döpke 2000; Yip & Matthews 2007). The present paper contributes to this debate. We investigate the pro-drop properties in Norwegian of Mandarin–Norwegian bilinguals born into Chinese-speaking immigrant families in Norway. The production data indicate that there indeed is cross-linguistic influence in this grammatical domain. The paper therefore supports the interdependent development hypothesis.

Cross-linguistic influence manifests itself not only in the form of transfer, but also in forms of acceleration and delay (cf. Paradis & Genesee 1996). Yip and Matthews (2007:37) further add that quantitative differences between bilingual and monolingual development is another form of cross-linguistic influence. Drawing evidence from Mandarin–Norwegian bilinguals' pro-drop in Norwegian, we examine the forms and patterns of cross-linguistic influence and demonstrate that the two developing grammatical systems in bilingual acquisition are interactive rather than autonomous.

The data in this paper were drawn from two recordings of transcripts from an ongoing project on Mandarin–Norwegian bilingual development. We acknowledge that the conclusions are tentative in nature, and that we need further monolingual and bilingual data to consolidate the results.

## 2. Pro-drop in Colloquial Norwegian and in Mandarin

### 2.1 Colloquial Norwegian

The canonical word order of Norwegian is SVO, as illustrated in (1a). Norwegian is also known as a V2 language, that is, finite verbs occur in the second position in root clauses. The standard analysis of V2 involves leftward movement of the finite verb to the C head of CP, and movement of a constituent into the Spec of CP (Vikner 1995). When the constituent moved to the Spec of CP is a non-subject, for example, an object, inversion of the subject and the finite verb is required in order to satisfy the V2 rule (cf. 2b).

(1) a. Jeg så *Titanic* i går.
      I saw *Titanic* yesterday
   b. *Titanic* så jeg i går.
      *Titanic* saw I yesterday
      'I saw Titanic yesterday.'

What is less known is that Colloquial Norwegian allows pro-drop, though with some restrictions. Nygård, Eide & Åfarli (2008) showed that subjects can be dropped in Colloquial Norwegian. The following are some of the examples they gave ([e] represents the empty argument).

(2) a. [e] gjør aldri lekser sjøl.
       do never homework self
       ' (I) never do homework myself.'
    b. [e] fikk ikke lov å herje som vi ville
       got not permission to act out as we wanted to
       'We were not permitted to act out as we wanted to.
    c. [e] var alltid sånn på barneskolen
       was always such in primary-school-the
       'It was always like that in the primary school.'

In the first two examples, the dropped subjects are personal pronouns. In (2c) it is the expletive subject *det* 'it' that is dropped.

Nygård, Eide & Åfarli (2008) also mentions that topic-linked object drop is possible in Colloquial Norwegian. Here is the example they gave:

(3) A: – Har du sett filmen?
       have you seen film-the
       'Have you seen the film?'
    B: – [e] så jeg i går.
       saw I yesterday
       'I saw (it) yesterday.'

In (3), B's utterance actually involves a topicalized null object, whose reference (the film) can be identified in the preceding discourse. The alledged existence of a null object in the sentence-initial position is manifested by inversion of subject and the verb, which is typical of a V2 construction. It should be noted, however, that null subjects and null objects have a very restricted distribution in colloquial Norwegian. The dropped subjects/objects typically occur in sentence initial position in V2 configuration on the root clause (Rizzi 2000).[1] Thus, pro-drop is prohibited in embedded clauses, as shown in (4):

(4) Han sa at han så *(filmen/den) i går.
    he said that he saw film-the/it yesterday
    'He said that he saw the film/it yesterday.'

Another point to be noted is that although subject drop is quite frequent in colloquial Norwegian, object drop is not frequent. Referential objects are normally realized, either in the canonical object position, as in (5a), or in the topic position, as in (5b):

(5) a. Jon liker den gule kjolen, men jeg liker den ikke.
       Jon likes the yellow dress, but I like it not
       'Jon likes the yellow dress, but I do not like it.'
    b. – Liker du den gule kjolen?
       like you the yellow dress
       'Do you like the yellow dress?'
       – Nei, den liker jeg ikke.

[1] Recently, Engdahl (to appear) observes that in Norwegian and Swedish declarative sentences, the expletive *det* can be dropped when it co-occurs with a topicalized referential *det*, even when the expletive *det* is not in sentence initial position. Here is one of the examples she gives:
Det$_i$ var [e] bra at du sa $t_i$.
it was good that you said.
'It was good that you said (it).'
We note, however, that the analysis of this construction remains to be investigated; hence we will not include it in our proposal at this point.

no, it like I not
'No, I don't like it.'

## 2.2 Mandarin Chinese

Compared with Colloquial Norwegian, Chinese allows pro-drop rather freely, both in written and spoken forms, and both in main and embedded clauses, as shown in (6):

(6) a. Wo zuotian kan [e] le.
       I yesterday see Asp
       'I saw (it) yesterday.'
    b. Ta shuo ta zuotian kan [e] le.
       he say he yesterday see Asp
       'He said that he saw (it) yesterday.'

In both sentences, the objects of *kan* 'see' can be dropped, as long as the previous discourse provides a topic to which the null objects can refer. In (6a) the null object appears in a root clause; in (6b) the null object occurs in an embedded clause. It should be noted that Chinese allows referential pronouns in object positions. However, overt pronouns in object position are possible only when they refer to animate entities; they are obligatorily dropped when referring to inanimate entities. In cases like (6), if the pronouns refer to inanimate entities (the film), it is ungrammatical to have an overt pronoun in the object position.

What is the nature of pro-drop in Chinese? Huang (1984) observes that the dropped arguments in Chinese are actually discourse identified null topics. It is well known that Chinese is a topic-prominent language. A sentence, such as (7), typically consists of a topic, loosely defined as 'what a sentence is about' (Li & Thompson 1981), and a comment, comprising the rest of the sentence, saying something about the topic.

(7) Zhe bu dianying, wo zuotian kan le.
    this CL film I yesterday see Asp
    'I saw the film yesterday.'

Particularly, Chinese permits discourse identified null topics. In a piece of discourse, a single topic licenses multiple null topics coreferential with it, forming a so-called topic chain construction (Shi 2000). This is illustrated in (8):

(8) Zhe bu dianying, wo zuotian kan le. [e] hen jingcai.
    this CL film I yesterday see Asp very good
    'I saw the film yesterday. (It) was very good.'

In (8), the topic of the second clause is co-referential with the topic of the preceding clause. It is then dropped. *Zhe bu dianying* 'this film' and the null topic thus form a topic chain. The result of this topic chain formation is that the second clause in (8) is seemingly subjectless. Null arguments in an embedded clause can also pick up their reference from the discourse, making pro-drop in embedded clauses a possibility (cf. 6b).

Pro-drop is rather frequent in daily discourse of Mandarin speakers. Wang et al. (1992) found that in adults' speech, subjects were dropped at the rate of 45.6% and objects at the rate of 40.1%, and that in (4-year-old) children's speech, subjects were dropped at the rate of 38.2% and objects at the rate of 26.0%. In both populations, the frequency of null subjects outnumbered that of null objects.

As we have shown, although both Mandarin and Colloquial Norwegian allow pro-drop, the distributional regularities in the two languages are fundamentally different. The similarities and differences between the two languages with respect to pro-drop make this a perfect grammatical domain to investigate cross-linguistic influence in order to gain insight into the differences between bilingual acquisition and monolingual acquisition.

## 3. Previous studies

In the pro-drop literature, the focus has been on early language development, typically in the period before 3 years of age, when pro drop in child language co-occurs with children's use of root infinitive structures. Many researchers thus link pro-drop in child language to the development of verbal inflections (see e.g. Sano & Hyams 1994; Blom 2008). In this paper, we look at later developmental stages, when the bilingual children under study have passed the root infinitive stages. Thus, pro drop in these bilingual children's Norwegian is less likely to be related to the development of inflections, but is more probably a reflection of their dual input in Norwegian and Mandarin Chinese. Therefore we will not consider the literature on pro-drop in early child language, but instead we will give a brief overview of the relevant literature on adult L2/L3 acquisition and bilingual acquisition.

Yip and Matthews (2005, 2007) are among the few bilingual studies involving a Chinese language. The subjects under study are Cantonese–English bilinguals whose upbringings are taking place under the one–parent–one–language principle.[2] Yip and Matthews examined the bilinguals' production of null objects in English and found that compared with monolingual English children, their English showed more frequent occurrences of non-target null objects. The frequency of null objects in the bilinguals' English ranges from 19% to 34%, as compared with monolingual English children, who drop objects at the rate of 2.8% to 9%. In addition, null objects are rather persistent in the bilinguals' English: Instances of non-target null objects are observed as late as age 6;11.

Yip and Matthews attributed the bilingual–monolingual differences to cross-linguistic influence from Cantonese, in which object drop is much more frequent than in English. The cross-linguistic influence is accounted for by two factors. One is language dominance.[3] Yip and Matthews observed that among the Cantonese–English bilinguals, Cantonese-dominant children are more prone to non-target object drop than English-dominant children. The other factor is referred to as input ambiguity, i.e. a surface string in the input for language A is compatible with both language A and language B. In case of null objects, optionally transitive verbs like *eat* are compatible with both the English analysis, as represented in (9a), and the Chinese analysis, as represented in (9b).

(9)  a.  eat β         b.  [TOPIC]$_i$ eat [e]$_i$
         [+generic]        [+definite]

In the target English analysis, the missing object is syntactically not present, but is semantically interpreted as generic. In the Chinese analysis, by contrast, the missing object is syntactically present, and it is coreferential with a null topic, and it is semantically definite. The bilingual children may be misled by the surface similarities and assume that English transitive verbs behave as in Cantonese, leading them to protracted production of non target null objects in English.

Cross-linguistic influence has also been attested in adult L2/L3 acquisition regarding the pro-drop properties. In a cross-sectional study of 7 groups of Chinese-speaking adult learners of English, Yuan (1997) found that the beginner group transferred the null subject and null object properties from Chinese to English, but in the more advanced groups, there is an interesting subject–object asymmetry: Null objects are more difficult to unlearn compared with null subjects.

---

2   It usually the case that each of the parents speaks his/her native language to his/her child(ren).
3   Language dominance in the study of Yip and Matthews (2005, 2007) is determined by mean length of utterances (MLU). Since MLU is not a reliable predictor for later stages of language development, which the present study is focused on, we instead use length of exposure to determine language dominance. The bilinguals under study have longer exposure to Norwegian as compared to Mandarin, so they are assumed to be Norwegian-dominant.

Similar findings are reported in third language acquisition. Jin (2008, 2009) investigate the acquisition of subjects and objects in Norwegian by adult learners of L1 Chinese–L2 English–L3 Norwegian. The Chinese speakers had acquired advanced proficiency in L2 English, and were learners of Norwegian as a third language at three proficiency levels (beginner, intermediate, advanced). Direct transfer from the L1 was observed even though the L2 is typologically closer to the L3. Like Yuan (1997), the studies also pointed to a prolonged duration of a stage of an indeterminate status of null objects in L2 and L3 interlanguages.

The above studies in L2/L3 acquisition and bilingual acquisition all indicate that pro drop in Chinese is an area where cross-linguistic influence tends to occur, and that the unlearning of null objects is particularly challenging. It is of interest to examine whether there is any cross-linguistic influence in the domain of pro-drop from Mandarin to Norwegian in the Mandarin–Norwegian bilinguals. If cross-linguistic influence is found, we will further explore whether the forms and patterns of the cross-linguistic influence is the same as in the previous studies.

# 4. Methodology

## 4.1 Data collection

The current study is part of an ongoing project on bilingual acquisition involving Mandarin and Norwegian. The project is a longitudinal case study of a Mandarin–Norwegian bilingual named Lele. Spontaneous speech data were audio recorded at Lele's home from when Lele was 5;11 years old until the present time, when he is 7; 2 years old. The data were collected both in a Mandarin language context and in a Norwegian language context. The main aim of the project is to record and investigate the later stages of bilingual development and compare it with monolingual development. So far, the corpus contains 7 Norwegian recordings which altogether last about 265 minutes. The present paper is based on two files of transcripts. Information of the two files is given in table 1.

*Table 1. Information on the files*

|  | Child | Interlocutor | Situation | Length |
|---|---|---|---|---|
| File 1 | Lele (5; 11) | HL (6; 2) | Lego construct | 0:34:13 |
| File 2 | Lele (6; 10) | NN (3; 9) | Lotto game | 0:57:38 |

## 4.2 Subjects

The principal protagonist in this study, Lele, is the son of the first author. He was born and brought up in Trondheim, Norway. Both his father and his mother are native speakers of Mandarin. Both parents speak English and Norwegian as well, but the language between the parents is mainly Mandarin. Lele is a so called second generation immigrant. Like many other second generation immigrants, his input conditions are situation-bound: Mandarin at home, Norwegian in the community. His Mandarin input is mainly from his parents, who are his main caregivers in Norway. The parents play no role in his Norwegian development, though. The parents rarely address Lele in Norwegian, and Lele speaks exclusively Mandarin to his parents, though occasionally his Mandarin is mixed with some Norwegian words.

Lele's Norwegian input is mainly from the daycare center which he started to attend on a full-day basis when he was 15 months old. Before that age, his Mandarin input was dominant. After he started to attend the daycare center, his Norwegian input caught up and became the dominant one. As people in Norway usually speak their own dialects, Lele has the opportunity to be exposed to many different Norwegian dialects. However, only two dialects represent his regular Norwegian input. One is the local Trønder dialect. That is the dialect spoken by the three caregivers working in Lele's group. The other is the Oslo-based, eastern Norwegian dialect. This dialect is closest to the written standard called *Bokmål* 'book language', and it is the one in which the stories are read in Lele's daycare center. It is also the language spoken by cartoon figures in TV cartoon programs, which Lele watched for about an hour daily.

Lele's interlocutor in file one, named HL, is a girl who is three months older than Lele. She lives in Lele's neighborhood and often comes to visit Lele. HL's parents are both native speakers of the local Trønder dialect. HL thus represents typical monolingual children, with little contact with other languages before school age.

Lele's interlocutor in file two, NN, was aged 3; 9. Like Lele, she is also a second generation immigrant born into a Mandarin-speaking family. She attended the same daycare center as Lele, though she started much later, at the age of 2; 8. Before she started the daycare, she only spoke Mandarin, though she had some Norwegian input from TV and from the people around her. At the time of recording, when she had attended the daycare for 13 months, she was using both languages. Her mother reports that Norwegian is her dominant language, and that she usually switches to Norwegian at home when she talks with her elder brother, who is also a Mandarin–Norwegian bilingual.

## 4.3 Transcripts

The Norwegian files were initially transcribed by a research assistant, who is a native speaker of Norwegian and specializes in linguistics. The transcripts were then double checked independently by the three authors of the paper. The first author subsequently integrated all the modifications into the final version of the transcripts. The authors acknowledge that it is a big challenge to transcribe children's speech. It is particularly challenging to decide whether a (light) subject/object is produced or not. In case there were questions or disagreement about a transcribed utterance, the three authors would repeat listening to the utterance several times and discuss the decisions until reaching an agreement. When there was doubt, the data were left out and not considered for data analysis.

## 5. Results

We first singled out the complete utterances produced by each subject in each file. The complete utterances were then divided into 5 groups according to sentence type. The distribution of sentence types in the two files is shown in table 2.

*Table 2. Distribution of sentence types*

|  | Child | Declarative sentence | Imperative sentence | Wh-questions | Yes/no questions | Embedded sentence |
|---|---|---|---|---|---|---|
| File 1 | Lele | 170 | 19 | 8 | 9 | 21 |
|  | HL | 58 | 6 | 21 | 25 | 7 |
| File 2 | Lele | 244 | 21 | 19 | 36 | 25 |
|  | NN | 125 | 10 | 14 | 44 | 1 |

Jin & Eide (2010) examined Lele's Norwegian production data and found that many aspects of his Norwegian syntax, including finiteness, V2, imperatives, wh-questions, yes/no questions, embedded clauses, fully converge on the target. The findings suggest that in the above mentioned grammatical domains there are few qualitative differences between Lele and age-matched Norwegian monolingual children. The present paper focuses on pro-drop and investigates whether there are quantitative or qualitative differences between Lele and HL (an age-matched monolingual Norwegian child) on the one hand, and Lele and NN (a Mandarin–Norwegian bilingual like Lele, but much younger in age) on the other hand.

We started with File 1 for data analysis, and then went on with File 2. We searched for null objects in Lele's production data, but did not observe a single instance of object drop. Objects were either in-situ, as in (10a), or they were topicalized, as in (10b).

(10) a.  Jeg har mista det.
         I have lost it
         'I have lost it.'
     b.  Den så jeg her et sted.
         it saw I here a place
         'I saw it somewhere here.'

We did observe 9 cases of subject drop, though. All of them occur in root, declarative clauses. Seven of them are targetlike, and in all of the seven sentences, the dropped subjects are self-referring personal pronouns such as *vi* 'we' and *jeg* 'I', and they all appear in the first position of root clauses. Three of the examples are given in (11).

(11) a.  [e] kan sette her på først hvis vi vil.
         can put here on first if we want to
         '(We) can put it here first if we want to.'
     b.  [e] vet hvor jeg kan finne den.
         know where I can find it
         '(I) know where I can find it.'
     c.  [e] trenger tre.
         need three
         '(We) need three.'

The other two instances of subject drop, shown in (12), are target divergent. [4] Native speakers will naturally use overt pronouns to fill in the empty positions.

---

[4] We noticed that the verbs (*låse* and *gått*) in (12b) were wrongly inflected for past tense. However, we did not correct them, as this is not an issue for the present study. This also applies to other examples cited in this paper.

(12) a. Den må være opp. Der skal [e] kjøre opp.
   it must be up there shall drive up
   'It must be up. (It) shall drive up there.'
   b. Men [e] tok nøkkelen, og [e] låse opp døra, og [e] gått inn det her.
   but took key-the, and lock up door-the and gone in this here
   'But (he) took the key, unlocked the door and went in here.'

In (12a) the topic is a toy car. In the first clause, an overt pronoun is used to refer to it, while in the second clause the subject is dropped. As the adverbial *der* 'there' is topicalized, the dropped subject is supposed to occur immediately after the finite verb. In this case, subject drop is ungrammatical in Norwegian, given the ban on subject drop in sentence middle position. In (12b) the topic in the previous discourse is a lego figure performing a series of actions, one action after another. Lele used *og* 'and' to connect the actions, and dropped subjects in each clause. The more idiomatic sentence would probably employ *og så* 'and then' and overt subjects, as shown in (13):

(13) Men han tok nøkkelen, og så låste han opp døra,
   but he took key-the, and then locked he up door-the
   og så gikk han inn det her.
   and then went he in this here

The two target divergent sentences in (12) have one thing in common: They seem to be cases of the Mandarin-like topic chain construction, in which a topic in the previous discourse licenses multiple null topics coreferential with it. The two examples thus constitute suggestive evidence pointing to transfer from Mandarin to Norwegian in the bilingual acquisition.

We will now compare Lele's pro-drop with his Norwegian interlocutor HL. We found that object drop is non-existent in HL's speech on this file, and that there is only one instance of subject drop, shown in (14).

(14) Kan ikke dele opp et hus nei.
   can not split up a house no
   '(We) cannot split up a house, no.'

The frequency of null subjects in Lele's Norwegian is quite low, but still it is high as compared to HL (5.3% vs. 1.7%). Thus this file suggests that there is a quantitative difference in terms of subject drop in Mandarin bilingual children and their Norwegian monolingual counterparts.

Turning to file 2, in which the conversation is between two Mandarin–Norwegian bilinguals, we found that both Lele and NN frequently dropped subjects, but they rarely dropped objects. Lele has three instances of object drop in declarative sentences, listed in (15).

(15) a. Ja, jeg vet [e]
yes, I know
'Yes, I know.'
b. Da har jeg [e]
then have I
'Then I have (it).'
c. Kunne ønska [e] en sånn, jeg òg.
could wish one such, I too
'I could wish myself a such thing, me too.'

In (15a), the Norwegian verb *vet* 'know' needs to collocate with an object *det* 'it', which is omitted in Lele's utterance.[5] Similarly in (15b) the object of the verb *har* 'have' is missing. In (15c) the verb *ønske* 'wish' should take two objects, i.e., a direct object and an indirect object, a reflexive *seg*. What is missing here is this reflexive indirect object.

NN also has three instances of object drop. They all occur in yes/no questions:

(16) a. Hæ? Fikk du [e]?
what got you
'What? Did you get (it)?'
b. Fikk du [e] av Jack?
got you from Jack
'Did you get (it) from Jack?'
c. Liker du[e] ?
like you
'Do you like (it)?'

---

[5] We observe that even Norwegian monolinguals may drop the object in (15a), possibly due to the influence from English. The object drop in this case then can also be due to such Norwegian input. In addition, the negated version *vet ikke* is fine without any pronoun.

The verbs in the above questions, *få* 'get' and *like* 'like', are both simple transitive verbs. So NN's utterances without an object sound a bit odd.[6] From the discourse context, we see that the missing objects are actually part of the discourse topic. To illustrate, the discourse context where utterance (16b) occurs is shown in (17).

(17)  (NN pointing to a toy)
    NN:    Har du laga den i skolen?
              have you made it in school
              'Did you make it in school?'
    Lele:    Nei, jeg har fått den.
              no, I have got it
              'No, someone gave it to me.'
    NN:    Fikk du av Jack?
              got you from Jack
              'Did you get (it) from Jack?'
    Lele:    Nei, jeg fikk den av en i familien min.
              no, I got it from one in family-the my
              'No, I got it from someone in my family.'

Recall that topic-linked object drop in sentence middle position is banned in Norwegian. So these target divergent utterances NN produced, though limited in number, suggest transfer from Mandarin. It should be noted, however, that except the utterances in (16), NN uses overt pronouns when necessary. Some examples are given in (18).

(18)  a.    Jeg har det i barnehagen, ja.
          I have it in daycare-the, yes
          'I have it in the daycare center, yes.'
    b.    Jeg fant den.
          I found it
          'I found it.'
    c.    Vil du se den?
          will you see it
          'Do you want to see it?'

---

6    However, the negative counterpart of (16a) is better. It may occur in contexts such as the following:
    A:  Jeg fikk ikke Snø-hvit bok.
         I got not Snow White book
         'I didn't get a Snow White book.'
    B:  Fikk du ikke?
         got you not
         'Didn't you?'

This indicates that NN has the knowledge that an overt pronoun is obligatory in Norwegian when the object has definite reference in the discourse context, and that she is not mixing Norwegian with Mandarin in this respect.

Unlike cases of object drop, which are few and far between, subject drop is quite frequent in both of the bilinguals' Norwegian. All cases of subject drop in Lele's and NN's Norwegian occur in root declarative sentences. So the present paper disregards the other sentence types in calculating the rate of subject drop. The missing subjects fall into three categories: Topic-linked inanimate referential pronouns, expletives, first/second personal pronouns. Table 3 gives an overview of subject drop in Lele's and NN's Norwegian.

*Table 3. Distribution of subject drop in Lele's and NN's Norwegian*

|  | Topic-linked inanimate referential pronouns | Expletives | Personal pronouns | Total declaratives |
|---|---|---|---|---|
| Lele | 2 | 3 | 17 | 244 |
| NN | 2 | 8 | 8 | 125 |

As shown in Table 3, there are 22 cases of subject drop in Lele's declarative utterances, accounting for 9.0% of the declarative utterances he produced. All the utterances are to a great extent target consistent. The missing subjects in (19a-b) are topic-linked inanimate referential pronouns. In (19c-d) they are expletives,[7] and in (19e-f), personal pronouns.

(19) a. (pointing to a candy)
  [e] Ligne på et sånn godterismykke.
  look like a such candy pearl necklace
  '(It) looks like such a candy pearl necklace.'
 b. Det er maling. [e] Går ikke bort.
  it is paint. goes not away.
  'It is paint. (It) doesn't go away.'
 c. [e] Mangler to faktisk.
  lacks two actually
  '(There) are two missing, actually.'

---

7 An external reviewer points out that the dropped element in (19c) and (19d) could well be a locative topic. We think, however, that only (19c), but not (19d), could be analyzed as having a dropped locative topic.

d.  [e] Var bare én sånn her.
    was only one such here
    '(There) was only one like this here.'
e.  [e] Skal rydde det her
    shall clean up it here
    '(We) shall clean it up here.'
f.  [e] Har brukt opp alle sjansene dine.
    have used up all chances yours
    '(You) have used up all your chances.'

As compared with Lele, NN has a slightly higher rate of subject drop. She has 18 instances of subject drop out of 125 declaratives that she produced, i.e. the rate of subject drop is up to 14.4% in her Norwegian. NN's missing subjects fall into the same categories as Lele's, but with a different proportion, which is 2:8:8. In other words, NN has a much higher rate of expletive drop than Lele has (44.4% vs. 1.4%). In Norwegian, the expletive subjects *it* and *there* usually take the form of *det*. NN drops *det* in both types, as we can see in the examples in (20).

(20) a.  Her ligger [e] dame.
        here lies lady
        '(There) lies a lady here.'
    b.  [e] Mangler bare én.
        lack only one
        '(There) is only one missing.'
    c.  [e] går an å tygge, ja.
        possible to chew, yes
        '(It, referring to the candy) is chewable, yes.'
    d.  Her var [e] rotete, her.
        here was messy here
        '(It) was messy here.'

It should be noted that in (20a) and (20d) the dropped expletives are supposed to occur in a sentence-medial position; omission makes the utterances ungrammatical in native Norwegian. We believe that the target divergent utterances produced by NN are development errors, because we did not observe any instances of sentence-medial expletive drop in Lele's Norwegian, though he has similar input conditions as NN. A plausible explanation is that younger Mandarin–Norwegian bilinguals, such as NN, have not yet internalized the knowledge that Norwegian does not allow expletive drop in sentence middle position. We expect that NN will stop making such 'errors' as she grows older in the bilingual contexts, just as Lele did.[8]

## 6. Summary and conclusion

In this paper, we have investigated the pro-drop phenomenon in Mandarin–Norwegian bilinguals' Norwegian speech. We have found evidence pointing to cross-linguistic influence in this grammatical domain. The cross-linguistic influence in terms of pro-drop has two instantiations: transfer and quantitative differences. The use of the topic chain construction in Lele's Norwegian and the instances of topic linked object drop in sentence middle position produced by NN constitute evidence for transfer from Mandarin to Norwegian in the bilingual children. As far as quantitative differences are concerned, we found that both bilinguals dropped subjects at a much higher rate when compared with monolingual Norwegian children. More interestingly, we observed that the frequency of subject drop in Lele's Norwegian showed great variation depending on who he was talking with. When his interlocutor was a monolingual Norwegian, Lele dropped subjects at a rate of 5.3%. When he talked with a Mandarin–Norwegian bilingual like himself, however, the frequency of subject drop in Lele's Norwegian increased to 9.0%. The younger bilingual, NN, even had a higher rate of subject drop, i.e. 14.4%. This result is consistent Grosjean's (1998) hypothesis about transfer and language mode, which claims that the bilingual child is more susceptible to cross-linguistic influence when both languages are activated. Although in file 2, the two bilinguals conversed almost exclusively in Norwegian, they were addressed in Mandarin by their parents just before they started talking with each other. So, there is reason to believe that their Mandarin was kept active as they talked. Such findings reveal the interactive nature of bilingual development. The autonomous development hypothesis is thus not supported.

Another striking finding in this paper is the extremely low rate of object drop in the bilingual children's Norwegian. Recall that both adult Chinese-speaking L2 learners of English/Norwegian and bilingual Cantonese–English bilingual children have great difficulty unlearning the Chinese-type topic-linked object drop, and that Cantonese–English bilinguals are still producing null objects in their English as late as age 6;11(cf. Section 3). It is thus surprising that

---

[8] An external reviewer suggests that a look at the occurrence of expletives in monolinguals of comparable age to NN's is needed in order to claim that NN's drop of expletives is a development error. As monolingual development can differ from bilingual development, we still hold that a longitudinal study of NN's later developmental stages will be more illustrative for this matter.

Mandarin–Norwegian bilinguals have overcome this challenge, at a younger age (especially in case of NN).

What makes Mandarin–Norwegian bilinguals behave so differently from Cantonese–English bilinguals in term of object drop? We suggest two explanations. The first explanation is concerned with a cross-linguistic difference between English and Norwegian. Although the two languages are similar as far as object drop is concerned, they differ as to the realizations of inherent (non-thematic) reflexivity marking. While non-thematic reflexivity marking is obligatory in Norwegian, it is optional in English. In fact McWhorter (2007) points out that inherent reflexivity marking is one of the aspects that make English contrast with all other Germanic languages, i.e. that all Germanic languages, except English, have obligatory realization of inherent reflexives. A big class of Norwegian verbs, such as *gjemme* 'hide', *vaske* 'wash', *forte* 'hurry', takes no-thematic reflexives that the English counterparts don't. The existence of such verbs makes the occurrences of optionally transitive verbs less frequent than those in English. This will trigger bilinguals to realize at an early age that an object is obligatory in Norwegian.

Another likely explanation is language dominance. The two groups of bilinguals indeed differ in terms of language dominance: While the bilinguals in this paper are Norwegian- dominant, the Cantonese–English bilinguals are Cantonese-dominant. As Yip & Matthews (2007) observed, the English-dominant Cantonese–English bilinguals seem to have a much lower rate of object drop as compared to their Cantonese-dominant counterparts. However, lacking the relevant data from Mandarin-dominant bilinguals in the present study, our explanation can only be speculative in nature. In any case, the contrastive behaviors between the two groups of bilinguals in terms of object drop is intriguing, and it calls for further research on exactly why Mandarin–Norwegian bilinguals unlearn object drop at an earlier age than Cantonese–English bilinguals do.

# References

Blom, Elma. 2008. *The Acquisition of Finiteness*. Berlin: Mounton de Gruyter.
Chang-Smith, Meiyun. 2005. *First language acquisition of functional categories in Mandarin nominal expressions: A longitudinal study of two Mandarin-speaking children*. Canberra: The Australian National University dissertation.
Chang-Smith, Meiyun. 2010. Developmental pathways for first language acquisition of Mandarin nominal expressions: Comparing monolingual with simultaneous Mandarin-English bilingual children. *The International Journal of Bilingualism* 14. 11-35.
De Houwer, Annick. 1990. *The Acquisition of Two Languages from Birth: A Case Study*. Cambridge: Cambridge University Press.

Döpke, Susan (ed.). 2000. *Cross-linguistic Structures in Simultaneous Bilingualism.* Amsterdam: John Benjamins.

Engdahl, Elisabet. (To appear). Vad händer med subjektsvånget? Om *det*-inledda satser utan subjekt [What happens to the subject requirement? On subjectless clauses introduced by *det*]. *Språk och Stil* 20.

Grosjean, François. 1998. Transfer and language mode. *Bilingualism: Language and Cognition* 1: 175-176.

Huang, C.T. James. 1984. On the distribution and reference of empty pronouns. *Linguistic Inquiry* 15. 531-574.

Jin, Fufen. 2008. Third language acquisition of Norwegian subjects and objects by Chinese-speaking learners. In Tor A. Åfarli & Fufen Jin (eds.) *Comparative Grammar and Language Acquisition in the Age of Globalization: Norwegian and Chinese*, 165-178. Trondheim: Tapir.

Jin, Fufen. 2009. Third language acquisition of Norwegian objects: Interlanguage transfer or L1 influence? In Yan-kit Ingrid Leung (ed.) *Third Language Acquisition and Universal Grammar,* 144-161. Bristol: Multilingual Matters.

Jin, Fufen & Kristin M. Eide. 2010. Contradictory parameter settings in one mind: A case study of a Mandarin-Norwegian bilingual's acquisition finiteness and V2 in Norwegian. Paper presented at Finiteness Fest Workshop, Norwegian University of Science and Technology, Trondheim.

Li, Charles & Sandra Thompson. 1981. *Mandarin Chinese: A Functional Reference Grammar.* Berkeley: University of California Press.

McWhorter, John. 2007. *Language Interrupted: Signs of Non-Native Acquisition in Standard Language Grammars.* Oxford: Oxford University Press.

Nygård, Mari & Kristin M. Eide & Tor A. Åfarli. 2008. Ellipsens syntaktiske struktur. In Janne Bondi Johannssen & Kristin Hagen (eds.) *Språk i Oslo: Ny forskning omkring talespråk*, 172-183. Oslo: Novus forlag.

Paradis, Johanne & Fred Genesee. 1996. Syntactic acquisition in bilingual children: autonomous or interdependent? *Studies in Second Language Acquisition* 18. 1-25.

Rizzi, Liugi. 2000. *Comparative Syntax and Language Acquisition.* London: Routledge.

Sano, Tetsuya & Nina Hyams. 1994. Agreement, finiteness, and the development of null arguments. In M Gonzalez (ed.) *Proceedings of the NELS* 24, vol. 2, 543-558.

Shi, Dingxu. 2000. Topic and topic-comment constructions in Mandarin Chinese. *Language* 76. 383-408.

Vikner, Sten. 1995. *Verb Movement and the Licensing of NP-positions in the Germanic Languages.* Oxford: Oxford University Press.

Wang, Qi, Dianne Lillo-Martin, Catherine Best & Andrea Levitt. 1992. Null subject versus null object: Some evidence from the acquisition of Chinese and English. *Language Acquisition* 2. 221-254.

Yip, Virgina & Stephen Matthews. 2005. Dual input and learnability: Null objects in Cantonese–English bilingual children. *Proceedings of the 4th International Symposium on Bilingualism*. 2421-2431.

Yip, Virgina & Stephen Matthews. 2007. *The Bilingual Child: Early Development and Language Contact.* Cambridge: Cambridge University Press.

Yuan, Boping. 1997. Asymmetry of null subjects and null objects in Chinese speakers' L2 English. *Studies in Second Language Acquisition* 19. 467-497.

Emails: fufen.jin@ntnu.no, kristin.eide@ntnu.no, tor.aafarli@ntnu.no

# The L2 Acquisition of the Mandarin Chinese Perfective Marker – *LE* by L1 English Speakers

Mónica Cabrera & Nicholas Usaj
*Loyola Marymount University & National Taiwan Normal University*

## 1. Introduction[1]

L1 English speakers learning Mandarin Chinese as a second language have many difficulties with mastering the perfective aspectual marker *-LE*. It has been suggested that this difficulty is due to the way in which some teachers, curricula, and textbooks present the aspectual particle *-LE*. As reported by Ma (2006), instructional materials incorrectly present *-LE* as the equivalent of the English past tense, or they fail to make an explicit comparison between these grammatical elements in order to clearly establish the similarities and differences between them. An additional factor that has not been explored in previous L2 studies is the way in which the context of learning influences the acquisition of the perfective marker *-LE*. The present study investigates the L2 acquisition of *-LE* by English native speakers at the college level in two different settings: a study abroad program in Beijing, China, and a classroom-based language program in a university in Los Angeles, California. The interaction of L1 transfer and context of L2 learning is also investigated.

## 2. Differences between the Mandarin Chinese perfective marker *-LE* and the English past tense

Differently from English, Mandarin Chinese has no actual tense markers. However, this is not to say that there are no ways to express time in this language. Mandarin Chinese uses different aspectual particles, adverbs, and resultative verb complements (Smith 1991; Sybesma 1999). As shown in (1a) below, *-LE* is a perfective

---

[1] We would like to thank Kathy Yang, Suzie Banda, and Loyola Marymount University RAINS Research Assistant Program. All errors are ours.

morpheme, i.e. it expresses a completed action. The English translation of (1a) and the example in (1b) show that, in this case, Mandarin Chinese -*LE* and the English past tense express perfect aspect or a completed action. However, these grammatical elements are different in at least the following two respects.

(1) a. Wo mai-le hen-duo dongxi.
 I buy-LE many things
 'I bought many things.'
 b. I bought many things.

First, in sentence (1a), it is clear that the action of buying things is completed. However, this is not always the case. Some argue that perfective -*LE* does not necessarily always encode completion, but rather termination (Smith, 1991). If -*LE* only referred to completion, (2a) would not be acceptable. Although (2b) sounds odd in English, it is an acceptable sentence in Mandarin Chinese.

(2) a. Wo zuotian xie-le yi-ge xin, keshi mei xie-wan.
 I yesterday write -LE one-CL letter but not write-finish
 'I wrote a letter yesterday but I didn't finish it.'
 b. #I wrote a letter yesterday but I didn't finish it.

Second, according to Smith (1991), the aspectual marker -*LE* has the perfective interpretation when it appears with non-stative verbs, such as achievements, activities (cf. 3a), accomplishments (cf. 3b), and semelfactives. When -*LE* does actually appear with predicates encoding states, its meaning is not perfective but inchoative, i.e. it refers to the beginning of an event. In (3c), if -*LE* were to be understood as the perfective morpheme, the sentence would mean that I was sick, and already got better. However, it means that I just got sick.

(3) a. Activity:
 Tamen zuotianzai gongyan chao-le yi-jia
 they yesterday in park quarrel-LE one fight
 'They quarreled yesterday in the park.'
 b. Accomplishment:
 Wo zuotian xie-le yi-ge xin.
 I yesterday write-LE one-CL letter
 'I wrote a letter yesterday.'

c.  State:
    Wo bing-le.
    I sick-LE
    'I got sick.'

On the other hand, the English past tense can appear with all verb classes, as the glosses in (4) show, irrespective of lexical aspect (or Aktionsart). The interpretation of the past tense in English is the perfective or completed event.

As we will see in the next section, the Mandarin Chinese textbooks that were consulted for this study do not provide an explanation of the aforementioned differences between English and Mandarin Chinese perfective morphemes. A topic that is emphasized, nonetheless, is the existence of two different -*LE*s: verbal and sentence final -*LE*. The first one has been exemplified in sentences (1a), (2a) and (3) above. According to Wen (1995), sentence final -*LE* has five basic uses: change of state (e.g. 4a), a new situation (e.g. 4b), correcting a wrong assumption (4c), advising or warning (4d), or closing a statement (4e).

(4) a.  Wo dong le.
        I understand LE
        'I understand.'
    b.  Xianzai xia yu le.
        now descend rain LE
        'It's raining now.'
    c.  Wo yijing gei ta liang bai kuai qian le.
        I already gave him two hundred CL money LE
        'I gave him $200 already.'
    d.  Bie xiyan le.
        don't smoke LE
        'Don't smoke anymore.'
    e.  Wo ba haizi dai lai le.
        I BA child bring VCOMP LE
        'I have brought the child here.'

Other researchers describe the meaning of sentence final -*LE* in more general terms. For example, according to Sybesma (1999), "sentence-*le* expresses that the preceding sentence denotes a state which is relevant for the present moment, implying that some change has occurred". In the next section, we turn to the learning scenario that the L2 acquisition of perfective -*LE* poses for the native speaker of English in different learning contexts.

## 3. The learning problem: Contexts of L2 learning

According to Ma (2006), some curricula, and textbooks present the perfective marker *-LE* as the equivalent of the English past tense. For the present study, we reviewed two Mandarin Chinese textbooks, which are the ones used in the Chinese Basic Language Program where we tested L2 learners: *Chinese Primer* and *Integrated Chinese*. Both textbooks present verbal *-LE* before sentence final *-LE*, and in different chapters. Although when verbal *-LE* is presented it is highlighted that it is not the equivalent of the English past tense, the differences between the properties of L1 and L2 are not explained. We actually visited two sessions in which perfective *-LE* was introduced in order to see whether this point was further developed by the instructors. We observed that the instructor, like the textbook, emphasized that this marker is different from the English past tense, but again no further explanation was given as to what the differences were.

Taking into consideration that explicit instruction as to the differences between in the L1 and the L2 is not clear, L2 learners in the classroom will need to rely on positive evidence, the L2 input, to grasp the L2 properties of the perfective marker. This situation in itself is not problematic as language learners rely on input in the target language to develop proficiency. Nevertheless, the amount of L2 input that a college student learning Mandarin Chinese in a context of foreign language instruction receives is limited, and, therefore, it is very likely that L2 learners will not have enough L2 input to not establish incorrect correspondences between L1 and l2 elements. In the particular case of our study, the participants received only 150 minutes of L2 instruction, while living in Los Angeles, California, a city where English and Spanish are predominantly spoken.

Our goal is to compare the L2 acquisition of the perfective marker *-LE* in two groups of learners exposed to different quantity and quality of L2 input: classroom, and study abroad context. It is widely accepted that the context in which an L2 learner studies the language is an important factor that conditions the development of her grammatical and lexical proficiency. However, as pointed out by Collentine & Freed (2004), not many studies exploring the comparison between at-home and study abroad contexts are available, and the existing ones present contradictory results. Collentine & Freed (2004) provide a multivariate study of the at-home (or in the classroom) versus study abroad contexts of learning with a group of L2 Spanish speakers at the college level. Their data indicated that the at-home context facilitated the development of grammatical and lexical features, whereas the study abroad group showed an improvement in narrative abilities and fluency.

Freed, Segalowitz, and Dewey (2004) compared three different learning contexts for French L2 acquisition of oral abilities. Their three main contexts were classrooms at home, study abroad, and intensive domestic immersion programs. The domestic immersion group made significant gains in oral performance. When compared to the at-home group, the study abroad learners made statistically significant gains only in terms of speech fluency but fewer gains than the immersion group. These studies still show mixed results as to the effects of context of learning in L2 acquisition. With the present study, we would like to contribute to the body of research on the acquisition of L2 grammatical properties in the classroom and in study abroad settings.

## 4. Previous studies on the L2 acquisition of perfective -*LE*

In this section, we look at the previous research about the L2 acquisition of perfective -*LE*. We should clarify that in none of these studies the classroom versus study abroad scenarios are compared.

Wen (1995) studied the L2 acquisition of the perfective -*LE* versus the sentence-final -*LE* by L1 English speakers in an at-home (classroom) context at the beginning, and advanced levels of proficiency. For three weeks, the subjects were interviewed three times. The interview consisted of three tests: answering questions in a conversation, answering questions about pictures, and describing pictures. The results showed that the subjects acquired the perfective -*LE* before the sentence-final -*LE*. This result is not necessarily surprising as we have seen that perfective -*LE* is taught before sentence final -*LE*.

Yang, Huang and Sun (1999) studied a corpus of written work by L1 English / L2 learners of Mandarin Chinese from Beijing Language University, i.e. in a study abroad context. They studied all of the sentences in which the aspectual particle -*LE* was used, and found out that the subjects generally overused it, i.e. they used perfective -*LE* in unacceptable contexts. They reasoned that the cause for the errors was the equation of -*LE* to the past tense in English, i.e. L1 transfer, since the learners used -*LE* in all contexts in which the English past tense would have been accepted.

More recently, Ma (2006) studied the acquisition of perfective and sentence -*LE* through discourse. In this study, following Yang (2003), it is assumed that these grammatical elements are the same. Three different tests were administered to U.S. college students who were studying Mandarin Chinese. The first test was the University of Iowa Chinese Placement Test-Grammar Section. The second test was a multiple choice knowledge test. The third test was a production test in which pictures were shown to the subjects and the subjects were asked to narrate the story the pictures told. A significant positive correlation between the target-like use of -*LE* in discourse and the increase in the level of instruction was found.

The studies presented in this section show overgeneralized uses of perfective -*LE*, which suggests L1 transfer from English. On the other hand, clear effects of higher exposure to L2 input and a better mastery of the use of -*LE* are evident. Our study seeks to explore the relationship between context of learning and L1 transfer in the L2 acquisition of -*LE*.

## 5. Testing contexts of learning: Hypothesis and predictions

Based on the results of Collentine & Freed (2004), which favored the L2 acquisition of morphosyntax in the context of study abroad, our central hypothesis is that L2 learners of Mandarin Chinese who have been in a study abroad (SA) setting will have a better mastery of the perfective marker -*LE* than L2 learners of Mandarin Chinese who have not been in a study abroad (NSA) program, and have studied Mandarin Chinese in the classroom only. The following predictions ensue:

(5) a. SA L2 learners will make significantly more correct uses of –*LE* than NSA ones.
 b. SA L2 learners will make significantly less incorrect uses of –*LE* than NSA ones.

## 6. Methods

### 6.1. Participants

The present study has a cross-sectional design with 3 experimental groups (n=5 each) of L1 English / L2 Chinese learners: Learners in the United States or non-study abroad (NSA), learners that had been to a Chinese speaking country for a summer (3 months) or less but did not study Chinese there (SA1), and learners that studied Chinese in a study abroad setting for a semester or more (SA2). We had a control (C) group (n=5) of Mandarin Chinese native speakers. Table 1 provides a summary of some of the characteristics of the experimental and control groups.

*Table 1: Information about the participants*

| Subject | Sex | Age | Group Type | Class Level |
|---|---|---|---|---|
| 1 | F | 19 | NSA | CHIN 203 |
| 2 | F | 19 | NSA | CHIN 102 |
| 3 | M | 19 | NSA | CHIN 102 |
| 4 | M | 19 | NSA | CHIN 102 |
| 5 | M | 18 | NSA | CHIN 102 |
| 6 | M | 20 | SA1 | CHIN 102 |
| 7 | M | 18 | SA1 | CHIN 102 |
| 8 | M | 22 | SA1 | CHIN 102 |
| 9 | M | 21 | SA1 | CHIN 102 |
| 10 | F | 21 | SA2 | CHIN 204 |
| 11 | F | 22 | SA1 | CHIN 204 |
| 12 | F | 21 | SA2 | CHIN 102 |
| 13 | M | 21 | SA2 | CHIN 101 |
| 14 | M | 22 | SA2 | CHIN 203 |
| 15 | M | 22 | SA2 | CHIN 204 |
| 16 | M | 60 | C | N/A |
| 17 | F | 55 | C | N/A |
| 18 | F | 27 | C | N/A |
| 19 | F | 79 | C | N/A |
| 20 | F | 55 | C | N/A |

## 6.2 Instruments

A test via a proctor was administered to the subjects individually. The participants were instructed not to use dictionaries, textbooks, or any other aid (i.e. asking questions). They were also told to answer "naturally" and to not think too long about any one sentence. The test consisted of two parts. The first part was a brief language profile. It prompted the subjects for pertinent information such as their highest level of Chinese course taken, their mother tongue, and where they have studied Chinese and for how long. The subjects were also prompted for their language spoken at home as a child, at what age they started studying Chinese, and if they had ever spent time in a Chinese speaking country and for how long. There were multiple other questions relating to the participants' perceived level of linguistic abilities in Chinese and any other foreign language, if applicable.

The second part was the multiple-choice translation test that assessed the subjects' use of the Mandarin Chinese perfective particle -LE. It consisted of twenty-eight English sentences. Under each English sentence there were two Mandarin Chinese translations that the subject had to choose from to determine the correct usage (each sentence was in both pinyin and Chinese characters, but for the purposes of this paper we show only the pinyin version). Fourteen of the sentences tested the use of perfective -LE. All of the sentences in English were in the past tense. Seven sentences included verbs that were achievements or accomplishments (correct use of -LE), and in the other seven stative verbs were included (incorrect use of -LE). (6a) is an example of one of the sentences in which the usage of -LE is required, and, therefore, "a" is the correct answer. However, not all of them require the use of -LE. (6b) is an example of one of the sentences in which the usage of -LE is not acceptable and therefore "a" is the correct answer.

(6) a. He wrote four characters.
 a) Ta xie le si ge zi. c) I don't know
 b) Ta xie si ge zi.
 b. He was very happy.
 a) Ta yi qian hen gao xing. c) I don't know
 b) Ta hen gao xing le.

The other fourteen sentences were fillers, which did not test the usage of the aspectual particle -LE. All of the fillers were in the present tense, and none of them require the use of -LE. (7) is an example of one of the filler sentences. Because the filler sentences do not require -LE, then "a" is the correct answer.

(7) I want to drink a cup of coffee.
 a) Wo yao he yi bei ka fei. c) I don't know
 b) Wo yao he le yi bei ka fei.

In general, subjects were instructed to choose which of the two Mandarin Chinese translations best fit the English sentence. Of each pair on Mandarin Chinese sentences there was one that used -LE and one that did not. There was also an

"I don't know" box that could be checked if the subject did not understand the sentence upon first glance. This option should help to compensate for error.

## 7. Group results

Means were calculated for all three types of sentences; those that involve the correct use of -*LE*, those that involve the correct non-use of -*LE*, and the filler sentences. For the means of correct -*LE*, the closer the mean is to 1 the better the subjects did. In contrast, for the means of correct absence of –*LE* and filler, the closer the means was to 0 the better the subjects did. The means are shown in Figure 1.

Using One-Way ANOVAs, it was determined that for the sentences involving the correct use of -*LE*, the differences between the means of the four subject groups were not statistically significant ($F(3,16)=1.073$, n.s.). Similarly, for the filler sentences, the differences between the means of the four subject groups were

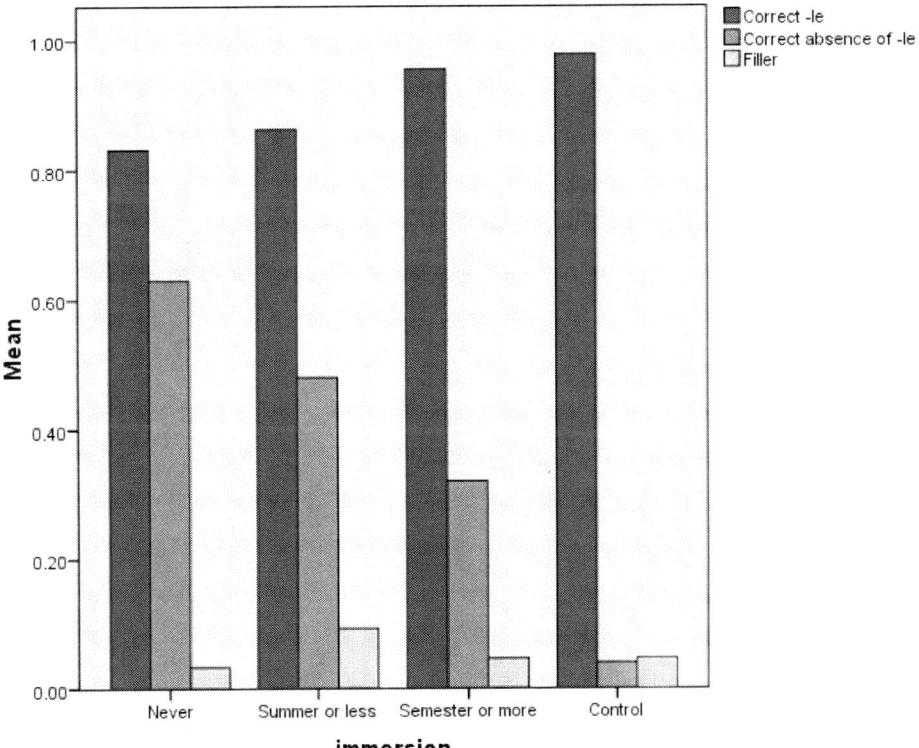

Figure 1: Group means

also not statistically significant (F(3,16)=1.056, n.s.). However, for the sentences involving the correct absence (non-use) of -*LE*, there were statistically significant results (F(3,16)=4.649, p<.05). According to the post-hoc test, the results were significant (p<.05) only between the means of the group that had never been in a study abroad setting (NSA) and the control group (Mandarin Chinese native speakers).

## 8. Discussion

Our central hypothesis is that L2 learners of Mandarin Chinese who have been in a study abroad (SA) setting will have a better mastery of the perfective marker -*LE* than those who have not been in a study abroad (NSA) program. The following predictions were presented in (5), repeated below as (8):

(8) a. SA L2 learners will make significantly more correct uses of –*LE* than NSA ones.
   b. SA L2 learners will make significantly less incorrect uses of –*LE* than NSA ones.

Prediction (8a) did not hold as they were not significant differences among the groups for the correct uses of perfective -*LE*. Nevertheless, prediction (8b) seemed to hold especially in the comparison between the L2 learners without any study abroad experience, and the Mandarin Chinese native speakers. In other words, when not using -*LE* is the acceptable choice, a difference between one of the experimental groups and the native speakers can be found. This result suggests that the NSA group tended to oversupply perfective -*LE* to contexts in which it is not acceptable. These learners still show L1 transfer effects; in other words, they tended to treat Mandarin Chinese -*LE* like the English past tense.

The means of the four main subject groups show that the more time spent in a study abroad setting the better the mastery of perfective -*LE*. Irrespective of whether the L2 learner was in China studying the language or not, the study abroad experience is the crucial factor that separates the NSA learners from the other groups. This could be due to exposure to more linguistic input when the subjects are in a study abroad setting.

The data shows that the subjects have an understanding of the cases in which -*LE* is equivalent to the past tense in English. All the subjects tested fairly high on the sentences involving the correct use of -*LE*. Similarly, all of the subjects also tested high on the filler sentences, which were all in the present tense and did not require the use of -*LE*. However, when it came to the sentences involving the correct non-usage of -*LE*, which were all in the past tense, there was variation between the individual subject groups. With these sentences, there was a trend that related the amount of time spent in China and the number of correct answers. Those who spent more time in an abroad setting had more correct sentences than those who spent less or no time in an abroad setting. The groups who spent less time in an abroad setting seem to overgeneralize the use of -*LE* to all contexts in which the verb is in the past tense.

It is interesting to note that when the subjects were compared according to the duration they spent in an abroad setting, those who studied five months or more seem to have very similar answers to those of the native speakers. This suggests that spending five months or more in an abroad setting greatly helps the L2 acquisition of grammatical features of the target language. Input plays an integral role in the success of L2 acquisition. Compared to the input in a classroom setting, the linguistic input in a native speaking country where the L2 is spoken is significantly more difficult to understand. In a classroom setting, teachers usually accommodate their speech to the students so that they will be more likely to understand. Teachers may slow their speech or choose simpler structures whereas native speakers in a country where the L2 is spoken might not accommodate their speech to the non-native speakers. They will probably speak just as fast as they normally do with the same level of sophistication. This quality of input along with the amount of intake, or actual input processed by the learner, seems to compound to help the learner acquire a second language.

## 9. Conclusion

The present study provides evidence in favor of the view that study abroad settings are more conducive to the development of L2 proficiency than at-home or classroom only settings. Data consistent with L1 transfer of English properties to the interlanguage of L2 learners of Chinese was found for the group of non-study abroad participants, whereas learners in a study abroad setting patterned with the native speakers. This study shows that study abroad helps develop grammatical competency in the target language.

# References

Collentine, J., & B. Freed. (2004). Learning context and its effects on second language acquisition. *Studies in Second Language Acquisition*, 26, 153-171.

Freed, B. F., Segalowitz, N., & Dewey, D. P. (2004). Context of Learning and Second Language Fluency in French: Comparing Regular Classroom, Study Abroad, and Intensive Domestic Immersion Programs. *Studies in Second Language Acquisition*, 26, 275-301.

Ma, L. (2006). Acquisition of the Perfective Aspect Marker *Le* of Mandarin Chinese in Discourse by American College Learners. Unpublished Ph.D. dissertation, University of Iowa.

Shi, Z. (1990). Decomposition of Perfectivity and Inchoativity and the Meaning of the Particle *Le* in Mandarin Chinese. *Journal of Chinese Linguistics*, 18(1), 95-124.

Smith, C. (1991). *The Parameter of Aspect*. Dordrecht, Netherlands: Kluwer Academic Publishers.

Sybesma, R. (1999). *The Mandarin VP*. Dordrecht, Netherlands: Kluwer Academic Publishers.

Wen, X. (1995). Second Language Acquisition of the Chinese Particle *Le*. *International Journal of Applied Linguistics*, 5(1), 45-62.

Yang, S., Huang, Y., & Sun, D. (1999). Acquisition of Aspect in Chinese as a Second Language. *Journal of the Chinese Language Teachers Association*, 34, 31-54.

Yang, Jun (2003). The Basic Function of Particle *le* in Modern Chinese. *Journal of the Chinese Language Teachers Association*, 38:1: 77-96.

Yao, T., & Liu, Y. (2005). *Integrated Chinese*. Boston: Cheng & Tsui Company.

Email: Monica.Cabrera@lmu.edu

# Appendix A

## LANGUAGE PROFILE

(This information will be kept confidential)

1. Sex: _____    2. Age: _____

3. What is the highest level Chinese course you have taken?
   Chin 101  Chin 102  Chin 203  Chin 204  Higher  N/A

4. Place of birth:    City: _____    Country: _____

5. Occupation: _____

6. What is your mother tongue? _____

7. What language(s) did you speak at home as a child?
   _____

8. What is your highest level of schooling?_____
   In which languages were you educated (i.e., language of instruction)?
   Elementary School: _____
   High School: _____
   University: _____

10. What language(s) do you use at work?   _____

11. Where have you studied Chinese?   _____

12. Estimate your level of Chinese on a scale of 1 to 5, where corresponds to "beginner" and 5 corresponds to "advanced":
    1   2   3   4   5

13. At what age did you start studying Chinese?   _____

14. Have you ever spent time in a Chinese speaking country? _____
If so, where?_____ when?_____ how long?_____
What other language do you speak besides English and Chinese?
_____

Estimate your level:
      1    2    3    4    5

# Appendix B

# TEST

**Instructions**: Please read each English sentence carefully and choose the best-fit Chinese translation. To mark your answer, simply circle the sentence of your choice. If you do not know which sentence sounds better, please circle "I don't know". Try not to think to long about your answers. You should mark the first sentence that comes to mind. Please do not ask anyone else for help or refer to any type of study material. I have provided an attached vocabulary list in case you do not recognize some of the characters. Remember, it is very important that you be brief in answering the questions. (N.B. There is a word bank on the last page for help with vocabulary)

1) He wrote four characters.
    a) 他寫了四個字。
       Ta xie le si ge zi.                      c) I don't know.
    b) 他寫四個字。
       Ta xie si ge zi.

2) He is dead.
    a) 他死。
       Ta si.                                 c) I don't know.
    b) 他死了。
       Ta si le.

3) He wanted to write three characters but he only wrote two characters.
    a) 他要寫了三個字，可是只寫了兩個字。
       Ta yao xie le san ge zi, ke shi zhi xie le liang ge zi.     c) I don't know.
    b) 他要寫三個字，□可是只寫了兩個字。
       Ta yao xie san ge zi, ke shi zhi xie le liang ge zi.

4) He arrives at ten o'clock.
    a) 他十點來了。
       Ta shi dian lai le.                    c) I don't know.
    b) 他十點來。
       Ta shi dian lai.

5) Did he finish eating?
    a) 他吃完嗎？
       Ta chi wan ma?                      c) I don't know.
    b) 他吃完了嗎？
       Ta chi wan le ma?

6) He wants to come back.
    a) 他要回來。
        Ta yao hui lai.
    b) 他要了回來。
        Ta yao le hui lai.
    c) I don't know.
7) He spoke Chinese yesterday.
    a) 他昨天說中文了。
        Ta zuo tian shuo zhong wen le.
    b) 他昨天說中文。
        Ta zuo tian shuo zhong wen.
    c) I don't know.
8) He wants to toast a slice of bread.
    a) 他要烤了一片麵包。
        Ta yao kao le yi pian mian bao.
    b) 他要烤一片麵包。
        Ta yao kao yi pian mian bao.
    c) I don't know.
9) Yesterday I ate food, read, drank coffee, and bought a book.
    a) 我昨天吃飯，看書，喝咖啡，也買了一本書。
        Wo zuo tian chi fan, kan shu, he ka fei, ye mai le yi ben shu.
    b) 我昨天吃飯了，□看書了，□喝咖啡了，□也買了一本書。
        Wo zuo tian chi fan le, kan shu le, he ka fei le, ye mai le yi ben shu.
    c) I don't know
10) They want to build a house.
    a) 他們要造一個房子。
        Ta men yao zao yi ge fang zi.
    b) 他們要造了一個房子。
        Ta men yao zao le yi ge fang zi.
    c) I don't know.
11) I liked to drink coffee before.
    a) 我以前喜歡了喝咖啡。
        Wo yi qian xi huan le he ka fei.
    b) 我以前喜歡喝咖啡。
        Wo yi qian xi huan he ka fei.
    c) I don't know.
12) I want to drink one cup of coffee.
    a) 我要喝一杯咖啡。
        Wo yao he yi bei ka fei.
    b) 我要喝了一杯咖啡。
        Wo yao he le yi bei ka fei.
    c) I don't know.
13) He was very happy.
    a) 他以前很高興。
        Ta yi qian hen gao xing.
    b) 他很高興了。
        Ta hen gao xing le.
    c) I don't know.

14) He resembles his father.
    a) 他像了他的父親。
       Ta xiang le ta de fu qing.
    b) 他像他的父親。
       Ta xiang ta de fu qing.
    c) I don't know.

15) He resembled his father.
    a) 他像了他的父親。
       Ta xiang le ta de fu qing
    b) 他以前像他的父親。
       Ta yi qian xiang ta de fu qing.
    c) I don't know.

16) He is very happy.
    a) 他很高興。
       Ta hen gao xing.
    b) 他很高興了。
       Ta hen gao xing le.
    c) I don't know.

17) He broke a cup.
    a) 他打破了一個杯子。
       Ta da puo le yi ge bei zi.
    b) 他打破一個杯子。
       Ta da puo yi ge bei zi.
    c) I don't know.

18) He likes to drink coffee.
    a) 他喜歡了喝咖啡。
       Ta xi huan le he ka fei.
    b) 他喜歡喝咖啡。
       Ta xi huan he ka fei.
    c) I don't know.

19) They built a house.
    a) 他們造了一個房子。
       Ta men zao le yi ge fang zi.
    b) 他們造一個房子。
       Ta men zao yi ge fang zi.
    c) I don't know.

20) I like eating food, reading, and drinking coffee.
    a) 我喜歡吃東西看書和喝咖啡了。
       Wo xi huan chi dong xi kan shu he he ka fei le.
    b) 我喜歡吃東西看書和喝咖啡。
       Wo xi huan chi dong xi kan shu he he ka fei.
    c) I don't know.

21) He burnt a piece of bread.
    a) 他烤焦了一片麵包。
       Ta kao jiao le yi pian mian bao.
    b) 他烤焦一片麵包。
       Ta kao jiao yi pian mian bao.
    c) I don't know.

22) He speaks Chinese everyday.
    a) 他天天都說中文。
       Ta tian tian dou shuo zhong wen.          c) I don't know.
    b) 他天天都說了中文。
       Ta tian tian dou shou le zhong wen.

23) He came.
    a) 他來了。
       Ta lai le.          c) I don't know.
    b) 他來。
       Ta lai.

24) Can you finish eating?
    a) 你吃完了嗎？
       Ni chi wan le ma?          c) I don't know.
    b) 你吃得完吃不完？
       Ni chi de wan chi bu wan?

25) He already arrived.
    a) 他已經到了。
       Ta yi jing dao le.          c) I don't know.
    b) 他已經到。
       Ta yi jing dao.

26) He wants to write three characters.
    a) 他要寫三個字。
       Ta yao xie san ge zi.          c) I don't know.
    b) 他要寫三個字了。
       Ta yao xie san ge zi le.

27) He died yesterday.
    a) 他昨天死了。
       Ta zuo tian si le.          c) I don't know.
    b) 他昨天死。
       Ta zuo tian si.

28) You write four characters!
    a) 你寫了四個字。
       Ni xie le si ge zi.          c) I don't know.
    b) 你寫四個字。
       Ni xie si ge zi.

Vocabulary List
完 wan: to finish
天天 tian tian: everyday
吃飯／吃東西 chi fan/chi dong xi: eat food
買 mai: to buy
一本書 yi ben shu: one book
以前 yi qian: before
像 xiang: to resemble
父親 fu qing: father
造 zao: to build
房子 fang zi: house

# Ultimate L2 Acquisition of the Chinese BA Construction: Two Case Studies

Fufen Jin
*Norwegian University of Science and Technology (NTNU)*

## 1. Introduction

In Chinese, the word *ba* can change the canonical SVO word order into SOV, as illustrated in (1) below:[1]

(1) a. Wo guan le men. (SVO)
   I close ASP door
   'I closed the door.'
 b. Wo ba men guan le. (SOV)
   I BA door close ASP
   'I closed the door.'

Traditionally, sentences like (1b) are called *ba* sentences, the corresponding sentences without *ba* (cf. 1a) non-*ba* sentences. The *ba* construction is complex and subject to a number of syntactic and semantic constraints, which I will present in section 2.

The *ba* construction is unique to the Chinese language; no corresponding construction has been found in any European languages. So the acquisition of the *ba* construction is of great interest to second language (L2) research. In this study, I will examine the ultimate attainment of the *ba* construction by two Norwegian speakers. One informant learned Chinese as an adult, the other learned Chinese in her early childhood. I test their acquisition of the syntactic and semantic constraints on the *ba* construction, and see whether all the constraints on the *ba* construction are ultimately acquirable. If not, it is of interest to find out whether the age of starting the acquisition of the second language makes a difference.

---

[1] The following symbols are used for the annotation throughout the paper. ASP stands for aspect marker, BA for *ba*, DE for *de*, the resultative marker in Chinese, CL for classifier.

The rest of the paper is organized as follows. In section 2, I present properties of the *ba* construction, focusing on its syntactic properties and its semantic constraints. In section 3, I review the relevant studies on L2 acquisition of the *ba* construction. In section 4, I outline my own study, including a detailed description of the informants' Chinese learning background, research questions and research methods. The results of the experiment will be presented in section 5. Section 6 discusses the findings and concludes the study.

## 2. Properties of the *ba* construction

The *ba* construction has been a central topic for Chinese grammarians, and it has been analyzed in different frameworks. A review of the different analyses is beyond the scope of this paper. The properties of the *ba* construction are summed up from influential works like Li (2001), Li & Thompson (1981), and Liu (1997), presented largely in a framework-neutral manner. I will first present syntactic properties of the *ba* construction, and then I present its semantic constraints.

A *ba* sentence can be schematically represented as in (2),[2]

(2)   NP* + *ba* + NP + V + X

where there is a subject (NP*), followed by *ba* and a NP, which is called the *ba* NP. Note that no element can intervene between *ba* and the *ba* NP. After the *ba* NP comes the verb, and then in turn something else (X) after the verb. The X is obligatory, that is to say, the verb cannot be bare in the *ba* construction. This property is referred to as the complexity constraint on the *ba* VP. Typically, the X can be an aspect marker (*-le/-zhe*), a resultative verb complement, a result clause (marked by *de*), a prepositional phrase (dative or locative), or a number expression (see Liu 1997 for a detailed discussion).

Following Li (2001), I assume that all *ba* sentences have a non-*ba* counterpart. Li argues that a *ba* NP corresponds either to a V-object or a V'-object in its non-*ba* counterpart. V-objects include direct objects, indirect objects, and instrumental/locative NPs. (1b) is an example where the *ba* NP corresponds to the direct object of the verb. The *ba* NPs in examples (3b) and (4b) below correspond respectively to the indirect object in the double object construction and to an instrumental NP in the (a)-version.

---

2   Li (2001) included another form, namely, NP* + *ba* + NP + X + V, where X is before the verb. While I acknowledge that this form exists, it is nevertheless rare. The typical form is the one where the X is after the verb. All the *ba* sentences in this paper have the form in (2).

(3) a. Wo fa le <u>ta</u> henduo qian.
       I fine Asp him much money
    b. Wo ba <u>ta</u> fa le henduo qian.
       I BA him fine ASP much money
       'I fined him a lot of money.'

(4) a. Wo yong <u>shui</u> jiao le hua.
       I with water water ASP flower
    b. Wo ba <u>shui</u> jiao le hua.
       I BA water water ASP flower
       'I watered the flowers.'

A V'-object is defined as "the object of a complex predicate consisting of a verb and its complement" (Li 2001:13). It can be an NP holding a possession or part-whole relationship with the V-object (cf. 5), or an NP identified with the subject/object of an embedded result clause (marked with *de*; cf. 6).

(5) a. Wo bo le juzi pi.
       I peel ASP orange skin
    b. Wo ba juzi bo le pi.
       I BA orange peel ASP skin
       'I peeled the skin off the orange.'

(6) a. Ta shao tie shao de meiren gan mo.
       he heat iron heat DE nobody dare touch
    b. Ta ba tie shao de meiren gan mo.
       he BA iron heat DE nobody dare touch
       'He heated the iron (so hot) that nobody dare touch it.'

In addition, in negating a *ba* construction, the negation word *mei/meiyou* precedes *ba* (cf. 7b). It is ungrammatical to put the negation word in front of the predicate (cf. 7c). In its non-*ba* counterpart, however, the negation word precedes the predicate (cf. 7a).

(7) a. Wo meiyou guanshang men.
       I not close door
    b. Wo meiyou ba men guanshang.
       I not BA door close

    c.    *Wo ba men meiyou guanshang.
         I BA door not close
         'I did not close the door.'

It is important to note, however, that the template in (2) greatly overgenerates. This is because the *ba* construction is subject to several semantic constraints. The first is called a definiteness constraint, according to which the *ba* NP must be definite or specific. Thus, (8) is ungrammatical, because the *ba* NP is indefinite. For the same reason, (9b) only has one (i.e. definite) reading, whereas (9a), its non-*ba* counterpart, may have two readings (i.e. definite and indefinite).

(8)    * Wo ba yi ben shu mai le.
       I BA a CL book buy ASP
       'I bought a book.'

(9)    a.    Wo mai le shu.
            I buy ASP book
            'I bought books/the books.'
       b.    Wo ba shu mai le.
            I BA book buy ASP
            'I bought the books.'

The second constraint is related to the notion of affectedness, that is, the *ba* construction describes something being affected.[3] This is a central characteristic of the *ba* construction, and as Li correctly points out, this special meaning is responsible for "the many constraints on the choice of verbs, the choice of *ba* NPs and the use of X in a *ba* construction" (2001:46). The notion of affectedness is illustrated in terms of the contrast between the two verbs *huan* 'to return', and *fa* 'to fine', both of which can take double objects (cf. 10a and 11a). The two verbs differ, however, as to which of the two objects can be preposed as the *ba* NP. For the verb *huan*, it is the direct object (i.e. *10 kuai qian*), and for the verb *fa*, it is the indirect object (i.e. *wo*), cf. (10b) and (11b), respectively. This is because (10b) expresses that the money is affected because of its displacement, whereas (11b) expresses that the speaker (*wo*) is affected by being fined 10 dollars. (10b) and (11b) contrast with the ungrammaticality of (10c) and (11c), where the *ba* NPs are not affected by the actions.

---

[3]    In the literature, the notion of affectedness is usually used on a par with the notion of disposal (see for example, Li & Thompson 1981).

(10) a. Ta **huan** le wo 10 kuai qian.
 he return me 10 CL money
 b. Ta ba <u>10 kuai qian</u> **huan** le wo.
 he BA 10 CL money return ASP me
 c. *Ta ba <u>wo</u> **huan** le 10 kuai qian.
 he BA me return ASP 10 CL money
 'He returned 10 dollars to me.'

(11) a. Ta **fa** le wo 10 kuai qian.
 he fine ASP me 10 CL money
 b. Ta ba <u>wo</u> **fa** le 10 kuai qian.
 he BA me fine ASP CL money
 c. *Ta ba <u>10 kuai qian</u> **fa** le wo.
 he BA 10 CL money fine ASP me
 'He fined me 10 dollars.'

To sum up, the *ba* NP corresponds either to a V-object or a V'-object in its non-*ba* counterpart. The verb following the *ba* NP cannot be bare. This is referred to as the complexity constraint. When negating the *ba* sentences, the negation word must precede *ba*. In addition, the *ba* construction is subject to two semantic constraints. First, the *ba* NP has to be definite or specific. Second, a *ba* sentence is a construction denoting affectedness. In the rest of the paper, I refer to these semantic constraints as [definiteness] and [affectedness], respectively.

## 3. Previous studies

Studies on L2 acquisition of the Chinese *ba* construction are few. So far as I know, there are only three such studies, namely, Jin (1992), Huang & Yang (2005), and Du (2006). I will review each of them in turn.

### 3.1. Jin (1992)

The study by H.G. Jin was conducted in the framework of Tsao (1987), who proposes that the *ba* construction is a topic-prominent feature of Chinese, treating the *ba* NP as a secondary topic. Jin examined learners of Chinese whose first language (L1) is English, a subject-prominent language, and investigated whether subject-prominent features are transferred in learning the Chinese *ba* construction. The study has a cross-sectional design involving learners of four proficiency levels, ranging from beginners to upper-intermediate (with three years of classroom learning).

Jin used three tasks to test learners' knowledge of the *ba* construction: grammaticality judgment, translation and story-telling. Here we only focus on the grammaticality judgment and translation tasks. The grammaticality judgment task consisted of 30 sentences, which were divided into three clusters according to the grammatical status of the *ba* NPs. The *ba* NPs were direct objects in cluster 1, attributives in cluster 2, and adverbials in cluster 3. In the translation task, learners were asked to translate 11 English sentences into Chinese using the *ba* construction. It was found that learners performed similarly in the two tasks: in both tasks they scored highest with cluster 1, and lowest with cluster 3, and this was true of learners at all proficiency levels. Jin explains this learning hierarchy as follows: learners go through a stage of first treating the *ba* NP as the preposed object, and then as either an object or a topic, and subsequently as topic of the sentence. Learners have no trouble with Cluster 1, because they simply treat *ba* as the marker of the proposed object. On the other hand, they have difficulty with cluster 3, because they do not have such structures in their native language. Jin thus takes this learning hierarchy as showing evidence of L1 transfer.

## 3.2 Huang & Yang (2005)

In their study, Huang & Yang are concerned with the delimited nature of the *ba* construction. Following Ritter & Rosen (2000), they assume that languages can be divided into Delimitation languages (D-languages) and Initiation languages (I-languages). In D-languages, telic verbs of accomplishments and achievements pattern together and the terminal bound determines eventhood; in I-languages, a grammaticalized event has an initial bound, and activities and accomplishments pattern together as events. Chinese and English are two examples of D-languages, whereas Japanese is an example of an I-language.

Huang & Yang included two learner groups of Chinese: learners with English as first language (a D-language, like Chinese), and learners with Japanese as first language (an I-language, different from Chinese). Each group included learners at four proficiency levels: beginner, low intermediate, high intermediate, and advanced. Treating the *ba* construction as a typical terminal bounding structure, Huang & Yang investigated whether the two learner groups show a difference as to the sensitivity to the telic property of the *ba* construction, and whether they syntactically express telicity in their *ba* sentences differently. They looked at the L2 written production data of the two groups. Any *ba* sentence with a bare verb was taken as atelic, and those whose verbs are associated with any delimiting elements were treated as telic. It was found that both groups demonstrate an overwhelming use (over 92% on average) of telic predicates in their *ba* sentences, indicating that they show a strong sensitivity to the telicity constraint on the *ba* construction. Huang & Yang thus conclude that the typological difference between Japanese and English does not have obvious effects on their acquisition of a telicity restricted *ba* construction.

Another point Huang & Yang observe is that the two groups show a similar pattern as to which delimiting strategies are preferred, the order being: Directionals & locatives > double object structure & resultative compounds > result *de* clause. The first two strategies account for about 80% used by the L2 learners. The use of result *de* clauses, however, is rare in the L2 *ba* sentences.

## 3.3 Du (2006)

Du (2006) intended to test whether English-speaking learners of Chinese have acquired the definiteness constraint on the *ba* NP and the complexity constraint on the *ba* VP (i.e. the verb in the *ba* sentence requires a complement, namely the X element in (2) above; bare verbs are not acceptable in a *ba* sentence). Due to design problems, only the complexity constraint was tested. So only this part of the experiment is reviewed here. Du investigated two types of X elements: the resultative verb complement (RVC) and an aspect marker *–le*. The learners were 65 English-speaking adults who were divided into three proficiency levels according to the number of weeks learning Chinese. The learners' knowledge of the complexity constraint was tested using two tasks: an oral production task using two-action video scenes as prompts, and a grammaticality judgment task, including grammatical sentences with RVCs/*le*, and ungrammatical ones without RVCs/*le* (i.e. verbs are bare). A group of 20 native speakers of Chinese served as a control group.

It was found that L2 learners produced significantly fewer *ba* sentences than native speakers. The differences across the three proficiency levels are not significant, suggesting that there were no strong developmental trends as proficiency level increases. Du interprets this fact as indicating that learners take the *ba* construction as a difficult structure, and that they try to avoid using it in their production. In contrast to the production data, the judgment task data indicate that L2 learners judge the *ba* sentences, both the grammatical ones and the ungrammatical ones, as well as native speakers. This shows that learners have good knowledge of the complexity constraint on *ba* sentences at an early stage.

## 3.4 Goals of the present study

As we can see, all the existing studies focus on the developmental stages in acquiring the *ba* construction. Though such studies are informative as far as the acquisition process during the earlier stages of learning the *ba* construction is concerned, they cannot address the question of ultimate attainment of the *ba* construction. In addition, the previous studies only investigate one or a couple of the properties associated with the *ba* construction. We need to investigate the acquisition of the whole set of properties and constraints on *ba* in order to obtain a more complete picture.

The present study intends to achieve such goals. First, the informants are at their endstate of acquiring Chinese, enabling me to investigate the final outcomes of acquisition of the *ba* construction. Second, the present study investigates both syntactic properties and semantic constraints on the *ba* construction, as presented in section 2. It will thus provide important information as to which properties are ultimately attainable, which are not.

In addition, the two informants differ as to the age of starting learning Chinese: one started as an adult, the other learned Chinese in her early childhood. This allows me to explore another important question in L2 research as to whether the age of acquiring a language has an effect on learners' ultimate attainment.

## 4. The present study

### 4.1 Informants

The present study includes two L2 informants, and 20 native speakers of Chinese as a control group. The native speakers of Chinese were all graduate students at the Norwegian University of Science and Technology. They come from different provinces of China, thus speaking different dialects of Chinese, but they all speak Mandarin as well.

The two L2 informants, JE and KH, were recruited in Trondheim, Norway. They were both native speakers of Norwegian, and according to their own reports, they were both perceived as fluent speakers of Mandarin. Considering their L2 Chinese learning backgrounds, which I will describe in some detail below, I assume that they have reached their ultimate state in learning Mandarin Chinese.

JE was 39 at the time of the test. She was brought up and educated in Trondheim, Norway. She had not learned any Chinese until she went to Taiwan at the age of 27. There she spent three years on intensive classroom learning of Mandarin Chinese.[4] She reported that she attended Chinese class four to six hours a day, five days per week. The Chinese training she received was comprehensive, involving listening, speaking, reading, and writing articles in Chinese. After she completed

---

4   Mandarin Chinese is used to refer to Modern Standard Chinese, known as *Putonghua* 'the common language' in Mainland China, and as *Guoyu* 'the national language' in Taiwan.

the Chinese learning program, she worked as a nurse in an international hospital in Taiwan. There the working languages were Chinese and English, but she reported that she spoke Chinese 90% of the time. After working there for four years, she returned to Trondheim and got a job in a medical profession. Even though she is now living in Norway, JE keeps frequent contact with her friends in Taiwan, and she finds some time to visit Taiwan, and cities of Mainland China each year. She also finds every opportunity to speak Mandarin with Chinese speakers she meets in Trondheim, all of whom perceive her as a fluent speaker of Mandarin.

KH was 27 at the time of the test. She was born in Taiwan, where her parents, both native speakers of Norwegian, worked as missionaries in a local church. At the age of two, KH was sent to a local day-care center, where the working language was exclusively Mandarin. There she quickly picked up Mandarin. She spoke Norwegian at home with her parents, and Mandarin outside home. This situation continued until she was seven, when she and her family moved back to Trondheim. There she attended Norwegian schools and had little chance to speak Chinese. In order to maintain her Chinese, her parents hired a Chinese tutor to teach her Chinese during the first three years after returning to Norway. Her parents also took her to Taiwan for a short visit every other year before she went to college. Shortly after she completed her university degree, she got married to a Norwegian man who worked in the Norwegian Embassy in China. The couple now live in Beijing, and come back to Trondheim only during holidays.

## 4.2 Research questions

In connection with the syntactic properties and semantic constraints on the *ba* construction, as presented in section 2, I address the following research questions:

RQ 1.  Do L2 learners have the knowledge that *ba* NPs correspond to V objects?
RQ 2.  Do L2 learners have the knowledge that *ba* NPs correspond to V' objects?
RQ 3.  Do L2 learners have the knowledge about the position for negation words in *ba* sentences?
RQ 4.  Are L2 learners sensitive to the complexity constraint on the *ba* VP?
RQ 5.  Are L2 learners sensitive to the semantic constraints on the *ba* construction, namely, [definiteness] and [affectedness]?
RQ 6.  Is there an age effect on the ultimate attainment of the *ba* construction?

## 4.3 The test

Each informant completed an acceptability judgment test. According to the syntactic properties and semantic constraints to be tested, the test sentences are categorized into the following six groups. In each group there is a control sentence, and one (or more than one) corresponding experimental sentence.

G1. *ba* NP=V object
    a.    Wo chi le pingguo.
            I eat ASP apple
    b.    Wo ba pingguo chi le.
            I BA apple eat ASP
            'I ate the apple.'

G2. *ba* NP= V' object
    a.    Ta zou de tui dou teng le
            he walk DE leg even pain ASP
    b.    Ta ba tui zou de dou teng le
            he BA leg walk DE even pain ASP
            'He walked so much that his legs became painful.'

G3. Negating *ba* sentences
    a.    Wo meiyou wang le ni
            I not forget ASP you
    b.    Wo meiyou ba ni wang le.
            I not BA you forget ASP
    c.    * Wo ba ni meiyou wang le.
            I BA you not forget ASP
            'I have not forgotten you.'

G4. Violation of the complexity constraint
    a.    Ta ti zhe ge qiou.
            he kick this CL ball
    b.    * ta ba zhe ge qiou ti.
            he BA this CL ball kick
            'He kicks the ball.'

G5. Violation of the [definiteness] constraint
    a.   Ta zuotian mai le yi liang che.
          He yesterday buy ASP a CL car
    b.   * Ta zuotian ba yi liang che mai le.
          He yesterday BA a CL car buy ASP
          'He bought a car yesterday.'

G6. Violation of the [affectedness] constraint
    a.   Wo gaosu le ta zhe ge hao xiaoxi
          I tell ASP him this CL good news
    b.   * Wo ba ta gaosu le zhe ge hao xiaoxi
          I BA him tell ASP this CL good news
          'I told him this good news.'

Each type has 10 tokens, making up 130 test sentences. In addition, 30 sentences are included as distracters. All the sentences are randomized using Random Number Generator. Informants were asked to judge the acceptability of each sentence on a scale of –2 to +2, where –2 means completely unacceptable, +2 means completely acceptable, –1 means probably unacceptable, +1 means probably acceptable, and 0 means "don't know".[5]

The test was conducted individually. All instructions were given in Mandarin. For the native group, the test sentences were presented in Chinese characters. For the L2 informants, the test sentences were presented in Chinese characters with pinyin annotations. Before the test, the informants were given a word list, containing the words used in the test. They were asked to read the list, and mark the words they do not know. It turned out that the two informants knew all the words in the list. After the informants completed judging the sentences, I singled out those sentences with scores of –1 and –2, and asked the informants to explain why they were judged ungrammatical, and to provide the grammatical counterparts. In so doing, I hope to make sure that the informants' judgments are relevant to the target properties. This procedure proved to be useful. To take one example, an informant judged a sentence as –1 simply because the negation word is *mei*, instead of *meiyou*. In fact, both forms are acceptable. When the negation word was changed to *meiyou*, she judged the sentence as +2.

---

5   The inclusion of a 0 score meaning "don't know» is problematic, because informants may assign "don't know» due to many different reasons. To single out those sentences assigned with a zero and to ask the informant to make an explanation after the test can be a remedy. For the present study, as we will see in section 5, it turned out that no informants assigned a zero score to any sentences in the experiment.

# 5. Results

The results of the judgment test are based on the corrected scores. No informants assigned a zero score to any sentences in the test, indicating that they understood all the sentences. In interpreting the test results, any scores above +1 are treated as acceptance. Conversely any scores below –1 are treated as rejection.

As we can see from table 1, the two L2 informants, like the native speakers, readily accept the *ba* sentences in G1. This suggests that they have the knowledge that *ba* NPs correspond to V-object in the non-*ba* counterparts.

*Table 1. Mean scores of judgment of G1:* ba **NP=V-object**

|         | JE  | KH  | NATIVE |
|---------|-----|-----|--------|
| control | 2   | 2   | 1.82   |
| ba      | 1.9 | 1.7 | 1.88   |

The judgment results of G2, shown in table 2, are quite surprising. It seems that native speakers do not show clear acceptance of the *ba* sentences in this group, whereas the two L2 informants accept them, judging them well above +1.

*Table 2. Mean scores of judgment of G2:* ba **NP=V'-object**

|         | JE  | KH  | NATIVE |
|---------|-----|-----|--------|
| control | 1.9 | 1.9 | 1.75   |
| ba      | 1.9 | 1.5 | 0.375  |

The native speakers' performance is unexpected, given that in the literature such *ba* sentences in G2 are assumed to be grammatical. This calls for a careful examination of the native speakers' judgment data on the *ba* sentences in G2. The data reveal that there is a variation among the native informants in their judgments of the *ba* sentences in this group. By variation, I mean that not a single informant consistently rejected/accepted all such sentences, and that not a single sentence was consistently rejected/accepted by all the informants. For illustration, let us look at sentence 160, the one that was judged with greatest variation.

S160.  Tianqi re de gou dou bu jiao le.
       weather hot DE dog all not bark ASP
       'The weather is so hot that the dogs are not barking.'

This sentence is taken from Li (2001: 29, her example 68), used as a good example "demonstrating that an intransitive V with a resultative complement can make an acceptable *ba* sentence". However, we see from figure 1 that only 3 out of 20 of native informants completely accepted the sentence, 6 of them weakly accepted it, while 9 completely rejected it, and 2 weakly rejected it.

This variation could result from dialectal differences among the native informants. Recall that the native control group came from different parts of China and spoke different dialects. It could well be that a certain sentence is good for speakers of one dialect, but bad for speakers of another dialect. Du (2006) also found some unusual patterns in native speakers' judgments on the *ba* construction in her study, and she suggested that dialect factors might play a role.

Whatever the reasons are causing the varied judgment given by native speakers on the *ba* sentences in G2, it is important to note that the statement that the *ba* NP corresponds to the V'-object is nevertheless valid. After all, almost half of the native speakers accepted such sentences. Given this, it is interesting to find that both of the L2 informants have good knowledge of this syntactic property of the *ba* construction, as can be seen from their mean judgment scores on the *ba* sentences in G2.

In judging *ba* sentences with negation words *mei/meiyou*, native speakers strongly prefer to have the negation word in front of *ba*, and thus reject the sentences with the negation word in front of the *ba* VP, as shown in table 3. The two L2 informants displayed a different pattern: while JE accepted the negation

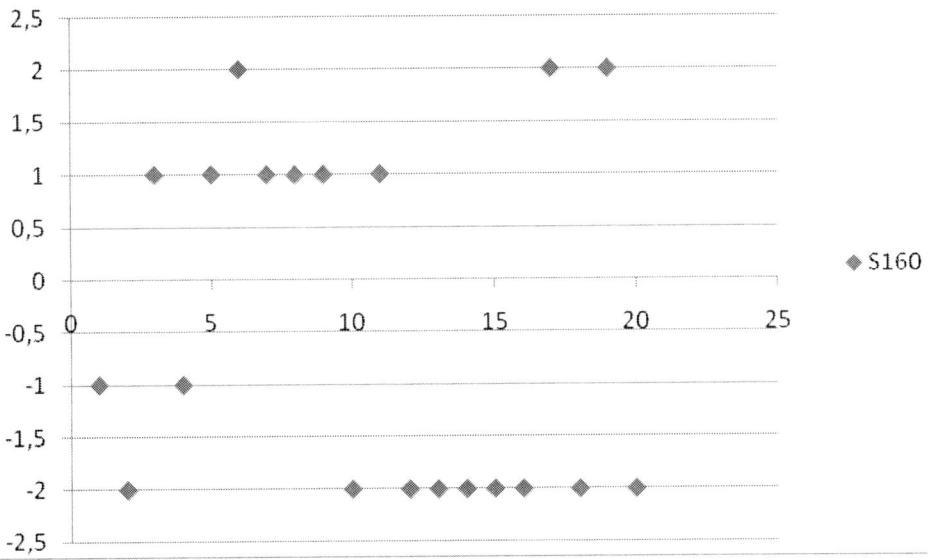

Figure 1. Native speakers' judgment on S160.

word in both positions, KH, like native speakers, only accepted the negation word in front of *ba*, and rejected the illicit *mei+ba* VP sequence.

Table 3. Mean scores of judgment of G3: negating ba **sentences**

|  | JE | KH | NATIVE |
|---|---|---|---|
| control | 2 | 2 | 1.7 |
| *mei+ba* | 2 | 2 | 1.47 |
| **mei+ba* VP | 1.6 | −1.8 | −1.01 |

The results of the judgment of control sentences and those violating the complexity constraint are presented in table 4. We see that the performance of JE and KH was nativelike, with both rejecting the *ba* sentences with bare verbs. This indicates that they are sensitive to the complexity constraint on the *ba* construction.

Table 4. Mean scores of judgment of G4: violation of the complexity constraint

|  | JE | KH | NATIVE |
|---|---|---|---|
| control | 1.7 | 1.9 | 1.73 |
| **ba*-complexity | −1.6 | −1.8 | −1.87 |

Table 5 shows the results of judgment of the control sentences and the corresponding *ba* sentences violating the definiteness constraint.

Table 5. Mean scores of judgment of G5: violation of the definiteness constraint

|  | JE | KH | NATIVE |
|---|---|---|---|
| control | 2 | 2 | 1.75 |
| **ba*-definite | 0.8 | −0.4 | 0.375 |

We see that native speakers' mean score on the judgment of the experimental sentences is around zero. This is surprising. Given the definiteness constraint, we should expect native speakers to show clear rejection of the experimental sentences. A careful examination of the test sentences and the judgment scores reveals that native speakers seem to make a distinction between *ba* sentences with *ba* NPs containing *yi ge* ('a + CL') and those containing modified numeral determiners, such as *san wu ge* 'three to five'. The former sentences were judged with greater variation, the latter sentences were judged more consistently.

For the sake of comparison, the mean scores of the judgments of sentences containing *yi ge* and those containing modified numeral determiners were calculated separately. There are seven *ba* sentences whose *ba* NPs consist of *yi ge* N, and three with modified numeral determiners. It was found that the mean score of judgment of the former type is 0.64, whereas the mean score of judgment of the latter is –0.77. T-test results show that the difference is significant [t (195)=5.65, p=.00], so we can conclude confidently that the two types of sentences were judged differently.

The following is one possible explanation for the differential treatment of the two types of *ba* NPs. Without larger contexts, 'a+CL+N' can have either a specific or non-specific interpretation. On a specific interpretation, it is a legitimate *ba* NP, making the *ba* sentence grammatical; when interpreted non-specifically, it is not a legitimate *ba* NP, making the *ba* sentence ungrammatical. This difference in interpretation thus gives rise to the variability of judgment of the *ba* sentences whose *ba* NPs consist of 'a+CL+N'. Modified numeral determiners (e.g. *san wu ge* 'three to five'; *shi lai ge* 'about ten'), on the other hand, are less likely to have a specific interpretation.[6] Native speakers thus tended to reject such *ba* sentences, as we can see from the mean judgment score (i.e. -0.77).

Turning the the results of the two L2 informants, we find that JE has a mean score of 0.8, and KH has a mean score of –0.4. Neither of them showed clear acceptance or rejection of the experimental sentences. Their judgment data indicate that both of them have varied judgment on the experimental sentences. At this point, we are concerned whether they show the same differentiation between *ba* NPs consisting of 'a+CL+N', and those with modified numeral determiners, as native speakers did. It is found that neither of them judged the *ba* sentences with a+CL+N consistently. Of the three sentences with modified numeral determiners, JE assigned +2 to two of them, and –2 to one of them, KH consistently rejected all three, assigning –2 to all three of them. Given the semantic complexity of 'a+CL+N', it is hard for me to interpret the L2 results. Besides, the number of the experimental sentences with modified numeral determiners is too small to warrant any strong conclusions as to whether L2 learners were sensitive to the definiteness constraint. It would require more careful design of experiments to test learners' sensitivity to the definiteness constraint.

---

6  See Liu (1997:85) where she argues that NPs with modified numeral determiner are non-specific.

Table 6. Mean scores of judgment of G6: violation of the affectedness constraint

|  | JE | KH | NATIVE |
|---|---|---|---|
| control | 2 | 2 | 1.95 |
| *ba-affected | 1.6 | −1.5 | −1.68 |

In judging the experimental sentences which violate the affectedness constraint, the native speakers showed clear rejection, the mean score being −1.68, as shown in table 6. The two L2 informants, however, performed differently. As we can see from the table, JE accepted the experimental sentences, whereas KH showed a clear rejection to them. This suggests that KH behaved like native speakers in showing sensitivity to the affectedness constraint. JE, on the other hand, showed a lack of knowledge of such a semantic constraint.

## 6. Discussion and conclusion

We first revisit the research questions addressed in this study.

RQ 1.   Do L2 learners have the knowledge that *ba* NPs correspond to V objects?
RQ 2.   Do L2 learners have the knowledge that *ba* NPs correspond to V' objects?
RQ 3.   Do L2 learners have the knowledge about the position for negation words in *ba* sentences?
RQ 4.   Are L2 learners sensitive to the complexity constraint on the *ba* VP?
RQ 5.   Are L2 learners sensitive to the semantic constraints on the *ba* construction, namely, [definiteness] and [affectedness]?
RQ 6.   Is there an age effect on the ultimate attainment of the *ba* construction?

The answers to the first five research questions, provided from the findings of the acceptability judgment test, are summarized in table 7.

*Table 7. A summary of test results*

|    | ba NP=V-object | ba NP=V' object | Negating ba | Complexity constraint | Definiteness constraint | Affectedness constraint |
|----|----------------|-----------------|-------------|-----------------------|-------------------------|--------------------------|
| JE | yes            | yes             | no          | yes                   | ?                       | no                       |
| KH | yes            | yes             | yes         | yes                   | ?                       | yes                      |

From table 7 we see that both L2 learners have good knowledge that *ba* NPs correspond either to V objects or V' objects. The finding that L2 learners can ultimately acquire the knowledge that a *ba* NP corresponds to the V' object is striking, because the relevant structure (e.g. result *de* clauses) is not found in their first language. Recall that both Jin (1992) and Huang & Yang (2005) found that L2 learners, including the advanced learners, had great difficulty with this structure in their production of *ba* sentences. Although we did not look at the L2 production data in this study, we did find that L2 learners show clear acceptance of such sentences in their judgments, indicating that they have acquired the knowledge that *ba* NPs can corresponds to V' objects of the non-*ba* counterparts.

It is found that the L2 learners are sensitive to the complexity constraint, consistently rejecting *ba* sentences with bare predicates. This should be expected, because previous studies (cf. Huang & Yang 2005; Du 2006) have attested that L2 learners are fully aware of the complexity constraint in the earlier acquisition stages.

The findings are inconclusive as to learners' sensitivity to the definiteness constraint. As mentioned earlier, this is probably due to a design problem. A more careful design of experiments, using *ba* NPs containing modified numeral determiners, should be included in future research.

From table 7 we observe that there are two areas where the two L2 informants performed differently. One is concerned with the position of negation words in the *ba* sentences, the other is concerned with the affectedness constraint. As far as negating *ba* is concerned, KH accepted the grammatical *ba* sentences with negation words preceding *ba*, and rejected the ungrammatical ones with negation words preceding the predicate. JE, on the other hand, allowed negation words in both positions in the *ba* sentences. I can see two reasons why JE persistently allow the illicit *meiyou* +VP sequence in *ba* sentences. First, this is the usual sequence in negating sentences with SVO word order. That is to say, in negating non-*ba* sentences, the negation word precedes the predicate. The L2 learners may remember the sequence as a common collocation, and apply it in the *ba* sentences as well.[7] Secondly, even for me as a native speaker of Mandarin, the positions of the negation word do not seem to make much difference as to the meaning of the sentence. Since it does not have an effect on interpretation and on communication, this illicit sequence may keep appearing in L2 interlanguage on a par with the grammatical *mei you+ba* sequence. N[8]

A similar contrast is found in JE's and KH's judgment of *ba* sentences that violate the affectedness constraint. While JE accepted the experimental sentences, disregarding whether the *ba* NPs are the affected ones, KH consistently rejected them. This finding seems to suggest that the affectedness constraint is ultimately acquirable for KH, but not acquirable for JE. The notion of affectedness is indeed elusive. As pointed out by Li (2001), affectedness need not be physical. It can be psychological or even imaginary. It is understandable that L2 learners have difficulty mastering this vague notion of affectedness.

The findings thus far also allow us to address the final research question as to whether there is an age effect in ultimate acquisition of the *ba* construction. The contrastive performances between JE and KH in the above mentioned areas point to a positive answer to the research question. As we see, KH, who started learning Chinese in her early childhood, has successfully acquired the whole set of properties of the *ba* construction. JE, as an adult learner of Chinese, on the other hand, has acquired only part of the properties of the *ba* construction. This suggests that the age factor indeed plays a role as to what is acquirable and what is not. A word of caution is in order. The present study only looked at one endstate informant in each case. A general limitation of all case studies is that the findings may not be generalizable. As no previous studies have tested the two properties of the *ba* construction, there is no way to make a comparison. Future studies involving more endstate learners of Chinese need to be conducted in order to consolidate the findings of the present study.

---

7  One of the reviewers suggests that this explanation may need further support from the informant's judgment on other sentence patterns, for example, the *bei* construction. I agree with the reviewer that this is worth exploring in the future.

8  One of the reviewers points out that in cases like the following, the position of negators does change the sentence interpretation:
   (i)  a.  bu da kai      b.  da bu kai
           not hit open        hit not open
           'not to open'       'not able to open'
   (2)  a.  bu neng lai    b.  neng bu lai
           not can come     can not come
           'not able to come'  'be allowed not to come'
This is true indeed, but the point remains that the position of negators does not change the semantics in the case of the *ba* construction.

# References

Du, Hang. 2006. The acquisition of the Chinese *ba* construction. Munich: LINCOM.

Huang, Yue Yuan & Yang, Suying. 2005. Telicity in L2 Chinese Acquisition. *Proceedings of the 7th generative approach to second language acquisition conference (GASLA 2004)*.150-162.

Jin, Hong Gang. 1992. Pragmatization and the L2 acquisition of Chinese *ba* constructions. *Journal of the Chinese Language Teachers Association* 28 (3). 33-52.

Li, Charles, N. & Thompson, Sandra. 1981. *Mandarin Chinese: A functional reference grammar*. Berkeley & Los Angeles: University of California Press.

Li, Y.-H. Audrey. 2001. The *ba* construction, http://www.cbs.polyu.edu.hk/tang/. (12 April, 2008.)

Liu, Feng-his. 1997. An aspectual analysis of BA. *Journal of East Asian Linguistics* 6. 51-99.

Ritter, Elizabeth & Rosen, Sara. 2000. Event structure and ergativity. In Tenny Carol & Pustejovsky James (eds.), *Events as Grammatical Objects—The Converging Perspectives of Lexical and Compositional Factors*, 135-164. Stanford & California: CSLI Publications.

Tsao, Fengfu. 1987. A topic-comment approach to the *ba* construction. *Journal of Chinese linguistics* 15. 1-54.

Email: fufen.jin@ntnu.no

# Index

Affectedness 194–95, 199, 201, 206–08
Atelic predicate 142, 145, 147, 149
*Ba* construction 12–13, 191–99, 203–04, 206, 208–09
*Ba* sentence 191–92, 195–97, 199–200, 202–08
Bare verbs 10–11, 131, 137–40, 144–45, 147, 197, 204
*Be*-type sentences 32–33, 36–37, 39, 48–49
Bilingual acquisition 153, 157, 159, 163
Cantonese 8, 15–17, 19–20, 23–24, 26–27, 75, 80–82, 85, 92, 106–07, 109, 157–58, 168–70
Catalan 133, 136, 145–46
Child Mandarin 10, 75, 78–80, 82, 85, 87–88, 97–99, 101–03, 105–06, 111, 131, 145, 147, 149
Chinese 7–15, 17, 20, 22, 25, 27, 29–33, 35–57, 59, 62, 64–65, 67–70, 72–75, 78, 80–81, 85, 92, 101, 105, 107–09, 111–14, 129–30, 150–51, 156–59, 170–76, 178, 180–85, 191–92, 195–99, 201, 208–09
Coda 9, 50–57, 59–62, 64–65, 67–70, 72–74
Complexity constraint 192, 195, 197, 199–200, 204, 206–07
Context of learning 12, 171, 175–76, 182
*Dao* ('to') 44, 118–19, 121–27, 129
*De*-nominal 88, 101–02, 104, 106
Definiteness 13, 15, 27, 43, 49–50, 54–55, 74, 82, 194–95, 197, 199, 201, 204–07
Definiteness effect 43, 49, 54–55
Descriptive clause 30, 51, 55, 59–60
Directional 10, 47, 111–14, 117–21, 125, 128–30, 197
Dutch 10, 75–76, 113, 131–39, 143, 145, 147, 149

English 7–8, 10–13, 27, 34–35, 38–40, 48–51, 54–56, 60, 62, 68–69, 74–75, 77, 108–09, 112–14, 129–33, 137–40, 142–43, 145, 147, 151, 157–60, 164, 168–76, 178, 180–81, 184–85, 195–97, 199
German 9, 13, 51–52, 54, 58–59, 63–64, 67, 69–71, 73, 75–76, 113, 131–35, 145–46, 150–51
Greek 75, 77, 108, 131, 138–39, 141–43, 151
IV2 51–54, 58–59, 63–64, 67, 69, 71–73
Indefinites-only restriction 54, 59–60, 67, 69–70
Italian 133, 136, 145–46
Japanese 151, 196–97
Kinship term 15–19, 21–23, 26, 86
Korean 150–51
L1 transfer 12, 171, 175–76, 180–81, 196
L2 acquisition 11–12, 171, 173–76, 181, 191–92, 195, 209
Locative 10, 30–31, 39, 43, 49–50, 55, 91, 97, 103, 111–15, 120–21, 124–25, 129–30, 166, 192, 197
Locus-DP 33–34, 38–41, 47–48
Mandarin 7–11, 14, 27, 29, 50, 74–75, 78–82, 85–88, 92, 97–103, 105–09, 111, 129–31, 144–47, 149–50, 153–54, 156–60, 162–76, 178, 180, 182, 198–99, 201, 208–09
Monolingual acquisition 10, 153, 157
Motion sentence 42–45, 47
Motion verb 9, 31–32, 42–45, 113–15, 118
Non-restrictive modifier 63, 65
Norwegian 7–13, 29–46, 48–51, 59, 153–70, 191, 198–99
Null modal 133–35, 142–43
Null object 155–59, 162, 168, 170

Null subject 76, 135–37, 145, 149–51, 155, 157–58, 163, 170
Past tense 12, 137–38, 140, 143–47, 149, 162, 171–75, 178, 180–81
Perfective 11, 131, 138, 140–43, 171–76, 178, 180, 182
Perfective aspect 11, 140, 182
Position verb 31–32
Post-verbal locative 10, 111, 124–25
Postverbal Constraint 36–37, 46
Predicate nominal 79, 84–85, 88–89, 91–92, 97–98, 102–03, 106
Presentative sentence 9, 29–32, 35, 42, 46–47, 49
Pro-drop 11, 136, 150, 153–59, 161, 163, 168
Proper name 15–16, 19, 21–23, 69, 75–76, 80, 82, 91–92, 103, 106
Restrictive modifier 52, 60–61, 63–67, 70, 72
Restrictive relative clause 9, 52, 62–65, 67, 70–71, 84

Root infinitive 10–11, 76, 131–32, 145, 150–51, 157
Russian 14, 133, 138–43, 150
Scalar implicature 63, 65–66
Secondary predicate 9, 52, 54, 62, 65–70
Small clause 9, 34–37, 39–40, 43, 45–46, 49–50, 56, 109, 132
Spanish 133, 136–37, 145–46, 151, 174
Study abroad 12, 171, 174–76, 180–82
Swedish 131–34, 151, 155
Telic 120, 139–43, 145, 147–49, 196–97
Telic verb 120, 139, 196
Temporal reference 11, 131, 139–41, 145–51
V2 9, 13, 52, 58–59, 69–70, 73, 133–34, 151, 154–55, 161, 170
*You*-sentence 9, 32–33, 37–38, 41–42, 45–47, 56, 61
*Zai* phrase 111–12, 114–21, 124–25, 127–30